WHISPER NOT

WHISPER NOT

The Autobiography of Benny Golson

BENNY GOLSON
AND JIM MEROD

TEMPLE UNIVERSITY PRESS *Philadelphia · Rome · Tokyo*

TEMPLE UNIVERSITY PRESS
Philadelphia, Pennsylvania 19122
www.temple.edu/tempress

Text design by Kate Nichols

Material from Chapters 1 and 2 appeared in different form as Jim Merod, "Benny Golson and John Coltrane," in *boundary 2*, volume 41, no. 3, pp. 93–122. © Duke University Press, 2014. All rights reserved. Republished by permission of the copyright holder, Duke University Press. www.dukeupress.edu.

All reasonable attempts were made to locate the copyright holders for the photographs published in this book. If you believe you may be one of them, please contact Temple University Press, and the publisher will include appropriate acknowledgment in subsequent editions of the book.

Library of Congress Cataloging-in-Publication Data

Names: Golson, Benny. | Merod, Jim, 1942–
Title: Whisper not : the autobiography of Benny Golson / Benny Golson and Jim Merod.
Description: Philadelphia, Pennsylvania : Temple University Press, 2016.
  | Includes index.
Identifiers: LCCN 2015044688 | ISBN 9781439913338 (cloth : alk. paper)
  | ISBN 9781439913352 (ebook)
Subjects: LCSH: Golson, Benny. | Jazz musicians—United States—Biography.
  | Saxophonists—United States—Biography.
Classification: LCC ML419.G635 A3 2016 | DDC 781.65092—dc23
LC record available at http://lccn.loc.gov/2015044688

♾ The paper used in this publication meets the requirements of the American National Standard for Information Sciences—Permanence of Paper for Printed Library Materials, ANSI Z39.48-1992

Printed in the United States of America

9 8 7 6 5 4 3 2 1

To all aspiring young musicians who are bent on moving ahead, following in the footsteps of those who preceded them, and making their own memorable footsteps, which will later be followed in by yet others who will come after them.

And to the myriad teachers who metaphorically offer up increments of themselves, and to the institutions, as well, that follow the same path as they light the way for "thirsting" aspirants.—**BENNY GOLSON**

To Maeve and our special gang, Karen, Pooh, Maya, and Paloma
—**JIM MEROD**

Contents

PART VIII VERSES AND A CODA

Illustrations follow page 142

Preface

FIRST HEARD Benny Golson's exotic sound my freshman year at Princeton when *Meet The Jazztet* was published. Two years later, *Turning Point*, his classic Mercury album with Miles Davis's rhythm section—Wynton Kelly, Paul Chambers, and Jimmy Cobb—appeared and I became a lifelong admirer. Across more than five decades my respect has grown exponentially. In human terms, that's a long time, merely a blink in eternity, which is what Benny Golson's music addresses with relaxed, artistically precise lyric means. Maestro Golson is a deeply philosophical man. When you know him—and readers of his autobiography will learn from and about him in greater detail than the majority of his peers and predecessors have revealed about themselves—you soon recognize that the serious, contemplative fellow is counterbalanced by a jubilant, at moments hilarious, fellow. For a good chunk of his eighty-six years, Benny Golson was a prankster extraordinaire, the guy in the hood and in road bands who kept things on track by keeping everyone loose. Someone has to do that, and our man was among the comically best at making a positive difference with Art Blakey's Jazz Messengers as well as with The Jazztet, which he co-led with Art Farmer. His presence was decisively felt, also, in Dizzy Gillespie's late 1950s big band and, before that, in Earl Bostic's aggregation.

For anyone not yet aware of the profound and seminal friendship that Benny shared to the very end with John Coltrane, the narrative of two young musicians who matured together across their formative years is utterly beguiling. The path here chosen to plot the swerves and unceasing surprises of Benny Golson's exceptional life is episodic. It traverses a kind of odyssey in which each part fits in place with the gentle click of unforeseen precision reminiscent of W. B. Yeats's definition of poetic elegance. Despite momentary setbacks and traumas, Benny's life is a study in human elegance. *Whisper Not* begins with the career-shaping, life-changing relationship between two adolescent saxophonists. It explores the urban setting where family and personal energies were constrained by Philadelphia's Depression and war years during the 1930s and 1940s. Benny's life has interacted with so many talented and influential people that we've grouped them into separate sections that reflect (a) intimacy, (b) professional significance, and (c) iconic partners and acquaintances who helped to make Benny's life and career adventurous without equal.

Born on January 25, 1929, Benny Golson has been alive almost from the outset of the de facto inauguration of the Jazz Age, when Louis Armstrong's mid-1920s Hot Fives and Hot Sevens emerged to create the genre with its ever-evolving ensemble protocols and improvisational expansion. Pops was twenty-seven and a half years older than Benny, but "jazz," as we know it across the past century, officially gained archival roots with Armstrong's November 12, 1925, recordings for Okeh Records. The art form that has consumed the whole of Benny Golson's life was barely three years old when he popped into the world in Philadelphia as an only child of a soon-to-be fatherless household. Benny's mother made his musical future possible by paying for piano lessons, buying his first saxophone, and tolerating the interminable (no doubt, at first, infernal) jam sessions that he and his musical pals honed their chops in. However, the prevailing truth of *Whisper Not* resides not merely in its hero's vastly successful and wildly eventful life, but in that life's significance beyond itself.

When you've known a genuinely self-effacing man like Benny Golson for as long as I have (fifty-five years of spiritual partnership; thirty years of shared experience in Los Angeles, New York, San Diego, Washington, D.C., Vienna, Pittsburgh, and La Jolla), you find yourself looking at it all closely. How can years disappear so quickly as joy becomes memories that haunt delight? One might take for granted so many good times as well as arresting moments of intimacy. That has never occurred between us. Benny Golson is so woven into my life and inner being that, more sobering than his constancy as a friend and mentor (as a colleague and a "party of one" beyond compare), I experience his presence in my existence the way I feel my hands and rely upon sight. He is naturally here like breeze in the cypress hedge around my waterfalls. My experience of Benny is defined by mutual understanding and overlapping sympathies. If I became angry or irritated with Benny Golson, it would be exactly as I irritate or anger myself, but I cannot recall once being irritated or angry with Benny. More than anyone I've known, Benny Golson approaches whatever secular sainthood may truly be. I do not know how else to characterize his humility and sensitivity, his glorious companionship and disarming candor. Was it Dwight Eisenhower who insisted that no man is a hero to those who know him well? As another eponymous guru once said, I resemble that remark. But Golson is not like the Ike some admired and others vilified. He's not like yours truly, who could irk a convention of undertakers just by showing up. Benny Golson makes people smile the moment he walks into a room. He lends something of his subtle but contagious karma to others. That's a good trick and likely draws its seduction from the joking prankster he was as a younger man. Benny's special quality of making people feel better for his proximity, the sense of blessing he seems to confer without effort or ambition, doubtless derives from habits he gave style to back in the 'hood. Street savvy was the coin of the realm in Philly, where he hung out with Trane, Jimmy Heath, Philly Joe Jones, Ray Bryant, and Bill Cosby. Those talented kids shared energy held in common as fledgling jazz cats.

This mysterious but affirmative influence that Benny Golson has enforced over the course of his ample life extends past borders of affiliation and friendship. He reshaped Art Blakey's professional modus vivendi. The Jazz Messengers and Art Blakey's unique pedagogical career were both strengthened by Golson's firm but gentle touch. Dizzy's big band songbook came to life with Benny's compositions and arrangements, which, together, crafted the emotional allure of that orchestra's sonic landscape. The Jazztet, which he and Art Farmer created and sustained in tandem, remains one of the most loved and respected "mini big bands" in jazz annals. The group was founded as a sextet to create space and harmonic layers for complex sonic colors beyond the possibilities of traditional quartets and quintets. These and other instances of Benny Golson's musical influence do not fully account for the larger significance of his life's work.

Whisper Not documents a long life's iconoclastic adventure. Benny Golson's memoir of an almost constant sequence of dramatic events traces the thrill of a protracted adrenaline rush punctuated with breathtaking climbs and gasping plunges. Rather than follow a worn-out chronological path, this narrative mirrors Benny's vivid recollection of his sustained roller coaster ride through a Technicolor global amusement park. The difficulty with that cartoon synopsis is its reductive shorthand. Unlike many in his generation, Benny disavowed drug use. In part that accounts for the good fortune of his healthy long life span. Seldom does anyone negotiate the zigzag course of a successful life's ups and downs by himself. For fifty years, Benny's wife, Bobbie, has shared the bracing ride. Their partnership is remarkable for its tender solidarity, which invokes Tolstoy's sardonic insight that all happy families are the same. Novelists characteristically search for malaise and purgatory. Lives such as Benny's with Bobbie do not attract novelistic suspicion. And yet what we find here is a tale defined by challenges endured, problems overcome, risks ventured, friendships celebrated, insights gained, hopes accomplished, and the unsuspected chaos of life's endless surprise steadfastly integrated with grace and artistic wisdom.

The large number and rare quality of the many people who've experienced Benny Golson's disciplined optimism emerge here as a veritable who's who of jazz masters along with seventy years of cultural cognoscenti: accomplished luminaries in cinema, sports, entertainment, and international business. Benny still flourishes and the startling aspect of his youthful geriatric-hood is the maniacal fact that he lustily seeks further, deeper confrontations with unknown waiting discoveries that (he feels in his bones) lurk at the edge of his awareness. Benny has both a child's affinity for mysteries and the confident abandon of unself-conscious genius. At the midpoint of life's ninth decade, which of us would not enjoy his undiminished glow against the horizon of the world's confusion? The survivors of a truly spectacular jazz generation still with us now—Sonny Rollins, Jimmy Heath, Kenny Burrell, Bucky Pizzarelli, Wayne Shorter, Charles Lloyd, Mundell Lowe, Ahmad Jamal, Benny Golson, and others (such as Phil Woods, Ornette Coleman, Gerald Wilson, and Joe Wilder, recently lost)—advance Zen-like artistic authority.

In the chaos of our era's interminable distractions—where we're perpetually at war, ensuring the constant waste of natural and human resources sacrificed to endemic paranoia; where fame is largely a product of promotional hype; where journalistic objectivity is a rumor within the self-deluding conformity that permeates too many professional enclaves—pretense and bombast often substitute for innovative creativity. Benny Golson's long-gestating artistic integrity exemplifies how one might confront the future—not with idealized hope or self-justifying farce or philosophical tragi-comedy, but with the flow of imagination's river of rivers, with spring's ageless welcome regardless of politics and place.

As a writer, no less than as a saxophonist, bandleader, and intervening collegial *tour de force*, Golson defied the odds of race and class. Growing up in a Philadelphia ghetto, he succeeded despite implacable impediments. He became increasingly relentless in pursuit of his goal: to make an archive of songs with indelible permanence. My belief that Benny Golson's life and work offer a viable model to encounter future challenges is not zeal in behalf of a friend. I've glimpsed the future. Civilization is vulnerable to false values, incalculable discord, and collapse. As Joseph Conrad noted without irony, civil society is the thinnest possible veneer of courtesy and reason protecting us from the worst in ourselves.

Jazz has provided humanity a century of profoundly annealing art. Nothing is certain as earth's exploding population collides with unremitting economic and territorial rivalries. Our collective need for examples of artistic power and human integrity seeks both intellectual and spiritual enlightenment. With the exception of Louis Armstrong, no one rivals Duke Ellington in jazz history. Like them, Benny Golson's time on earth has embodied nobility, generosity, and eloquent aesthetic feeling. *Whisper Not* reveals the courageous complexity of a uniquely elevated life.

—Jim Merod
May 2015, La Costa, California

Benny with Jim Merod. (Photo by Joe Wilder.)

Introduction

THIS BOOK'S INTENTION is not in league with the many volumes that have been published describing the errant behavior of some jazz musicians. The proliferation of such accounts is overwhelmingly depressing. They do not represent the complex humanity of the music and the people who create it. There are stories to tell of much greater consequence in the world of jazz than vivid recollections of the lapses, degradations, and unfortunate circumstances that often dog talented people whose success is thwarted by poor judgment. The human condition is a continual test of individual and collective will power. In telling my tale, I proceed in hopes that the reader agrees that people are free to decide their life's course as best they are able, consciously trying, with sustained energy, to attain their goals and avoid the pitfalls.

Why revive tales of deceased musicians' detrimental habits? When we think of extracurricular drug use, we are usually aware of the deleterious outcomes that often follow. When we think of jazz musicians, a doleful parade of negative clichés confronts us. The jazz lineage is dotted with tragedies rationalized with somber platitudes. And yet, if you lined up everyone who ever drifted from the straight and narrow—breaking laws or engaging in other destructive behaviors—standing before you would be people from every profession and persuasion, many holding important positions and held in high esteem by their peers. Dante's *Inferno* is populated by this comical, sad cast: religious leaders, doctors, lawyers, learned men and women of every rank, venal politicians, judges taking bribes and payoffs, business leaders and military leaders vying for power. Our public "watch dogs," journalists, succumb to these temptations, as do the overseers of charities who siphon funds to benefit themselves instead of those in need. Defense lawyers and prosecutors include many who supplement their already large salaries with dirty tricks. Are we to believe all lawyers and judges are committed to justice?

Perhaps the most despicable in our desultory line-up would be the "religious leaders" who perpetrate covert sex acts against the children they have sworn to protect and mentor. Big-name sports figures would also appear, as would individuals from all strata of police and law enforcement. Not to be overlooked are those we would least suspect, the grandmothers and occasional "nice neighbors" who give you hope the world is not as scarred by fraud and evil as it may seem on your most pessimistic days.

Given the prevalence of dereliction, and worse, all around us, time is wasted chronicling the deviance of musicians in particular. The world of jazz resembles any other human arena, peopled by the good, the bad, and the not so ugly. And so my book, like my life, chronicles music and events across more than half the length of jazz history to date. This is my world, what I have done, where I have lived, and the people I have come to know with varying degrees of care and solidarity.

Why did I write this book? Because I'm a jazz player, a jazz composer. I'm still ensconced within the richly divergent, often glorious jazz world, where I came to know a large contingent of its most significant members. I've passed my time with and worked alongside many of its characters, some of its charlatans, but also, serendipitously, most of its luminaries. Because for more than six decades I have functioned within a shared and frequently intimate artistic realm (partly public, mostly private) where I see and hear everything, I have stories I want to bring to light for the benefit of those who are truly interested. So, to clarify my authorial position, let me point across the human spectrum to the ubiquity of those who do terrible things in the name of false ideals. My task is not to single out people I have known, and sometimes admired, for vilification. If my assignment were only to expose or belittle musicians, my pen would refuse to move. This is not a book of titillation and exposé. I'm aware that these prefatory comments may sound dark, despite the fact that, across the span of my long life, fun and good luck have prevailed for me over disappointment and lament. I do not feel superior to anyone, and I refuse the role of moralizer. Instead, I note this divergence so that I can focus unobstructed on the wealth of talent I have encountered among the amazing people who have defined my life's trajectory. As I recall events and experiences, I witness again my life's blessings at every point. My aim is to recount moments and events with my peers that few others have had access to: serious and humorous events, happy times and sad, triumphs and failures. When I have encountered some in our profession who present themselves as self-affirmed "geniuses," I indict the unnamed posers with conviction. It is not for Benny Golson to harm or destroy anyone. Time is a corrosive to falsehood; lies cannot live forever.

Too frequently jazz has been treated as an inferior stepchild to supposedly "elite" art forms. But it has overcome profound problems without disguising lies as truths. Jazz is a relatively small community, but the art of jazz possesses an extraordinarily large democratic spirit. Jazz is inclusive of everyone with talent, regardless of social taboos and prejudices. I have aimed at total candor here. I originally wrote more than is offered here, but tact and discretion demanded courtesy. Bulk has not been my objective. The truth of the music's many parts and elements, as I have lived with them, is my focus in this volume.

In sum, I present something negative here only if it is not harmful. If it bears upon me directly, I have sought to take complete responsibility for my actions, good and bad. I have done things that few would easily suspect. While I am not proud of these actions, I must be honest or why bother to write this book at all? Why bother readers with evasions?

Youth carries enormous ignorance. But ignorance is not to be confused with stupidity. Ignorance indicates only that one does not have information or knowledge that might be useful. I now see that, as a young person, I did not have access to information and knowledge that would often have made things better or easier. I thought I already had everything needed for my journey. Time proved me wrong. I was not able to make consistently grounded decisions with adequate judgment. I made many mistakes. Thank goodness, however, for blind luck. Experience turned out to be a harsh yet loving teacher. My tenacity and ferocious determination to mature overcame my ignorance. Eventually, I learned what to do and what not to do, and knowing how to make such distinctions shaped my adulthood.

Looking back, I see that my life was a continuous struggle, and yet it was neither cruel nor excessively difficult. My life never seemed fundamentally unfair or too much to bear. I understood early in life that the rewards I sought depended wholly on my own efforts. Maybe that belief rendered me impervious to bodily hurt, mental pain, and spiritual grief. Then, too, when I was young, my mother was an analgesic. Lovingly, she absorbed much of my pain (alas), preventing me from developing an accurate sense of life. I see now that whatever I endured was worth the difficulties imposed. I eventually arrived where I wanted to be. Perhaps I can be considered a successful musician. My dream was not the age-old quest for riches. I would not turn my back on wealth now, nor would I had wealth come to me earlier. But my dream was simple: to play my B-flat tenor saxophone and write and play my music for the entire world. And that has happened. I was one of many who aspired to such heights. That banal fact makes my success not so special, after all, but that is as it should be. Cumulative success over a life's duration is one's greatest victory.

I hope the reader will come to appreciate the musicians who emerge in these pages as ordinary human beings who just happened to pursue the innocent endeavor called jazz, encountering inevitable failures, frustrations, triumphs, and rewards. When I was a boy, my heroes inspired me as I moved forward, gleaning scraps of musical insight wherever I could. I dedicated myself to jazz with my whole being. Such inspirations and opportunities were rungs on a ladder I climbed to accurately survey the landscape of my profession. In the beginning I made advances and suffered setbacks, but my burning desire—shared by a gaggle of musically dedicated kids, aspiring jazz novices in 1940s Philadelphia—drove me on with continually fresh strength. My mother, who was truly great, is now gone. She was always my champion. She made me and my teenage buddy John Coltrane feel as if we were her heroes. Musicians never stop needing encouragement. My wife, Bobbie, and our daughter, Brielle, have lived with me through the good, the bad, and everything else. Their love and encouragement have been infinite. The successes I have been able to share with them mean the world to me. I never take any of it for granted; I remember everything that made it possible. The long trek required strength from me, but also from those who traveled alongside me. For me, the ultimate reward has been the appreciation and acceptance of my writing and playing from audiences. If I became arrogant about even a small slice of this, I should be eligible for banishment.

In the early years, negative criticism caused me stress, until I understood what the criticism meant. Critics, some good, some bad, do what they do, just as musicians do. I needed to learn how to overcome negative discourse directed at my self-centered expectations. Some critical comments were useful. Others I discarded because the critical energy was (at least in part) mistaken or degrading. One status-seeking writer found an opportunity to gain advantage at my expense. No artist has time to linger with hurt feelings. I moved on, a useful habit that brought with it both emotional refinement and comfort.

Whatever accolades I receive today, whatever elevated names and titles are conferred on me, whatever awards are granted, I cannot permit myself to bask in their well-meant momentary glory. It is dangerous to do so. I never want to feel comfortable with praise or glory. That erodes creativity. I'm not exaggerating. My imagination must be kept free, to permit me to move in any direction at any time. Praise and glory are shackles.

Students often ask me which of my own compositions is my favorite. My answer is always, "I haven't written it yet." I doubt I ever will. The horizon is ahead. My skiff, like Odysseus's, knows no other destination but the next one. I hear the Sirens calling. They never tell the truth. Creative work is often lonely and wearying, a test of endurance not unlike an aging warrior's ennui. Perhaps a sense of renewed embattlement is inevitable. I do know that seductive diversions are strewn along the route home, wherever self-doubt and exhaustion are most likely to find them. After two decades away, Odysseus arrived home to rout pretenders vying for his wealth and authority. The *Odyssey* had no sequel, but I'm sure the warrior who invented the Trojan horse, permitting his army to enter Troy's gates with the adversary's help, was too restless to keep his head on the pillow when he got back to Ithaca. I'll bet that Odysseus—who tricked the Cyclops, faked out Circe, avoided the Sirens, and rafted the hellish seas between Scylla and Charybdis—had one more adventure in him. No truly creative person ever arrives home without immediately beginning to long for the next gig. Art is a lifetime commitment. It is the beautiful agony of striving to discover new things. Like Odysseus, an artist tries to improve on his best achievements, to outrun his own shadow.

Now I push my book into the world, while moving onward. *Whisper Not* is me here today, and it is also the other "me" who lived it. Everyone is a potential book. The writer and his text are the same and also different. Any well-lived life furnishes a trove of material for stories, recollections and accounts of improbable events that make up any life worth living—lives lucky enough to reflect on their own experience. Funny stuff: survival, wonder, and knowledge.

Just to be alive, to have been alive at the peak of one's best energies and inspirations, is everything to be hoped for: a dream worth dreaming and reliving. This book is my testament and my pledge to the future. I have chosen to recall my life as vividly and honestly as I can, to include details that may seem excessively bold and sharp, others edged in periwinkle. I've done my best. I now go on. I cannot reasonably think I know all there is to know, even about myself and my voyage through life. My views in this book are far from sacrosanct. I do not present them as a covert argument for any outlook or ideology, unless it is the transcendent fact of artistic power, of imagination's unfettered participation in a universe that allows humans to thrive, if they know how, on our much besieged, but still gorgeous orb. Is not life, at its deepest, about knowledge and creation? Should not that awareness enlarge fellow feeling and strengthen what is best in us as individuals?

My sincerest appreciation goes to Jim Merod. Our shared feeling has grown deep across many decades. I am proud of our work together. *Whisper Not* accurately presents the people, events, and aspirations that shaped me. One last wager: time will bear the truth of what I tell here.

—Benny Golson,
2015

PART I *John Coltrane*

CHAPTER 1

One of a Kind / JOHN COLTRANE

ONE COMPLETELY NORMAL July day, with no warning that anything in my universe might be askew, I headed over to the musicians' union, local 802, in New York City. Floyd, who worked the disbursement window, where I picked up my checks, asked if I had heard about John Coltrane's death. My heart jumped. I told him no and left. As when I learned about Clifford Brown's death eleven years earlier, I hoped this was one of those unfortunate rumors with a life of its own.

I walked down 52nd Street, my mind and memory turning over and over as I made a right turn onto Broadway, heading for a check-cashing place. I ran into a fellow musician. "Isn't it a drag about Trane?" he blurted. I stood dazed, impervious to reality. Was it true? My dear friend was gone?

My thoughts whirled. Was John really dead? Why now? Why him? How much further would John have advanced had he lived? A million questions raced through my mind. "This can't be true—it must not be true," I thought. "But what if it *is* true?"

I continued to my destination, half-hearted, in an emotional netherworld. I cashed a check, caught the IRT subway at 50th Street, and traveled uptown to my apartment. This ride, usually pedestrian and uneventful, was now monumental. On this day—July 17, 1967—John Coltrane went the way of all things on earth, to join his forefathers, gone forever. As the subway train roared angrily on, my mind drifted to a better time, to precious memories and to our aspiration-filled hearts in years past.

Suddenly, in my mind, it was 1944. I could even smell my house on Page Street in Philadelphia: fresh Kem-Tone paint on the walls, and on the floors cheap new linoleum. Their painted patterns never stood the test of time. My mother was always trying to make our house look better. I thought of Howard Cunningham, who played alto saxophone and attended my high school, Benjamin Franklin High. He stopped me in the hall one day, and told me excitedly that a new guy had just moved into the projects across town, on the east side, where he lived. "Man, you should hear this guy," Howard crowed. "He plays alto and sounds just like Johnny Hodges! His name is John Coltrane."

I had never heard such a strange last name, but that didn't matter. At that time Johnny Hodges was the barometer for alto saxophonists in jazz. "How old is this fellow?" I asked. Howard said the new guy was eighteen years old and had just come home after a short stint in the Navy. I knew I couldn't wait for happenstance to bring us together, so I begged Howard to bring him to my house the next day right after school. He agreed. Now as the IRT rattled uptown, I recalled the irony that, just next door to Howard lived a young tenor saxophonist, Bootsie Barnes, who later became—and still is now—a mainstay on the Philadelphia jazz scene. There is no accounting for life's harsh quirks and cruel twists.

True to his word, the next day Howard rang my home doorbell at precisely 4:00 P.M., an hour after school ended. I found Howard standing on the top step, near the door, but down on the sidewalk at the bottom of the steps, looking like a country bumpkin, stood this fellow holding his saxophone case in one hand and biting his thumbnail on the other. He looked like a shy little sheep. That was my first sight of John Coltrane.

They came in. Howard sat on the couch while John just stood in the doorway to the living room looking lost, as if waiting for me to tell him what to do. Kids can be awkward, lacking in social graces. I'm sure I was just as gauche. "Play something," I ordered my new acquaintance, as if I were the local jazz authority. I couldn't think of anything else to say. But this was precisely what John was waiting for. He whipped his horn from its case and assembled it in a flash. He played (what else?) his version of Johnny Hodges's famous recording, "On the Sunny Side of the Street."

We were all amateurs, of course, but I had never heard a sound that big emerge from any of our horns. This guy did, indeed, sound like Johnny

Hodges! I was in the habit of having young musicians come to my house for jam sessions (if one could really call them that). But never had anyone sounded as professional as this new guy, Coltrane. When he finished, my mother, who was busy upstairs with household chores, shouted downstairs, "Who was that?!" John sounded better than anyone or anything she had heard from the rest of us. I told her it was a new friend named John Coltrane. That first hesitant, immature meeting was the beginning of a life-long friendship between two eager young musicians.

Before long, all of the aspiring local amateurs knew who John was. Soon, John met Jimmy Heath, whom I already knew. John was elated because, as he put it, Jimmy, who played the saxophone, was really "on it." Jimmy possessed substantially more knowledge about jazz than the rest of us and we all desired to emulate him. For example, Jimmy knew how to play solos that followed the chords correctly.

John and I soon began to meet almost every day, just the two of us. Intuitively, we were preparing for our "full flight"—our world debut, which we were sure would happen someday without fail. Somehow we were confident. In the meantime, we tried to figure out what this thing called jazz was all about. We played piano for each other, after a fashion. Sometimes I would play the old upright piano in our living room, which I wore out with my lessons. I played piano along with John's alto sax, attempting to accompany him and make a genuine jazz duo. My knowledge of jazz was nil, so my piano thumping must have been torturous for John, learning to play his first horn. (My performance was a travesty, but his accompaniment to my playing was even worse.) We didn't care; all we had was each other. So we struggled. We were not to be thwarted. It was us against the world! Imagine that naïveté. Imagine that good luck. Think of the profound good fortune each of us gained from our chance meeting, and from our subsequent long friendship.

Sometimes John sat in the overstuffed chair by our living room window, his horn braced between his legs on the chair cushion, one leg slung over the arm of the chair. I loved to hear him play "There's No You," which he played in the most beautiful way. It is not sentimental recollection on my part to say that John produced a fantastic sound on his alto sax from the beginning—rich and full and haunting. I have always contended that his sound, from the first time I heard it, was distinctive, even then challenging the strength of any professional saxophonist. John Coltrane's sound, then and always, was unique.

John often dropped old southern expressions on me. Referring to his tired feet, he'd say, "Feets hoits, mind hoits, everything hoits." I'd laugh every time he said that because the way he said it was hilarious, perfectly matching the miserable look on his face.

Early on, John became a regular member of jam sessions at my house. Ray Bryant played piano. His brother, Tom, played bass. They were also regulars. Sometimes Steve Davis, a bass player who later played in John's quartet, joined us, as did William Langford, a boogie-woogie pianist whose name later became Hasaan Ibn Ali. We tolerated Hasaan, I suppose, because we were all just beginning to learn how to play jazz. Later he became known as the "Legendary Hasaan" because his style eventually went way "out there." He became a sort of Thelonious Monk in his own strange way. Tom and Ray Bryant were quite advanced players even though they were only fifteen and fourteen years old, respectively—young geniuses. I still marvel at their youthful talent. But the largest truth, defining everything we did, was that we were all heavily invested in our musical futures.

As I rode the IRT train north in Manhattan on that sober July day in 1967, traumatized by what I still hoped was only a rumor of John's death, I recalled the sights, sounds, and feel of our cheerful adolescences in Philadelphia. My mother played an odd but wonderful role in our jam sessions. Before we began those sessions we could always depend on her calling downstairs. "Is John down there yet?" she'd ask. He'd answer, "Yes, Miss Golson!" Mother's inquiry meant that John had to play "On the Sunny Side of the Street." This went on week after week. One day, after one of our sessions, I said to her as nicely as I could, "Mother, I know you like the way John plays, but this calling downstairs for 'On the Sunny Side of the Street' every time we get together is a drag. Know what I mean?" Her reply was quick and sharp. "This is my house. I'll ask whatever I want."

So my mother had frustrated my attempt to be hip. Poor John had to play "On the Sunny Side of the Street" every afternoon for months, even though he was now well beyond his Johnny Hodges phase. I was embarrassed, but John never complained. He was always cooperative and mellow. Sometimes we recorded our efforts. One of our habitués, who played vibes, had a wire recorder. These were the early days of portable recording, during the Second World War. The government had banned oil-based products, and recording tape was such a product. To record in your own home, you needed a wire recorder. Charlie Parker had a fan, a man named

Dean Benedetti, who followed him around with a portable wire recorder to capture his solos in clubs and concerts. Our personal recordings were not for posterity. We wanted to hear whether we were any good. After each recording, the wire had to be rewound with a finger inserted into the spool. We didn't care about the slight delay, because we wanted to hear what we sounded like.

This period was one of risk taking and reward seeking for us. We had to prepare ourselves for the road ahead, wherever it might lead. We simply wanted to play, and to be a meaningful part of the jazz scene. John and I were explorers. We felt as if we were on our own seeking answers to musical questions we could barely discern. My living room "studio" helped us accomplish a great deal, in truth. I now see that our compulsion to search for the inner secrets of jazz was almost pathological. Our minds sought discipline, while our souls were on fire. We were free. That combination— discipline and passionate risk taking—is the essence of artistic freedom, and John and I felt free and profoundly lucky to have one another. We knew very little technically, but we searched constantly for new songs and fresh ideas, as well as for any technique we might use to improve our playing. We were young but we were honest, hard-working, naïve adventurers. We devoted as many of our waking hours as possible to progressing musically. What would tomorrow bring? We always wondered how our journey would evolve.

We were lucky. Those were the good old days. In some ways they were genuinely better times, a more tolerant and supportive era, for young mavericks determined to find their instrumental voices. We played in jam sessions at many clubs. The majority took place in North Philly, where John and I lived. Since I was not an accomplished soloist, I copied recorded solos that I liked, and I trotted them out in jam sessions. I didn't care what the instrument was. If I liked a solo, I memorized it. Then I played it over and over *ad nauseam*. That's all I had to offer: regurgitation.

On jam days—Saturday afternoons between four and seven—John and I started at one end of Columbia Avenue, where most of the clubs were located, and proceeded toward the other end. We played at each club for an hour, then moved to the next. If we didn't get to a particular club, we started there the following week. These clubs were small, on the ground floor of apartment houses or in storefront slots, long and narrow. With so many musicians ready to play, instruments in hand, one would think chaos ruled. Everyone was an amateur, and the scene was frantic. But chaos seldom occurred, at least not at the beginning of a song. Significant negotiation was usually required to agree on what tune we would play. Precisely when a tune seemed to be chosen, someone would confess he didn't know it. We would negotiate again, eventually settling on a song that someone else had previously shot down. As a result, we played a lot of blues. Everyone seemed to know the blues. The first chorus wasn't bad, even with fifteen or twenty guys plowing forward. Some played the melody, others harmony. One or two other musicians filled in around the edges of the melody. Those who didn't know what was going on or couldn't keep up fingered their horn without playing a note: an all-star impression of musical hipness. Nobody could tell the difference anyway.

That routine worked for the head, but when solos got launched, mayhem ensued. All of us practiced at home all week for this fleeting moment of self-assertion. Fifteen or twenty kids, all aspiring to be the first soloist. We all launched our solos simultaneously, with a musical roar. Our collective elbow-jabbing horn blasts redefined counterpoint. If only old man Bach could have heard us! Too many horns blaring at once, everyone aiming to take the first solo—that was our jazz apprenticeship. This madness went on for at least half of the first blowing chorus. Eventually the most determined and aggressive player emerged, as others petered out. Darwin was right: the fittest survive.

John and I often laughed about this comedy. The soloist who held the spotlight would play until he exhausted all he knew how to blow—which was often not much. He then often started over, to perpetuate his moment out front. This routine was enormously time-consuming, selfish, and maddening to everyone itching to play. Of course, such selfish logic eventually crashed and burned. When the heroic soloist drew a deep breath, near the end of a chorus, he was toast. Instantly, someone else intervened with a pickup, even if they were two or three and a half bars early. The next self-appointed solo star was off and running.

The time allotted for each set was fairly strict. Forty minutes were "on," and intermission was twenty minutes. Therefore, one tune consumed each set. Everyone played greedily and no one exercised self-restraint. I look back and marvel at how those young rhythm sections endured. Nonetheless, tired drummers also wanted solo space, to end a set—which made for further interesting elbow jabs. John and I haunted as many of these sessions as we could. They were our training ground.

These ferociously enjoyable events and desires defined our years together. I doubt anyone ever had a better pal than John Coltrane. John was self-contained. He could be a torrent without boundaries, but he also offered friendship without limits. He helped me find my way as an artist. He always appreciated anything I did for him. We helped each other in more ways than can easily be told or recollected. Looking back at those magical years of searching and hoping, I feel both awe and kinship with those two trusting kids who were John and me, although they are "us" no more.

On that fatal day in 1967, when I arrived at my stop on 103rd Street in Manhattan, I walked over to 102nd Street, where I lived. I looked south toward 100th Street where John lived. Time had closed a door. History sealed itself against further glory from my dear friend John Coltrane, but he was part of me, a force of nature who was inscribed forever within me. I made my way into the building where I lived, numb and enfeebled, drained of the energy necessary to recall more vivid memories from our past. Thoughts and images, once pleasant, now haunted me. I entered my apartment, not knowing what to do. I leaned against the door and cried.

CHAPTER 2

John and I Meet Diz and Bird

JIMMY JOHNSON AND HIS AMBASSADORS was a fairly popular big band in Philadelphia in the 1940s. As fate would have it, John and I, along with Ray and Tommy Bryant, came to Johnson's attention. He asked us all to join his band, a real surprise because the band was composed of older players. One of the trombonists, Gino, had been on the road with Andy Kirk and His Twelve Clouds of Joy. To us, that was the big time. The band's repertoire was entirely stock arrangements, crafted mostly by Spud Murphy, "the king of stocks," and Van Alexander. The arrangements were very well done and made young players sound professional—as polished as we were as yet capable.

Each night paid eight dollars, twice as much as I later received for my first "genuine" gig. Unfortunately, since we were supposed to be "ambassadors" (of what, I have no idea) we had to rent tuxedos, four dollars each time we played. That left four dollars for the night's wages. We didn't care. We were playing, and we were allowed a solo now and then, even if it was only four or eight bars. John played third alto. I played fourth tenor. The experienced saxophone players took the bulk of the solos. Zack Wright, a tenor saxophonist, was well respected and someone I looked up to. He was old enough to be my father (about forty!) and he played very well, indeed. I felt I could learn a lot from him. His sound on tenor made me conscious of mine, which I was working hard to refine, along with how I expressed notes and phrases. Sound has always been extremely important to me. Anyone who plays an instrument should strive for the best possible sound, or else the instrument's full range and the player's chops both suffer. A young musician must learn to listen to everything: to what he or she plays, what the music means, and how it sounds. Constant awareness constitutes the indelible heart of jazz creation.

Jimmy's gigs took place mostly on weekends, perfect for a kid in high school. Oh, how we lived for those gigs! They were opportunities to play before *people*. John and I often played for a lonely audience of two, ourselves. We felt that we were moving onward and upward, nonetheless.

One day, a few hours before one of these gigs, Jimmy's son came by our houses. (Neither of us had a telephone.) He informed us that the gig that night had been called off. John and I were extremely disappointed. That evening we listened to our good old seventy-eight-rpm albums in my living room. My mother asked why we looked so dejected. We explained that our gig had just been canceled. In her infinite wisdom, she knew the truth. "No job is called off that late, so I bet they're playing without you," she asserted. John and I looked at her in disbelief. "Oh no, Miss Golson," John protested, "Jimmy wouldn't do anything like that." Her reply was directly to the point: if she were the one who had received this bad news, she would go to the gig to find out for herself.

John and I were out the door immediately. The gig was scheduled for the Civic League, six or seven blocks from my house. When we were half a block away, we heard live music: a big band. "That's our music! That's Jimmy!" John said. I thought it might not be Jimmy's band, since every large group in town played stock arrangements. We went right up to the entrance. When the door opened for a customer, we heard everything clearly. Still, we were not sure. We needed to see the band. The ballroom was in a basement with steps leading down to the dance floor. The bandstand was at the far end of the hall. Through the open door, we could not see the musicians on stage. Our solution was stealthy but simple. When the door opened again, we fell on our stomachs at the entrance. People looked at us like we were crazy, but we saw everything. The evidence was before us. We couldn't believe our eyes: Jimmy Johnson was playing his heart out. The band was doing fine without us. A stranger sat in John's chair. Another stranger occupied mine. We had no words to express how badly we were affected by this insult. It was as if we'd been dropped down an elevator shaft or locked out of Christmas. We stood there on the street completely forlorn. Jimmy had iced us. He had not even given us the courtesy of a personal word, a thank you or an apology. His wordless message told us we that weren't good enough; we were miserable failures.

As soon as we entered the front door of my house, John blurted, "You were right, Miss Golson!" Both of us felt humiliated, and I think both of us would have cried had the other not been there. We stood, immobilized, in the middle of my living room. Mom put her arms around us both, and neither of us ever forgot her warm hug or her prophetic words. "Don't worry," she said. "One day both of you will be so good they won't be able to afford you." At that moment, we couldn't grasp the significance of her reassuring message. John Coltrane and I had just been rejected. Snubbed. Dumped.

In 1945 a very special concert was scheduled to take place in Philadelphia. Dizzy Gillespie and a musician named Charlie Parker were coming to town. John and I knew who Dizzy was but nothing about this Parker fellow. We wondered how he would play. I was happy because my idol, Don Byas, was scheduled to play at the same event, along with Slam Stewart, Al Haig, and Big Sid Catlett. On the same bill, Elliot Lawrence's local band featured a seventeen-year-old trumpet player named Red Rodney. Lawrence's father was a prominent radio announcer who hosted a talent show every Sunday for the Horn and Hardart restaurant chain. Along with two friends, Jules Greenberg and Don Rapaport, we competed in the talent show as a quartet called The Hot Spots. We lost, even though our friends and families sent hundreds of cards to the station voting us the best act. In other words, we cheated, but to no avail; I always felt somebody at the station figured out our scam. Regardless of setbacks, a lot of us looked forward, with great anticipation, to the Dizzy Gillespie–Charlie Parker concert. For John and me, the first live jazz concert that we had attended since we began playing together was momentous.

The concert was staged at the Academy of Music, home of the Philadelphia Orchestra. We took our places, greatly excited, in the cheap seats in the uppermost level. Diz's band kicked off with the strangest Latin-sounding tune we had ever heard. John thought it sounded "like snake charmer's music": Dizzy's "A Night in Tunisia" was weirder than anything we had heard before, but intriguing. The band moved through the melody, dove into an interlude, then opened into a bravura set of riffs, or glissandi, a sustained high-octane break by the alto player, Charlie Parker. To us, the sound was way out there. Parker was dressed in a double-breasted suit with all of the buttons closed. He looked like an adult stuffed into his grade school graduation suit. I thought he might explode at any moment, especially when he bent over, reaching for inspiration, conjuring the next amazing phrase from his horn. Layers of notes and tones spilled out, some blurred but all articulate, melodic lines of impossible pure imaginative intensity. These were epochal musical statements. John and I were as astonished as we might have been had the musicians on the stage begun to levitate.

We both nearly fell over the balcony rail, all the cells and nerves in our bodies wild with abandon. Their music was crazy and we went into an exuberant delirium, doubtless a form of higher awareness and pure joy. John tried to crawl up my gyrating body while I was grabbing onto him with barely contained amazement. We were both screaming like schoolgirls. We had heard strong performances in our young lives, but nothing like this. This was beyond "good." It was completely new, innovative, and profound. We were drunk with happiness and bewilderment. I felt like crying. We didn't know it then, but our musical world changed that night. For me, my hero Arnett Cobb began to fade, and John's idol, the elegant Johnny Hodges, soon drifted from John's psyche forever.

Diz played like a brilliant whirlwind. No less than Charlie Parker, Diz transported us to strange and unfamiliar musical territory, wonderful, previously unheard but astounding, even miraculous. This was a landscape we did not understand. We loved it, nevertheless. We were agog, incapable of immediately apprehending this music with our senses or intellects. Neither John nor I could decode what we heard. It was over our heads but in our faces. Its glory was "for" us—we felt that we were *supposed* to be there, first to witness, then to carry on what took place that magical night. I loved what Don Byas played that evening, but Charlie Parker and Dizzy Gillespie stole our youthful souls and returned them elevated. The two of them changed the feel and sound of the musical future. That night in Philadelphia, we had no idea where that future would take us or what would await our arrival. But we wanted to go there. We knew we had no choice. Our ears and hearts pulled us ahead, ablaze with curiosity and desire, determined to follow wherever this energy took us. Bird and Diz became our heroic mentors.

As I look back, the rhythm section that night did not match Dizzy's drive or Charlie Parker's soaring heights. Everything that had been "traditional" in jazz came under assault that night in Philadelphia. I remember hearing a bit of stride in Al Haig's piano work. Slam Stewart, bowing a solo, simultaneously hummed or "scatted" the same notes. Big Sid Catlett (who was the drummer that night, I believe) anchored everything with a strong groove. But what did John and his youthful pal know about anything? Our ignorance and innocence gave us impetus to move ahead with dispatch. Nonetheless, we were amateurs and that night we could not yet understand that the way in which someone arrives at success is as important as the arrival itself. Later I realized that the *how* and the *what* are firmly intertwined.

A new musical world was developing far beyond the one we had previously been trying hard to master. We had to recast our thinking and our playing. Something new and wonderful was coming on the scene and we were there! John and I both felt in our bones that the Gillespie-Parker approach was a decisive break from orthodox ways of defining harmony and rhythm. Was it ever! We were intoxicated by what we heard that night. Newness for its own sake often stumbles or dies out. Sometimes, too, what is "new" is merely trivial or worse. The world is a cruel and sometimes foolish judge of art and creative talent. But Bird and Diz were planting seeds of their own rare creation. John and I realized our vast good fortune to watch fresh musical growth burst from the soil of overworked tradition.

When the concert was over, we stumbled backstage to get our heroes' autographs. We were thrilled to stand in front of these giants from a world we now wanted to inhabit, to hear their voices in conversation and their confident remarks. John and I were overwhelmed by proximity to jazz heaven. I wanted to grab their words and wrap them in my handkerchief, keep them safe in my pocket. If their spoken words had held tangible substance, we would have stolen them all.

As these musical pioneers prepared to leave the theater, John and I latched on. We followed "Mr. Parker" up Locust Street. The concert at the Academy of Music had been held in the early evening. Mr. Parker was now on his way to play at the Downbeat Club, four or five blocks away, where a local rhythm section consisting of Red Garland, Philly Joe Jones, and Nelson Boyd was waiting for him. He invited us to walk down the street with him. "Wow," I thought, "why can't some of our friends happen along so they can see us walking side by side with Charlie Parker?" As we walked up Broad Street, John asked if he could carry the great man's horn case. Mr. Parker handed his case to John, who carried it as if it were the Ark of the Covenant. From the other side of our threesome, I asked Mr. Parker "what kind of horn" he played. He said it was a Selmer. What kind of mouthpiece, I asked, and then what brand and strength of reed? I mentally catalogued this information and felt as if I had the upper hand on something. Just what, I wasn't sure.

When we arrived, all too soon, at the club, "Mr. Parker" took his horn from John and, before disappearing up the steps to the club on the second floor, thoughtfully turned to us. "You guys stay on it," he said. "Maybe one day I'll be hearing about you." Those words reached our ears and our hearts. We sealed them within and bid our new hero good-bye.

John and I were too young to gain access to the club, and we certainly did not have the admission fee for an extravagant night at a jazz club. So, from 9:00 P.M. until the final note of the last set at 2:00 A.M., we stood outside, listening from the sidewalk below. John and I underwent a slow baptism that night. We barely regained enough sanity to intermittently change our standing positions. When the music finally stopped, we were as tired as any musician on that bandstand. John Coltrane and I played every note and every beat in our emotional cores. The hour was late. We had been gone from our homes since late afternoon. We knew our parents must be worried, but we took no account. We risked their ire because something miraculous had happened this night and we were there—in person!

Our conversation walking home from South Philly to North Philly, where we lived, was filled with "What if ..." and "Do you think . . . ?" We contemplated ourselves into a stupor, not the slightest bit aware of how long we had been walking. We were somewhere else, our minds and emotions prevailing. Our bodies floated home. From this sublime evening, we received not technical know-how, but something more important, artistic inspiration.

When we got far enough north, John headed east over to 12th Street and I headed west to 17th Street. We did not yet know what we were searching for. The laboratory of imagination does not always reveal what it seeks—at least not right away. Nonetheless, if the mind moves ahead, insight and direction often follow. John and I wanted to reject the past, throw away all false starts and amateur errors, and rush headlong and heedless into the future. We deeply desired new things. We were hungry and brash but respectful of genius before us. We would embrace enlightenment at any cost.

For every master there are many apprentices. Like us, all of the aspiring young musicians in Philly were soon to become apprentices to Dizzy Gillespie and Charlie Parker. Where would they lead us? We knew it would be far beyond where we stood at that moment. I don't think sleep paid John or me a visit that night. Our minds were too full to cooperate with something as meaningless as sleep.

John and I were in the habit of seeing each other almost every day. Since neither of our families had a telephone, John would call me from a telephone booth near his home. He used the number of the public telephone at the cigar store on a corner not far from my house. If there was a kid hanging around the store, the owner sent him over to my house. In turn, I gave the kid a nickel and rushed down to the store to await John's call.

Our first conversation after Bird's concert with Diz was on the phone. John sounded confused. "Did you try any of that stuff Mr. Parker told us about—his horn and mouthpiece and his reeds?" I told him yes. "Did anything happen?" I told him no. "Me neither," he agreed. Kids can be stupid; we both had a lot to learn. None of the things Bird told us that fabulous night helped us to play the way he did—darting and soaring, fast yet precise. We had to find that out for ourselves. Entering musical terra incognita, John and I plunged in together, with all our energy, innocence, and hope.

CHAPTER 3

John Becomes a Dynamo

JOHN COLTRANE AND I were fortunate. Our musical careers were progressing, and we hoped soon to take flight under our own power, no longer merely imitating players who preceded us. We felt the stirrings of artistic liberation and professional ambition. As kids with talent and ambition, on occasion we pondered our future successes. What would be our jazz legacy, our place in music history? The question "How long will it take for us to get there?" often dominated our thoughts. Our artistic efforts became herculean. Both of us sought maximum understanding of this new music delivered to our hungry souls by Bird and Diz. Of course, we wanted to hear more of their live performances, since we had experienced how powerful their music was on stage, alive and direct. We wanted to see our heroes in action, but we would have been satisfied to see them walking or talking together in our neighborhood. We intuited, however, that we would likely never see them again on Philadelphia streets.

John Coltrane and I decided we had to go to New York. We had no other option. A friend who played the alto sax, Joe Stubbs, had a clean 1941 two-door Buick. If we paid for the gas, we inquired, would he drive us up to New York on his day off? He agreed and off we went. We had no idea what to expect in New York, especially since we would be arriving in the middle of the week. We didn't even know where to find our heroes. It didn't matter. Just being in New York would be a thrill, because this was where all of the great jazz players lived.

We arrived during the day. All the clubs were closed. The Apollo Theater, on 126th Street, came to mind. Maybe we would meet someone backstage. We traveled up to Harlem but that idea was foiled. Nothing hip was happening there. However, standing backstage wondering what to do, we saw someone vaguely familiar walking toward us. Wait. Holy moly, it can't really be Thelonious Monk!

Indeed it was Monk, but we had a problem. Which one of us would approach the great man? John was too shy. We couldn't let Monk walk by undisturbed. Trying to appear hip, I blustered, "Hey, Mr. Monk, what's hap'nin'? Is there any action?" He looked at me, annoyed, and scolded us. "You kids are too young to be lookin' for drugs." We quickly explained that we were aspiring saxophone players from Philly. We were not looking for drugs. We just wanted to hear some of the musicians we loved from our records. Monk told us that we'd have to come back that night, which was impossible for us, he thought, because we had to go home. Joe Stubbs did have to get home, ready for work the next morning. Monk was right about that part.

I chuckle about that day. There we were introducing ourselves to Thelonious Monk, as if we were part of his world. Consider where we were all soon headed. Monk was already a great pianist and a great composer. Not many years later, Monk, who sent us home and warned us away from drugs that day, requested John's partnership in a groundbreaking quartet that ran for nine months at the Five Spot Café down in the Village. Amazing! Our place in the stream of time—did it begin with Bird's arrival alongside Diz that glorious night in Philadelphia, or did it start in Harlem, when we waylaid a very patient Thelonious Sphere Monk?

I look at all these moments, their mystery and generosity, and cannot get to the bottom of time's meaning. It is elusive. John Coltrane was unusually serious minded and extremely talented. Time made John Coltrane its confederate. John devoured each challenge as it presented itself, and his career took quantum leaps. That day, we drove back to Philadelphia incredulous that we had actually seen and talked to Thelonious Monk. We had been to the mountain. We became heroes to our friends in Philly after word emerged about our meeting with the enigmatic Thelonious Monk.

Philadelphia boasted many jazz clubs at that time, and John and I continued to gig often. John, however, soon got a very strange gig. Word came to me that John was working at a club called The Ridge Point. We called it The Point because of the street configuration there, where instead of bisecting each other, three streets crossed—Columbia Avenue, 23rd Street, and Ridge Avenue—such that the shape of the building at that intersection resembled a large slice of pie—much like the famous Flatiron Building in Manhattan. The bar's shape mimicked the building. The bandstand was at the wide end of the pie. The tip, or the point, was the main entrance. All that was interesting, but The Point was not a bona fide jazz club. Eddie Woodland, a tenor player, usually held forth. Woodland was a "boot 'em up" tenor player with a circus aura, who held audiences in the palm of his hand by walking the bar, with bravado. Crowds loved him, but for some reason, he took a leave of absence. Maybe he was sick. Then word went around that my pal John was playing at The Point, and I knew John wasn't that kind of saxophone player. The Point was definitely not a hip jazz club, and the regulars expected every artist to walk the bar. Our families both had telephones now, but I decided not to call John and ask him about his odd gig. I would just walk in during the matinee on Saturday afternoon, without telling him I was coming.

I remember walking to the club that day. The music was clear even from the street, at a distance. First, I heard the persistent loud drum back-beat. Next I heard the saxophone. It was clearly Eddie Woodland doing what he did so well, pleasing the people, walking the bar, revving the crowd. I figured John wasn't there after all. Another false rumor. Eddie was playing extremely well that afternoon. He was really "on it," as Tommy Flanagan would have said. The sax was hollerin', the joint was rockin'. The groove, though different than usual, had me swaying in time as I stepped in the door.

I could not believe what I saw. This wasn't Eddie at all, but John! John Coltrane was up on the bar at the small end, at the tip of the mud pie, honking, grooving, preparing to go down to the far end and back to the bandstand again. He was cranked up, playing low B-flats, nimbly stepping over drinks like a mountain goat on slippery terrain. He didn't see me right away. But when he came up from one of his low horn-swooping move-ments, he looked in my direction. His eyes got wide and he stopped right in the middle of a group of low B-flats. He took the horn out of his mouth, stood straight up, and said, "Oh, no!" I fell against the wall, dying with laughter. I'd busted him. He was humiliated, but he finished his slumming bar performance.

When John came off for intermission, he was remorseful. "Oh, why did you have to come? I thought I could get through the week without you guys knowing." The hidden irony, of course, was that John did not really breach any etiquette or protocol. Many of us so-called hip jazz musicians were soon doing the same thing. Gigs helped pay bills. The rent man cares not a jot about styles of music, only his remuneration. Such gigs were not a waste of time or talent. Despite John's momentary embarrassment, that type of work also rounded us out musically, giving us experience with the broad expanse of jazz. These gigs showed us how to make a living. So we did our work and catalogued our lessons. I am a broader, better musician for having done similar gigs. John came to feel that way, too, something you can hear in his playing, if you know what to listen for, especially when John plays the blues.

John later took a job with Daisy Mae and the Hepcats, who did not play jazz at all, but John made good use of the experience and played authentically what Daisy Mae required. Daisy was a singer who played a cocktail drum with a foot pedal. She had to stand when she played the long, vertical drum, using only brushes on the top. Wearing floppy ties, the group sang together, rocking and swaying side to side, rendering their version of "Rag Mop." They were an entertaining group, but you'd never hear "Cherokee" or "Hot House." John took the job seriously and did it well. Looking back, I can say that we all played non- and sub-jazz modes and styles when we had to. Necessity breeds creativity and success.

In retrospect, I see that we all advanced rather well. Certainly Philly was good to two hard-working young saxophonists. The days of jam sessions at my house came to an end. The musicians who used to gather there for the most part moved on successfully. Percy Heath soon played with a trio, The Hollis Hoppers, headed by pianist Bill Hollis. They were terrific. Percy came out of the Army Air Corps as a pilot in the Tuskegee unit, an all-black experimental fighter unit during World War II. He made the fastest progress of anyone I've ever known on the bass. I think what he accomplished was virtually impossible. In a few years he left for New York. Percy Heath became one of the most recorded bass players in jazz history, especially after he joined The Modern Jazz Quartet. In my opinion, he was a genius.

In 1947 John got an offer to join King Kolax, a midwestern traveling band that used a tractor trailer (for hauling horses) that had been converted into a bus with seats and several beds. The trailer was low to the ground (for easy entrance of the horses). The band toured the central states and then went on to the West Coast. Earl Coleman, the vocalist on Charlie Parker's version of "Dark Shadows," told me that he was at a West Coast private jam session with John Coltrane when Bird walked in. John, who was still playing alto at that time, handled it extremely well. He sounded so good that Bird inquired about the alto player tearing it up. When I asked John about this, he confirmed it. Did he tell "Mr. Parker" he was one of the two young guys who followed him to the Downbeat Club in Philly, I asked. He laughed and said no. John was shy about such things. However, when he returned home from Los Angeles, he had a few things to show us. We wanted to hear everything step by step, note by note.

John enjoyed regaling us with his adventures. He had played with Bird in a live session and met a whole raft of musicians we had heard only on records. He also brought back a new tune of Bird's, "Relaxing at Camarillo." When he played it for us in my basement, the first couple of bars sounded out of kilter. The upbeat was where the downbeat should be and vice versa. The guys listening thought it was just not right, so it took us awhile to get how hip this new song was. Most of us were still learning, with John now in the lead.

While we were together in Philly learning how to play, John Coltrane was always a bit ahead of the rest of us (except for Jimmy Heath, who was also brilliant in his own way). I always admired how quickly and gracefully John took on new challenges while the rest of us were still considering what he had just taught us. As I look back, it's as if John were not exactly from our time period. John's mind was always on tomorrow. He looked forward constantly, asking, seeking. How could he improve today in order to discover things belonging to the future? John never lingered in one place. History failed to earn his attention. John was a searcher, consistently ahead of his time. He reached for musical excellence and artistic perfection in absolutes—ironic, in retrospect, because he was already in the process of creating jazz history.

The fact is that John Coltrane was restless, always stretching and reaching, always *supposing*, just as we did together walking home that night in Philly after listening to Charlie Parker outside the Downbeat Club. On the deepest level, perhaps more than Bird and virtually all others, John was never satisfied with what he accomplished. He always knew something else was possible, in the cosmic vastness or in the depths of his own mind. He constantly probed, pushed, analyzed, and rethought everything. John knew he'd eventually get to it—whatever "it" was. Later in his career, some musicians put John down, and others misunderstood him, because he embraced a sound that seemed too "far out." To some, John was attracted to outlandish ideas. But consider the way a diamond looks upon first discovery: rough, in need of chisel and polish. John Coltrane was such an unsculpted original, raw and authentic. The source material of artistic history is inevitably carved from granite quarries and nearly inaccessible diamond mines. When an avant-garde innovator unearths something previously unknown, often he is thought to be a fool. Later when the idea achieves widespread acceptance, the outcast becomes a god or a genius. Sometimes such accolades are true. John was a genius of musical exploration. At least once, on stage, John removed the horn from his mouth, let it hang around his neck, approached the microphone, and beat his chest, adding animalistic sounds as punctuation. After that set, his drummer asked him what had inspired the chest thumping. John replied that he "couldn't think of anything else to play." Apparently, he had depleted his mind's inspiration and the limit of his instrument—but only for a moment.

Most student saxophone players in Philly schools also received clarinets. When John got his clarinet, he disappeared for several weeks, as he often did. Tom and Ray Bryant had moved into the projects across town on Parrish Street. When John returned from seclusion, he brought his clarinet to our gig. When we played "Body and Soul," he played a heartfelt rendition on clarinet. We were all amazed that he had mastered that difficult instrument so quickly.

As John and I became professionals, we lost the habit of spending all our time together. Instead of practicing together almost daily, we received "on the job training" as the demand for our playing steadily increased. Soon John briefly joined a quintet led by Johnny Lynch, who played trumpet in Dizzy Gillespie's first big band. Lynch was a good trumpeter and landed decent gigs after he came back to Philly. One such gig was at the South Philly roller-skating rink every Sunday afternoon. (There was no roller-skating on Sundays, only his quintet's music.) The band had a good repertoire and sounded terrific. Nonetheless, John left that job for a three-week gig touring the East Coast with Eddie "Cleanhead" Vinson. Cleanhead played alto sax and sang the blues. When he left Cootie Williams's band, Cleanhead decided to use East Coast musicians instead of bringing a band out from Kansas City. He hired John on alto, Johnny Coles on trumpet, Louie Judge on tenor, and Shuggie Otis on bass. The drummer may have been Charlie Rice. I don't recall the pianist.

One night Cleanhead and Louie had a significant argument. After the intermission, all of the musicians came back out on stage, except Louie. He decided to demonstrate his anger by showing up late. Cleanhead kicked off the second set without him. At that point a beautiful thing took place. When they had left for intermission, the musicians had placed their instruments on their stage chairs. Not long after the music resumed, a tenor sax solo was in order. With Louie Judge nowhere in sight, Cleanhead told John to grab Louie's horn and take Louie's solo slot. It wasn't John's horn. He was reluctant and refused to pick up the horn. After a few more bars, Cleanhead repeated his demand louder, more urgently. John remained noncompliant, so Cleanhead yelled out loud. "Pick up the horn! Pick it up now!"

John picked up Louie's horn just in time for the solo. Johnny Coles told me that John sounded fantastic. His sound was not unlike Dexter Gordon's. Louie, who had been in seclusion pouting, emerged running across the dance floor. He jumped up onto the bandstand and belligerently grabbed his horn from John's neck strap. The scene must have been a combination of Keystone Kops and outright weirdness. Coles reported not only that John Coltrane's sound on tenor was unique but also that John told him those few bars gave him an entirely different feeling for the horn, and he was fascinated. Soon after, John bought a cheap tenor sax and hauled it to his gigs (along with his alto) at the skating rink. Though he regarded the tenor sax at first as a novelty, he came to rely on it more and more. The alto became the novelty and then was gone completely.

In short, somewhere around 1950 a new musical birth took place for John, and from then on John Coltrane was a tenor saxophonist. From that moment forward he was on a mission, trying to accomplish something unearthly and eternal before time ran out. Increasingly his practicing was spartan, rigorous, unbroken, consuming him from early morning until past midnight. Mary, John's cousin, said that when they were living in the same apartment, neighbors complained about his interminable practicing. The ensuing solution was perfect. His pastor gave him keys to the church so that he could practice undisturbed. Seeking something beyond style, John explored the enormity of the unfamiliar, the unknown. In the years that followed, although his restless spirit did not permit him to play with complete satisfaction, he played with a sense of exploration and adventure where no limits existed. John pushed his music into an undefined terrain of previously undiscovered elastic possibilities.

During this time, I went to hear John at a club called Emerson's, at 15th and Catherine Streets in Philly. I heard his powerful horn outside the entrance. The huge sound of his horn suffused every brick of the building. I stepped inside and felt his blast of monomaniacal, immoderate creativity rip through the dimly lit, smoked-filled room. John's playing was an erupting volcano, its uncontained authority raging over everyone. He had covered an enormous distance in a short time. He was launching himself across artistic and cultural history by the sheer force and demonic beauty of his talent.

During this transformative time in his life, John accepted an offer to play with Johnny Hodges, his earlier hero. He replaced Al Sears, who played on Rabbit's hit "Castle Rock." Sears also played with Duke Ellington but was not up to Ben Webster's level even though he seemed to fit Duke's artistic concept. Johnny Hodges's septet added Lawrence Brown on trombone and John on tenor sax alongside the alto/trumpet front line. Al Sears was a "boot 'em up" player very different from John. For some enigmatic reason, John never told Johnny Hodges that he had been John's boyhood idol.

Not long afterward, in 1955, John landed a job for me on a special tour with Billy Eckstine's band. John's style then carried a sort of hopping and skipping attack, musical pointillism perhaps. His style changed, of course, as he kept driving to find something unique, unlike anyone else's approach to horn playing. Do I need to say that John finally achieved his goal?

Because we were old friends and neither of us was making much money, during the Eckstine tour John and I decided to stay at YMCAs all along the route. We shared one bed to save money. It was a drag trudging to a common bathroom for everyone on the hallway. But it put a few more dollars in our pockets. Since we liked southern cooking, and the tour was in the South, every morning we headed out to find a restaurant that served brains and eggs, sausage, grits, gravy, and biscuits. To us, that was the breakfast of champions. Also, we both loved southern-baked sweet potato pies. One day we discovered a place with six-inch pies, perhaps fifteen in the showcase. I bought three or four. John bought the rest. When John and I found food we liked a lot, we ate until our stomachs protested.

The next morning, all our sweet potato pies were gone. John ate at least twice as many as I did, which made the bus ride a special experience for him that day. We had to stop over and over for John to take care of personal business. I have a photo of this band, labeled "South Carolina, 1955," but John isn't in the picture. He was in a restroom.

When I first met John Coltrane, he played his alto saxophone exactly like Johnny Hodges. John liked a song called "There's No You," by Hal Hopper. Every time John came to my house, he played it with a big, beautiful sound. If John had continued to play his alto, he would have become one of the strongest possible alto players. I've heard few on that horn perform the way he did. What a sound! Not long after he picked up the tenor sax, his favorite tune became "Time Was." Could he ever play that song! As usual, John was reinventing music.

Later that year, Miles Davis added drummer Philly Joe Jones to his group. Soon, he needed a tenor player for his increasingly famous quintet, because Hank Mobley was leaving to perform on his own. Miles asked Philly Joe for a recommendation. John Coltrane's name came up, but Miles had never heard of him. Pressed for more details, Philly Joe probably made the understatement of his life; when asked, "Can this guy play?" he replied simply, "Yes."

When John left Philadelphia to join Miles, all the rest of us left, vicariously, with him. The new quintet began to rehearse and I ran into John on Columbia Avenue some time later, where most of our matinee jam sessions had taken place a few years earlier. John told me that everything was going great but that Miles needed material. "Do you have any tunes?" he asked.

Did I have any tunes? Does Ford make cars? Since I passed my compositions around like calling cards (nobody paying any attention), I had many to choose from. I decided to give Miles only one. Too much of a good thing creates confusion. One good song, I felt, might have more impact. Recently, I'd written what I called the "crazy tune" because the structure was somewhat aberrational, just possibly strange enough that Miles might like it. So I gave John the song. Two weeks later I ran into him again. Before I could say anything, John blurted enthusiastically, "Remember that tune you gave me? Miles recorded it. He really dug it!"

I couldn't believe my ears. Miles Davis recorded one of my songs! Wow! Not long before, James Moody had recorded another one of my tunes, "Blues Walk," and that earned me a little bit of attention. This time, Miles's version of my crazy tune "Stablemates"—with my name listed as composer—put me on the map. After that bit of good luck, many to whom I had given lead sheets now retrieved them from the trash pile or from under their beds or from the backs of desk drawers. Miles's recording one of my pieces prompted people to look at my writing again. Before long, it felt as if everybody were recording my tunes. Within a few years, innumerable recordings of my compositions were in circulation. I owe that success to John Coltrane, who initially took my oddball song to Miles Davis. "Stablemates" was the song that did it for me, simply because Miles Davis recorded it. Not long after, John told me that he liked the way he handled my quirky new song on Miles's Prestige recording better than his playing on Paul Chambers's Contemporary Records session soon after.

During the period he was working with Miles, John wrote a song and sold it to Miles. "Weird Blues" was a chromatic-inflected tune in the tradition of Monk's "Straight, No Chaser." John told me how he arrived at the strange melody. He was working with a guitar player who wasn't very good. In fact, he was just plain bad—so bad that it was difficult for him to stay in the same key throughout a tune. In order to find his way forward, he would play ascending chromatics (notes ascending step by step) until he found the key again—thus, John's "Weird Blues." All kinds of things inspire tunes, it seems.

Working with Miles was a good move for John's phenomenally fast-advancing career. But John remained restless. When he finally decided to form his own group, a quartet, he chose McCoy Tyner on piano, Jimmy Garrison on bass, and Elvin Jones on drums. This quartet, impressive from the start, became legendary. It's humorous for me to recall how McCoy joined that group. I was working in Philly one Sunday afternoon with a local rhythm section. Nineteen-year-old McCoy Tyner was the piano player. He could really play! To find out how good he was, I called a tune in a strange key—one of the keys jazz musicians usually neglect or avoid, such as E, F-sharp, or B (I don't remember which). But McCoy played it as though he were in B-flat, a familiar key. Then and there I knew this young pianist was ready. I didn't forget him after that gig. When Art Farmer and I were forming our Jazztet, I wanted McCoy to be our pianist. John heard him somewhat later and stole him from me—at least that's what I laughingly told him. McCoy told me that John struggled with his decision to ask him to join his group. Our long friendship tugged at John's conscience, but John's quartet was where McCoy belonged; he and John were on similar, equally exciting, wavelengths.

John had now gained a stature neither of us would have guessed possible in our early, struggling days in Philly. He wound up exactly where he deserved, on the top rung of tenor saxophonists. He continued his self-denying, labor-intensive, excruciatingly difficult practice regimen. The reward, however, was even greater than the effort to attain it. If you rang the bell to his apartment while he was practicing, and if Naima, his wife at the time, was not home, there would be no response because John refused to stop his routine to answer the door. No one could interrupt his obsessive practicing.

Some have noted a thin line between genius and madness. The kind of intensity found in Vincent van Gogh, Pyotr Tchaikovsky, John Keats, Jackson Pollock, Budd Schulberg, Robert Schumann, and Vaslav Nijinsky offers an object lesson in artistic focus.

I don't know about madness in John's dedication to his craft, but I do know his genius. He functioned with immense scrutiny of his horn, of musical structures, and of his own technique, and out of his passion he created the greatest possible music during his time on earth. John moved forward with Judas Maccabeus's stride. His energy achieved the nearly impossible—a truly new way to write and play music. I suppose all of us, in seeking our best individuality, are creative components of larger forces. John epitomized that fact, documenting past and present possibilities even as he created his (and our) artistic future.

In the end, I wonder how creativity can be measured. Psychological examinations of inspiration and influence aside, creativity is doubtless measured by the way an artist's work is accepted: by the persuasive reach of meaningful things he or she coaxes into existence. Inevitably, the arbiter of artistic worth is the extent to which a creation lasts past its creator's lifetime. Permanence, longevity, and endurance are the ultimate, implacable measures of artistic worth. Seeing or hearing new shapes come to life out of nothingness can be an overwhelming experience. Successful artistic achievement brings pressure to create and perform at even greater intensity. Such inner fire goads not only the artist but his audience, too. Great artists create their own spotlight. People are attracted to bright light. Such a brilliant luminosity was John Coltrane.

Though John's approach to the saxophone was quite different from mine and from that of most of our predecessors, he genuinely appreciated the older masters, such as Don Byas, Ben Webster, Johnny Hodges, and

Willie Smith. All of us respected our forebears, but even after John gained a wide reputation as a saxophonist, he was prompted to write a five-page letter of powerful appreciation to Coleman Hawkins. Hawkins was so pleased that he called his drummer, Eddie Locke, and asked him to read John's letter. Jimmy Heath heard about the letter after Hawkins's death and asked Eddie if, just possibly, that letter could be found. It would have been a treasure, but unfortunately the letter was by then long gone. However, a funny thing soon happened. John went to see Hawkins and took Eric Dolphy with him. Hawkins spoke to both of them for a while, and then, looking at Eric, said, "I don't worry about you. I can out-melody you." John and Eric laughed that night and long after.

I have spoken with many young players on the scene who have expressed deep appreciation for those who came before them. Joshua Redman and Joe Lovano are two. John had it right. Musicians are frequently encouraged, influenced, and inspired by their predecessors.

In the summer of 1957, John and I were warming up in the same tent at the Newport Jazz Festival in Newport, Rhode Island. John was preparing for a performance with his quartet, and I was warming up to perform with Dizzy Gillespie's big band. Suddenly, John took his horn out of his mouth and laughed. "Do you remember what your mother said that night when we were so dejected about being thrown out of Jimmy Johnson's band?" he asked. "Sure," I replied. "Well, we're here and they're still there." Our laughter filled the tent.

During the many days, months, and years John and I spent together, we never competed with each other. We were pals, plain and simple. Each of us admired the other. In 1957, to my surprise I won the Downbeat Poll in two categories: best "new star" saxophonist (though I felt Johnny Griffin deserved it) and best new star arranger. The next year I won it again as best new star saxophonist! I don't recall if or when John won a "new star" award. It didn't matter to either of us, because something far more significant awaited us both, especially John.

Stan Getz had been acknowledged as the number one tenor saxophonist for a few years. Stan was always one of my favorites, but everybody finally had to acknowledge that John was a phenomenon walking in nobody else's footsteps. John searched in places never before visited musically, uncharted musical territory that contained ideas defying the banality of names. No one walked with him; we all merely followed if we could, or watched him forge ahead by himself. I do not consider it an overstatement to say that John Coltrane had entire constellations of ideas within him.

Hearing John on a recording was one thing. Hearing him in a club was another. The first time a person heard John perform live, something profound must surely have taken place for that listener. This was an experience that would change the way anyone heard his music. What a humbling experience to apprehend genius directly.

No matter how fast he played, no matter how many ideas he articulated, you always heard the blues—not the structure of twelve bars, but the feeling of the blues itself. If any element of the world's force or complexity entered John's music or his playing, it was solely a byproduct of his artistic intention. John was about music, not the world—only art. John's solos eventually took on qualities beyond the structures of the tradition he inherited. They sometimes explored arabesque musical concepts and complexities rivaling the Pythagorean theorem. John's playing could seem to be factoring irrational numbers or topological space. How can we account for these qualities? Perhaps John's intellectual curiosity, his artistic desire, and his ferocious emotional commitment—alongside his insatiable attraction to the esoteric—launched such passionate forays.

My son Reggie and Duke Ellington's nephew, Stephen, both loved Elvin Jones. They never missed an opportunity to hang out with Elvin wherever he was playing. Both were aspiring drummers. One day at Rudy Van Gelder's studio in Hackensack, New Jersey, they were awaiting John's arrival from Philly to finish an album. John was two hours late, extremely apologetic, and went to work right away, "so quickly," Reggie told me, "that he recorded the first tune without removing his overcoat."

My friend of many years, this former North Carolina country bumpkin, had traveled a million miles and would travel another million in pursuit of his elusive goal: artistic perfection. John knew that absolute artistic perfection was not possible, but I sensed that he was at war with his own mortality. John wanted to accomplish as much as humanly possible in one lifetime. He derived a certain satisfaction from reaching for this elusive perfection. That endeavor, more than an inclination but a kind of maniacal affinity for an Ultimate, fired his creative imperative. In his quest for perfection, John Coltrane made discoveries that laid the foundation for the future of music. John Coltrane was a musical pioneer with the force of a constantly enlarging tsunami.

I suspect that I knew John better than most because we grew up together and were inseparable as teenagers. In retrospect, I see that John was like a crouching tiger always ready to pounce. His mind never rested. I've never known anyone so bonded to a skill or goal as John Coltrane or seen elsewhere such otherworldly devotion to an art. Unforeseen occurrences terminated John's quest, yet his accomplishments prevail across the nearly half a century since his death. His accomplishments challenge us today and will surely remain a permanent legacy in jazz history. John is gone, but his life continues as an inextinguishable example of spiritual nobility.

PART II
The 'Hood and Youthful Reckonings

Composer supreme, tenor man supreme, jazz man supreme, good guy supreme: that's BENNY GOLSON!

    —SONNY ROLLINS

CHAPTER 4

Uncle Robert and the Man

A S A YOUNG BOY, I quickly came to understand that there were differences between white people and black people that went beyond skin color. Injustices against black people did not make me angry. They made me feel inferior. That feeling followed me until the time I entered junior high school. The terrible racist things I saw and read about were overwhelming, wrong, and thoroughly unfair. I thought they would never end in my lifetime.

When I was eight years old, in 1937, a small group of us visited Georgia, the graciously unenlightened South. My mother's brother, my Uncle Robert, came with us. Uncle Robert was a man who could be pushed only so far, and then he became somebody else, potentially violent. I did not yet understand the tense situation between blacks and whites in the South. Nor did I understand that the tensions between black people and white people were legal and economic as well as social and political differences, but I soon found out. We drove all night on our trip and found ourselves lost, in a small, unfamiliar town in Georgia. Uncle Robert sought directions from a nearby policeman on a street corner. The cop was a very large white man. Uncle Robert pulled the car up beside him, leaning out to inquire, "Hey, bud, how do we get to—" He was stopped roughly, mid-sentence, by an unfriendly voice: "What did you say to me?" Uncle Robert started to repeat his question: "How do we get to . . ." "No," the cop insisted, approaching the car. "That's not what you said, nigger!" Uncle Robert stuttered, discombobulated. He couldn't figure out what the policemen wanted and I didn't understand why the glowering officer was angry. I'd never seen my fearless uncle so confused.

An arm's length from Uncle Robert, the cop demanded an answer. "What did you call me?" Pulling back, my uncle retraced his linguistic steps. Apologetically, he replied haltingly. "Oh . . . 'Bud'!" The policeman stepped even closer, polishing the dirty car with his clean blue uniform, his club at the ready. "If you even think of calling a white man 'Bud' again, someone like me will bash your head in. Understand?" My uncle cringed like a kid about to take a beating from his father. I didn't understand the whole thing. A strong black man was humbled before my young eyes. He doubtless felt humiliated, too, his behavior thoroughly self-erasing, as he apologized in a blatantly "Uncle Tom" manner. Uncle Robert had no choice. He was trapped. When we pulled away, I knew that something was completely skewed. The world was very different in this part of our native land.

I have since heard, seen, and experienced many things like that. Eventually I came to understand Uncle Robert's on-the-spot transformation in the presence of that intimidating white Georgia cop. Everything would be all right for us as long as we "stayed in our place." Over time, I learned what that *place* was. We were subordinated to white power, capricious but fearsome. It disturbed me deeply. The entire situation was wrong. Couldn't the law do something about it, I wondered?

As I matured, I discovered that the law itself perpetuated racism. The law was frequently blind, and frequently retreated from the cause of fairness. The law and justice, I realized, are entirely different things. In the South, when black and white clashed, when an accusation was hurled against a black man, law and justice were never coordinated. Repeatedly, the law was employed indiscriminately as a weapon against black people. When a black man stood accused, whether he was the guilty party mattered not at all: Things could always be improved with one less nigger.

All this was bad enough, but I soon became aware of something unhealthy within the black population, too. The lighter a black person's skin, the better the person regarded himself. Darker-skinned blacks treated lighter-skinned blacks as if the latter were, in fact, better. I remember the pride black men often displayed if their wives or girlfriends were lighter skinned. This was false pride; establishing a relationship with a lighter-skinned woman was a conquest or accomplishment. Why? Because a person with jet-black skin was at the bottom of the social ladder. I remember comments from people in my community ranking one another in this manner. A neighbor or acquaintance might be said, derogatorily, to be "too black."

Lighter-skinned blacks ranked higher socially simply because their skin color was closer to that of the white man, who was king. A popular movie appeared during that vexed time when skin color was so self-consciously important within the black community. Louise Beavers, a black actress, starred in a film called *Imitation of Life*. Beavers played a black domestic servant who had given birth to a child fathered by a white man. The child, named Peola, looked white. After this movie, which virtually every black person saw, it became common to refer to a light-skinned black person as a "Peola." More than a designation of personal identification, the name came to characterize a subrace within the black population. (The previous term for these "fortunate," light-skinned blacks, "high yellow," was not abandoned; both designations were used.) Understanding very little of all this, as a boy I thought that lighter-skinned blacks must be genuinely superior in some way I could not grasp. In short, I absorbed a mythic view of color and rank held by others who were even more perplexed than I was. After all, I was a kid. How could I think through this communal confusion? One thing was clear, however. Some light-skinned black people had naturally straight, soft hair. They did not need the hot straightening combs or curlers that other blacks used to treat their hair. These blacks were the ones who could most easily pass for white, particularly if they spoke "like a white person." If a "Peola" married a white person and the couple had children, they were disliked intensely by darker-skinned "colored people," as we were called in those days. Why such disdain? These lighter-skinned folks denied—in fact, sought to obliterate—their racial origins. For selfish reasons, they left others of their native race behind socially. They had no sense of brotherhood with their own people. "Peolas" thought they were better than the rest of us, we felt. They strove to prove their "superiority," and living as whites they faced fewer obstacles in life than darker-skinned folks. They felt, without guilt or conflict, that their lighter skin elevated their intrinsic worth.

Such racial self-inflation is not as widespread in black communities today, but it still persists. As strange as it may seem, a black person almost always recognizes another black person no matter how light the person's skin, how narrow the nose, how thin his or her lips, how perfect his or her diction, or how "elegant" the person's lifestyle. Over time, many black people have "passed" for white, both male and female. Some may have enjoyed happy and productive lives, carrying their secret to the grave. Seeing them passing among whites, other blacks often wonder why the white community does not see the subtle truth before them. White people sometimes ask how we recognize racial kinship. Some answer, truthfully, that they don't know how they know—they just know. Apparently, in Eastern Europe, gypsies are able to identify other gypsies immediately. Doubtless, in both of these cases, it's intuitive.

In the mid-1930s, I became aware that Uncle Robert was an avid baseball fan. I had no interest in sports at the time. (Much later, in the 1980s I became obsessed with boxing, a sport—the "sweet science," it is sometimes called—that absolutely intrigues me). In my youth, baseball was racially segregated. Blacks who had talent and wanted to play professionally had to join the Negro League, formed in 1920. Knowing nothing about baseball, and having little interest, only slowly did I acquire superficial knowledge of the sport. In my neighborhood, I constantly heard the heroic name, Satchel Paige, a pitcher with the Kansas City Monarchs. (Jackie Robinson was revered, too, but that came later.) Another prominent name uttered often was Josh Gibson, a power-hitting catcher for The Homestead Grays. By the time Paige went to the majors, with the Cleveland Indians, he was past his prime. In fact, when he played his final game in 1965, he was fifty-nine years old. He was the oldest player in the history of major league baseball. In fact, many old timers regarded the wily Satchel Paige as quite possibly the best pitcher in history. Maybe so, but Gibson hit 972 home runs, a feat no one else ever achieved, including Hank Aaron, Barry Bonds, and Babe Ruth. That rare accomplishment took place over the span of a relatively few years. When Gibson died of a stroke at thirty-five years of age, he was still a young man who should have achieved much more.

Many black teams played the baseball circuit during my formative years. I don't remember their names, but I do remember that many of them played in Philadelphia. While they never played at famous stadiums, but on naked fields, they drew large crowds. Baseball was a huge focus in black neighborhoods in the summertime. One field where blacks played in Philly was located at the corner of 25th and Diamond. I never went to a game there, but I often rode past that field in the car with my family. I saw and heard joyful crowds watching black baseball heroes whose fame was sadly limited by the prejudices of an otherwise inspiring era of American sports. Heroic baseball adulation in our world usually began with the uniquely great Satchel—and, unfortunately, it nearly ended there. Finally, in the mid-1950s, the Brooklyn Dodgers' Branch Rickey found the courage to buck racial exclusion. He signed Jackie Robinson, who eventually awed many white players, including the baseball commissioner, and touched white fans, although in his first years of playing in the majors, he endured insulting, brutal treatment. He heard every derogatory term a man can encounter and was the victim of the dirtiest tactics that could be perpetrated against him in broad daylight. I remember how tough it was for Robinson. I was a teenager wholly aware of bigotry, segregation, subordination, and the stress they cause.

Life's lessons are often ponderous or difficult to absorb. Many people avoid grappling with problems or seek merely to dull their pain. Yet, of this I'm certain. People in my neighborhood enormously resented the treatment of blacks in all areas of American life. Black people were no less loyal to their country, no less patriotic, than whites, and blacks went to war for their country, for ideals they believed in even if those ideals were not honored to the benefit of black people. Blacks were shut out from professional sports for much too long to experience it as "justice" when the supposedly free commercial market of "open" competition was finally established. When Joe Louis won a fight, however, doors all along our block burst open, and people ran wild through the neighborhood, singing over and over: "Joe Louis, world champion!" Hilarity and joy took over the streets. Our block became animated like the best MGM musical on the finest Hollywood soundstage. People danced with abandon, from the happiness born of honor long denied.

But even a joy such as this was short lived. Through that era, we lived day by day with the terror of bigotry, sometimes subliminal. Racism is an aberration, terror in its subtlest, most insidious form. Such negative energy could not be fully contained; we all felt it. Racism was triumphant because its deepest wounds were hidden. To whom could we complain? The blues were our constant companion, and with the blues, you're supposed to pick yourself up. No question: everyone who reveled in the euphoria of Joe Louis's heroic victories entered a momentarily altered state of consciousness, an involuntary but visceral response to deep, pent-up emotions. I am certain now that those essentially ritual celebrations of black athletic accomplishments were transitory escapes from the constant, nearly unendurable pain in our brave world. Such spasms of victory no doubt offered profound if fleeting hope to black people. Briefly, redemptively, all black hearts sang as one.

CHAPTER 5

Two Heroes and a Night at Minton's

ANYONE WATCHING a small boy walking with his father soon notices that he imitates his father's gait and gestures. The little guy wants to be just like the big guy. Imitation is not just the sincerest form of flattery, but a sign of admiration and love. I was once a little fellow whose dad didn't come around as often as I wished he would. My father, therefore, never really understood what I was up to musically. He never encouraged me. That mattered not in the least because, whenever he appeared, my heart leapt with joy. I didn't know about the problems he and my mother suffered. I knew only that I loved him. When my father came to the house, he would shout out the nickname he gave me: "Dick! Oh, Dick!"

Dick was my name, in his world, until I started high school. I didn't know why it was conferred. I didn't know why it disappeared. I didn't care because my father was my hero. That nickname conjured all sorts of fantasies—mainly that my dad was back! But it wasn't true; he wasn't back to stay. My parents separated well before I knew anything about the experience of having a mother and a father at home together. After my father returned from the Second World War, he suggested to my mother that they might get together again. I was beside myself at that prospect. Instead, they divorced. My dream of having a father who lived with us at home was shattered. Vicariously, I enjoyed the wholeness of family life when I visited school pals who lived with both parents. Kids endure.

Some of my most vivid memories date to when I was seven or eight years old. My Uncle Robert was working as a bartender at the New Deal Café in Philadelphia. One night he got into a heated argument with a customer, who stormed out shouting, "I'll get my gun and blow your head off!"

Philly was plagued by a gang called The Forty Thieves. They were notoriously vicious thugs. The outraged customer who threatened my uncle was one of them. Every bartender working at the New Deal Café knew that the owner kept a gun under the bar. When the gangster returned, angrily bursting through the door, Uncle Robert shot him in the chest. Fortunately, the shot was not fatal. The police did not arrest Uncle Robert because everyone heard the customer threaten him. I learned of this incident not long after it happened, and I regarded Uncle Robert as a hero. I had seen many bad guys and good guys shoot it out in Saturday afternoon movie matinees. The good guy *always* won. Uncle Robert won. He was a hero—a completely good guy. Over and over, I thought to myself, "Nobody better mess with my Uncle Robert." I needed a hero and he was my hero.

In fact, Uncle Robert was a very nice guy who would go to any length to make, and then keep, peace. I didn't understand that then. After the shooting, I assumed he would shoot anybody who got in his way. Bang! The end of troubles. Actually, my uncle was a bad guy only when there was no other way out of trouble; the rest of the time, he was a quiet man whom very few sought to take advantage of. Eventually my nice-guy heroic uncle moved to New York and took a job tending bar at the iconic Minton's Playhouse in Harlem. I learned a great deal from my uncle and fortunately that relationship continued after he moved.

While I was growing up I discovered the genuinely encouraging fact that, if the odds were fifty-fifty in a serious dispute or confrontation, you could count on bullies, thieves, killers, intimidators, and gangster henchmen to scurry like rats out of danger. Their strength lay in manipulating situations so that the odds were on their side. Gangsters were cowards who depended on superior firepower, counting more thugs on their side than on the other guy's side, or stacking strength against any individual who became their enemy. When such low-life characters did not run off, it was usually because their own anger or fanaticism blinded them. I saw evidence of this many times in my neighborhood. Toughness is not an absolute quality. It usually depends on group support. That's why gangs are so prevalent. Gangs allow a group of otherwise cowardly young men to feel like big shots. Even on an international level, you see that cowards look to escape when they become anxious or fearful. A lack of courage is apparent both on the playground and in military combat, when the stakes of aggression are much higher.

A fairly ordinary incident cemented my understanding of street politics. One night on his way home, when Uncle Robert was well into his seventies, he was assaulted by four teenagers. Since he always carried large sums of money as a numbers runner, they found a bonanza. A few weeks later, on his way home once more, the same teenagers pushed their luck. Uncle Robert was carrying two bags of groceries. This time when they grabbed him, he was ready for them; he dropped the bags, a gun ready in his right hand. Before they could flee, my uncle put a slug into one kid's stomach. The kid screamed but kept running in pain. More shots were fired, to no avail. The kids disappeared like scared rats into darkness. Apparently no one reported my uncle's shot fired in self-defense, and he had no further trouble from these teenagers or from anyone else. The word was out. Uncle Robert was gloriously "crazy."

All of that provides a preface to my uncle's ongoing and somewhat zany influence on my maturation. When I was thirteen years old, in 1942, my mother took me to New York City to visit him. Uncle Robert had moved to Pittsburgh, trying to scratch out a living during the Great Depression, but he had found little success there, so the big city called his name. In Harlem, 125th Street was a sort of a cultural and racial crossroads, the center of black activity in uptown Manhattan. A pluralistic society, Harlem was far more integrated racially than elsewhere. It was a microcosm of the nation's future. Many people, living happily or unhappily in Harlem, never went downtown. They were parochial. They felt safe uptown. Why stretch their luck?

Uncle Robert worked at Minton's Playhouse, legendary for jam sessions that sometimes ran through the wee hours into daylight and early breakfast. Those sessions brought many great musicians together. In 1942, bebop was gaining energy and style at Minton's. The entire scene was avant-garde, an enormously exciting time for jazz and for artistically inclined people of all kinds. The United States was at war in Europe and across the Pacific Ocean, but a musical renaissance was happening in Harlem. I had no particular interest in jazz then; I wanted to be a concert pianist. But Uncle Robert promised that he would take me to Minton's to "dig the scene" and to hear the new music evolving there. I was introduced to Teddy Hill, the manager in charge who, in earlier times, had had his own band. He sat me in a corner out of the way. Soon, musicians began arriving. I remember a trumpet player named Joe Guy. Oran "Hot Lips" Page also showed up, as well as a fellow named Thelonious Monk, playing stride piano.

Years later, I would come to know Monk and learn that he was a master table tennis player. The only reason I recognized Monk's stride piano style was the prominence of his strong left hand, veering back and forth like Uncle Robert's and Uncle Dewey's when they played their versions of stride. A tenor player named Jack McVea appeared, too. I recalled his name soon after on a recording from Norman Granz's *Jazz at the Philharmonic*. Sugar Ray Robinson, the great prizefighter, came in and Uncle Robert introduced me to him. Neither Sugar Ray nor the musicians meant much to me at the time, as I had no idea who they were. I now realize how ironic it is that while my first visit to Minton's allowed me to witness history unfold, I had no sense of the importance it would have to my own career, soon to take root. Unawares, I experienced an early moment of the artistic heritage that the majority of my life has now traversed. Fortunately, my memory of that evening is still crystal clear.

Fourteen years later I played on that overcrowded stage myself, as many of my predecessors had done. I began my musical travels across New York's clubs and dives with rhythm-and-blues groups. We often worked the Apollo Theater, which meant my late nights were free for jam sessions. I met a wonderful saxophonist, Musa Kaleem, one night when he was a leader at Minton's. Musa had a "big sound" in the tradition of Don Byas. He invited me to join him on stage. The first tune we played was "Whispering." That was a big deal for me. Musa Kaleem, now all but entirely forgotten, was a beautiful tenor sax player. Many years later, Jackie McLean remembered him. I was surprised to hear Musa's name because I had heard nothing of him after that jam session. He played so well that anyone would surely think his playing was memorialized on recordings. Not so, but at another of those Minton's sessions, I met Gildo Mahones, a ferocious pianist who held his own across the years. Even though I was not yet living in New York, I frequently met wonderful musicians there. I never told Teddy Hill (years later still managing Minton's) that I was the nephew of the bartender who brought me to his club as a juvenile observer one night when Sugar Ray was in his prime and Monk was deep into stride.

CHAPTER 6

Early Tragedies and Victories

I BECAME AWARE OF DEATH in grade school, but only when someone died of old age, sickness, or an auto accident. Other kinds of death were unknown to me. One summer vacation when I was nine or ten, I learned something new and shocking. A schoolmate who lived nearby, Sam, was about a year older than I was. He was a bully who tormented anyone who tolerated it. I hated to see him coming down the street because I knew he would threaten me. Although he never laid a hand on me, his threats were weapons that elicited my fear. He knew that. No doubt because he was not a good student, his tough guy attitude brought him needed attention and street credibility. He earned that deformed version of respect from many of us.

Most of us came from poor families, and our parents couldn't afford to send us to summer camp or to visit distant relatives. Spending summer outside the city was just a dream. In lieu of vacations, we did sometimes take day trips in the city itself, sometimes spending whole days wandering in Philadelphia's vast Fairmount Park. The park is beautiful during the summer months, and dotted with ponds. Exploring the park one day on his own, Sam-the-bully found one of the large ponds, lost his footing, and fell in. He couldn't swim. No one heard his cries for help, and he drowned, a victim of bad luck and his inability to swim.

Although Sam had been a constant bully who caused considerable strife, I wasn't happy to be suddenly released from the problems Sam caused me and others. He was dead. We would never see him again. I might have imagined I'd be glad to see Sam dead, if the thought had ever occurred to me, but instead I was sad. When we went to see him laid out in the funeral hall, he looked as if he had never been a living, talking person. Lying motionless in the silk confines of his casket, Sam wore a neat, clean new suit, his face washed and powdered like someone on his way to an important engagement. It was Sam-the-bully, and it was no one at all. It was like a horrible dream. *Why did people have to die?* I thought. His death must have been painful—yet the object who lay before us no longer felt pain. We passed his bier and saw his parents sobbing. They felt pain. He did not. I resolved that such an accident would not happen to me. But how to control such a thing as death? For weeks my stomach felt like a bowl of Jell-O. How I hated death. But more was to come.

Charles Spotts was a bright student in our school, quiet and never threatening to anyone—completely unlike Sam—and a model of good behavior. Yet he too met a shocking end. Doubtless, there were things we did not know about Charles. Apparently, a white man—a total stranger—talked Charles into participating in a robbery. Charles told his older brother, but his brother wasn't able to stop him, and one night, Charles and his acquaintance robbed a jewelry store in our neighborhood. Both Charles and his white accomplice escaped.

The story did not end there, however. The accomplice must have become afraid that Charles would report him to the police. A couple of days after the robbery, Charles was reported missing. The police searched for him and questioned everybody in the neighborhood, but found no leads. Separately, however, through a fluke someone reported strange behavior on the part of the man involved with Charles. Although I cannot recall what drew the police's attention to him, when they went to the accomplice's home, they met a sickening sight. Charles's body had been hacked to pieces and left in the bathtub for the blood to drain. The killer was about to dispose of Charles's remains when the police arrived.

The gruesome news hit the local newspapers. The neighborhood was aghast and enraged. Unbelievably, the man was sentenced not to death but to only a few years in prison. As we all knew, there was no semblance of justice between whites and blacks. I assume, but do not recall, that Charles Spotts's murderer was released from jail early—for "good behavior," perhaps. In the early 1940s, if a white person killed a black person, punishment was mild—usually a slap on the wrist. Of course, if a black man killed a white man, he drew the maximum punishment. I've never forgotten the horror of Charles's murder and the barbarity of the entire incident.

Murder, I later came to see, is a crime not only against society but also against God and life. No one has a right to take a life except God. An eye for an eye means anyone taking a life should forfeit his own: a life for a life is divine justice. I only know that now.

Another schoolmate, Herb Townsend, matured earlier than most of us. He enjoyed the inevitable spurt into manhood that most of us still eagerly awaited. Prior to adolescence, we were all curious about life's joys and possibilities, and there was nothing different about Herb. Around sixth grade, we heard our voices change. Some began exploring realms we had no previous knowledge of—alcohol, smoking, and sex with willing girls. Some of the guys, including Herb, tried everything. Herb had turned into someone I could not identify with. He began hanging out with rough crowds. As he grew tall and manly looking, he started manhandling others. As long as "his boys" were with him, he would challenge grown men. The rest of us were still engaged in innocent pastimes.

On the street just behind ours, there was a man who had a fairly high position in the city administration. He had a severe limp in one leg, but he always dressed neatly and treated everyone in the neighborhood courteously. To me, he seemed like a real gentleman. Somehow he and Herb crossed paths and an argument ensued. Herb threatened bodily harm. Looming over this mild-mannered, partially disabled man, Herb set out to make an impression on onlookers. He wanted to be seen as a tough guy. The quarrel unresolved, the two parted. Everyone knew where this gentleman lived. Herb soon showed up on his porch and rang his doorbell. When the door opened, Herb lunged at the man with a knife and missed. No doubt surprising to Herb, however, his intended victim was ready with a knife. Stepping to one side, this otherwise mild fellow drove his knife deep into the left side of Herb's chest, directly through the heart. Herb died in a pool of blood on the man's doorstep. Our schoolmate could not have been more than fourteen years old. The police let the assailant go because he was defending himself against an attack, but we were horrified at how Herb met his end. Wanting to be a man, he acted like a fearless brute. Unfortunately, he did not understand that manhood demands wisdom. Many of his youthful friends are still alive. Herb's tragic notion of how to be a man cheated him of more than fifty years of precious life.

I cannot overlook my own thuggish behavior. Across the street from our house lived a large but very shy boy. We used to call him a sissy. I had no trouble keeping him "under control"; I considered myself to be pretty tough. At the end of the summer one year, Wilbert Butler had suddenly grown much larger. To our surprise, he had also begun to "talk funny," like a white person. He was, in fact, speaking perfectly correct English, but that made him sound strange in the ghetto. "Who does he think he is?" I wondered. I sneered that he probably considered himself better than the rest of us, who spoke "normally," without "ing's" at the ends of our words. My accusation triggered more than I bargained for. Suddenly one day, Wilbert asked me menacingly, "Do you remember how you bullied me, before this summer?" I nodded assent. "You want to try it now?" he asked me. I looked at him more closely, then sheepishly backed off. The last word regarding Wilbert? He became a policeman—a *big* policeman.

I scratched various soils, hoping to strike spiritual and emotional pay dirt. Music was at the heart of the best moments of my youth. I remember arriving one afternoon at the Earle Theater, at 11th and Market Streets, just as the feature picture finished. Lionel Hampton's band was ready to kick off. The lights dimmed, and the innocuous house music came up. Seventy-five percent of the audience was teenagers like me, playing hooky. School was irrelevant that day. A backstage voice announced Lionel Hampton and his band. The band roared suddenly into gear, the curtain still closed. My breathing quickened. I was at the center of the universe, hearing live music that had previously entered my life only through recordings. The curtains opened slowly. First, saxophones across the front row; trombones right behind them; then, those magnificent drums, complete with shiny cymbals, speaking a language I did not yet comprehend. Trumpets blaring from the back row announced a joyful tumult to come. Milt Buckner was on piano; Earl Bostic, alto; Arnett Cobb, tenor. I don't remember the others; they melded into one great moment of erotic musical excitement, the likes of which I had never previously imagined. Hamp's ferocious aggregation was far more forceful than the majestic pipe organ that was often played between shows at the largest theaters. The audience was screaming. I screamed too; I felt like I'd been let out of confinement. What is an ordinary day of school if not, for most kids, prison? Hamp's band and its ecstatic, self-confident vibe was an emotional eruption. We were all, for the moment, suddenly free.

Over the years, as I heard more bands perform live, I began to notice that musicians often wore sunglasses even indoors, on stage. Some were shaped like aviator goggles, wrapping around the side of the face. Obviously, I thought, they wore shades to protect their eyes from the bright stage lights. Later I discovered my false assumption. Shades were cool, but they also hid signs of certain illegal private habits.

Hamp whipped his band into a frenzy. The players were beside themselves and we were in awe of their raw power. Just as I thought my emotions had climaxed, Earl Bostic stepped to the microphone playing "snakes," running up and down his horn with enormous precision, performing instrumental acrobatics. Only much later did I learn what a master he was, a preview in some ways of John Coltrane, fifteen years after him. Bostic received only a moderate crowd reaction that day, and the band segued into an interlude that seemed destined to lead to something significant. Arnett Cobb then rose from his seat with smooth aplomb and took the microphone.

This was an era of jazz giants. Ben Webster came on the scene along with Coleman Hawkins; Lester Young, Don Byas, Leon Brown ("Chu Berry"), and Dexter Gordon; Johnny Hodges and Bird along with Eddie "Cleanhead" Vinson. Here I was, enthralled before Lionel Hampton's surging power. It was all for me!

I'll never forget that pregnant moment. The band made a two-bar break and left a memorable interval of silence for Cobb to fill as he chose. Cobb played one note. He started well below the pitch, then slid soulfully up, with a moan that defied sound or speech. When he hit that first note of his solo and plunged into the famous tenor solo on "Flying Home," originally crafted by Jean Baptiste "Illinois" Jacquet, the theater exploded with deafening screams. I probably screamed the loudest. I was on the verge of physical spasms, my heart pounding against the walls of my young chest. If I had not exercised real self-control, I would have cried shamelessly with joy.

Looking back, I realize I was no different from the teenage girls at Sinatra concerts, or the crazed fans at Beatles gigs two decades after I swooned over Lionel Hampton. The heart dilates and the mind enters an altered state. The outcome is almost certain to be complete departure from one's normal character and behavior. Lionel Hampton's orgiastic concert was a historic event for me. This event preceded that concert in Philly when Bird and Diz took no prisoners, almost destroying me and Coltrane. The Hampton concert revamped my musical aspirations and helped to define my life's entire course. It was an ordinary day in Philadelphia, and I was incorrigibly naïve. My dream of becoming a concert pianist began to lose its appeal that day. This lyrical thunder, this majestic, joyful sound, changed my life. My present life was inaugurated that day, in the jazz church of Monsignor Lionel Hampton. I remain glad with all my heart that I was present to accept communion from him.

Of course, with radical change, consequences ensue. The piano, which I was still studying, was a significant force in my young life. After hearing Hamp's explosive band, I came home and did my homework as quickly as possible in order to spend the rest of the night listening to the radio in search of a four- or eight-bar saxophone break. The maximum length of seventy-eight-rpm records was three minutes. A full solo chorus was impractical, unless it was the peerless Coleman Hawkins laying down his classic "Body and Soul," in 1939. I was aware how trite radio programs were, but I had no choice except to succumb to the tastes of radio disc jockeys. I heard Bud Freeman with Benny Goodman, Tex Beneke with Glenn Miller, and Ben Webster with Duke Ellington. I had no idea who I was listening to; my aesthetic savvy was still gestating. My confused search for saxophone majesty and mayhem continued for months, until finally my mother noticed. Why my sudden interest in these broadcasts, she asked. I told her the truth: that I had heard Lionel Hampton's band and had developed a passion for the saxophone. She replied with an embarrassing question. Even the sweetest interrogation can feel like an accusation. "What kind of saxophone?"

I had no idea. I was caught like a deer in headlights. My reply was rudimentary: "The one with the curve at the top." I felt stupid, but at least I described the horn correctly. I knew we couldn't afford even an old sax from the pawnshop. I did not ask for one; I figured this was a dream never to be fulfilled. *C'est la vie.* I was sad about that, but not excessively discomfited by life's limits. I accepted that we were at the bottom of the economic ladder. We were poor, but I was a happy kid, and I didn't mope or lament.

We lived in a three-storey house that my mother had found the means to rent when we got off welfare a few years earlier. A furnace warmed the house in winter, and coal for the furnace was delivered to the basement. Originally, horse-drawn wagons made these deliveries, but that changed during the years we lived there. The truck that brought coal supplies to the neighborhood had three sections, each holding a ton of coal. Most people got one ton at a time. The truck backed up to the house, and the entire carriage was mechanically lifted up, then down at a thirty-degree angle. The coal slid through a small basement window into bins in the cellar. The sound of coal sliding down the chute was like an announcement to the neighbors. When any house received a three-ton delivery, everyone knew it, for the noise lasted a long time. I watched to see how many sections went into our neighbors' bins. A three-section delivery was a status symbol. Mother bought one ton at a time. She couldn't afford more and status was irrelevant to her.

Back in 1943, collectors came every month for rent payments. Each landlord owned several houses. One winter month, our landlord came to collect the rent just after a heavy snowstorm. A few days before, I had noticed a leak in the ceiling of my room, which was on the second floor in the rear. Our house had three storeys, but my room was the only one of the rooms we occupied that did not have a room above it. A roof needing repair sat over my room. Mother surmised that melted snow was seeping through holes that needed patching. She told the rent man this when he came to collect his money. Instead of offering to repair the roof, he told her to climb out onto the roof herself, and push the snow off with a broom. He offered this warped advice with a straight face. He meant what he said. We were appalled. Imagine how dangerous it would have been for my mother to crawl out with a broom onto an icy, sloping, snow-covered roof, two storeys above the ground. That disingenuous advice reflects the disregard the moneyed class held for those from whom they collected rents. Our payments made their bank accounts fat, but they held us in contempt. If we didn't like their accommodations, we could leave. Someone else would pay them on time, next month.

The crook who stuffed mother's payment in his breeches never repaired our roof. Mother never climbed out onto the roof with a broom. We endured the leak. This neglect and disdain defined black lives in black neighborhoods. Black folks were, at best, tenants and rent payers for the fraudulent privilege of living on The Man's property. We were treated like squatters, inconveniencing whites in their haughty self-inflation. The 'hood was, in truth, an extension of pre-Civil War conditions. Blacks took what we could get; we had few alternatives. Like it or get out. Whatever rights we thought we had were ignored or finessed by those who held power, property, and privilege. Our substandard living conditions were at the pleasure of landlords. Authorities with city, state, or federal jurisdiction rarely, if ever, supported us in any way or even acknowledged complaints of abuse or wrongdoing. Such reports were deferred endlessly until the complainant gave up. Life in the 'hood was framed by infinite versions of Catch-22. If we were not dead, what was the problem? If we were about to die, it was too late for anyone to help anyway.

In truth, black landlords were seldom more compassionate or helpful than white landlords. Luckily, mother found "roomers" who rented part of our house. Their payments helped defray our monthly costs. She worked every day, so it was my job to make the roomers' beds every morning and to change their linens once a week, usually Fridays. It was also my job to keep the house clean. I did that every Friday after school. I hated housework: scrubbing floors, sweeping carpets, and making beds. I would have been embarrassed if any of my pals had known, but at home there were only the two of us. I saw how hard my mother worked to see that I got a good education, and to make sure I had everything I wanted and needed, so I did my utmost to ask for very little. Our circumstances were sometimes precarious, though mother did everything in her control to hide those occasions from me.

If I hated housekeeping, I did enjoy cooking. It gave me great pleasure to see my mother walk home from the streetcar stop, take her shoes off, and sit down at our table to eat a meal I had cooked. She often told me I was a good son. She was a great mother long before I became a good son.

During the winter months we had no problem with hot water for baths. However, because our hot water pipes ran through the heater, which was part of the central heating system, in the summer we had no hot water. Friday night was almost always "bath night" in black neighborhoods. So, on Friday evenings after school, I kept three very large pots filled with water on the stove. I heated them to boiling, then lowered the flame so that the water stayed hot for anyone in our house who wanted to take a bath. This privilege, of course, demanded that each person take his turn in an orderly manner. Our house had protocols, and usually they operated smoothly. Maybe I *was* a good son. But determination and hard work were personal mantras from which my mother never deviated. My mother was my champion. She worked her fingers to the quick to support me in anything I cared about. I always knew that she would give her life for me. Nonetheless, with all of her love and unceasing encouragement, by today's legal strictures upon parental behavior, she would have spent time behind bars for the beatings she imposed on me when I strayed from her demanding tutelage. As a child, I was a handful. I remember vividly the exact thoughts and actions that got me into trouble. With anyone except my mother, my deeply selfish inclinations would have delivered me to far greater trouble. All by herself, my mother kept me on the right path. Her ironing cord, which she grabbed in fury, left me appearing (under my clothes) like a wounded zebra. After such beatings, which I sorely deserved, she nursed my welts. We were co-dependents in a melodramatic educational romance. I was the student who suffered, yet appreciated his lessons. She was the strict enforcer of the straight and narrow. I cannot remember ever having a negative feeling or thought against her tough love.

Today I flinch in disbelief when parents say, "I can't do a thing with little Johnny." During the early days of my childhood, no parent I knew made such a statement. Most parents in the 'hood had something heavy in wait for errant behavior. I owe everything I am today to that brave, selflessly loving, tireless woman who spent most of her life swimming upstream. For many of those years, I was in her frail arms or bouncing around jabbering at her side. My mother weighed perhaps one hundred and ten pounds. Slight of frame, she was a spiritual giant. Every lick she gave me was for my benefit. She inculcated the vision and self-discipline that have been axiomatic to me for most of my life and which I fall back on when I make decisions or accept responsibilities of every sort. Mother had to be 100 percent certain that I understood those principles. It is immensely fortunate for me that she was successful. Bless her over and over!

When mother was near the end of her life, after a long bout with cancer, I spent nights beside her hospital bed in a beach chair. She felt she was taking too much of my time and told me she was sorry I felt I had to do this. I told her it was simple: she carried me for nine months and nursed me from the bosom of her existence. She sacrificed her life so that I could have a good education and a successful career. She held my life above her own when disappointment and despair threatened to overwhelm me. She was, indeed, my greatest source of strength and encouragement. I wished I could do more, much more, I told her. Later she told one of her lady friends, "I guess Benny told me a thing or two."

The story of my life and how it was shaped by my mother's stern yet profoundly caring love is a story without a conclusion, for where I go today, her spirit goes. When I awaken in the morning, her life stirs inside me still. But one day in our lives together stands out. I clearly recall the morning my mother left for work, a day like any other, yet when she returned home that evening, the world tilted radically and unexpectedly in my favor.

I was sitting on the front steps as I often did when mother came home from work, and that afternoon, as usual, I saw her walk up our block from the streetcar. On this remarkable, ordinary day, however, she had what looked like a suitcase in her hand. I was puzzled. She hadn't had a suitcase with her when she left that morning. The case was elongated. My heart almost stopped. In a flash, a million reasons crossed my mind why she shouldn't and couldn't possibly be carrying this particular long, narrow case. But she was. As she drew closer, I saw her smile, a big and (for her) quite unusual smile. That smile lit up the entire block, and made me tremble with disbelief and anticipation. All the day's negative thoughts dissolved. Finally, she chuckled happily, "I've got somethin' for you, baby!"

I leaped from the steps, a newly minted Olympic sprinter. She uttered the immortal words I had only dreamed of: "I've got a saxophone for you." On this, the greatest afternoon in mankind's long saga, my mother had a new horn for me—a *brand new* saxophone! I wanted to shout. I wanted to hug her. I wanted to tear into this priceless package. We went inside. She put the case on the couch and let *me* open it. My excitement was beyond comprehension. My hands shook as I fumbled with the latches that fastened the case. I opened it and a chorus from Mount Olympus flooded the room. My brain was afire. Soon I would play with Coleman Hawkins and Ben Webster, a new star bursting from an ancient egg. Here we were at the dawn of an unprecedented era in humanity's continual advancement. I stood on the threshold of a musical career without rival, a horn player whose chops had never before been heard. I was flying inside myself.

After a microsecond of indulging these slippery fantasies, I was actually holding my saxophone. Here was the thing without which I remained unborn, isolated, desolate—a nude, slithering protoplasm without access to expression, uplift, enlightenment, aspiration: the instrument was my true DNA. *With this stately gift, I thee offer my plaintive hopes and pledge that never shall I, one Lord B. Golson, ever fail the codes of Louis Armstrong, Charles Parker, or any of the musical warriors who have gone before and may (if I allow) come after.*

Yes, here it was: my saxophone in my hands. I was a kid with enormous, but raw artistic hope and musical aspirations, and now I felt like a grown man in a maternity ward holding his newborn son or daughter after long uncertainty, doubt, and anticipation. My first genuine "ecstasy" had been deferred, luckily, until this precise moment. Moments later, as I looked at this unexpected new arrival, I suddenly became disheartened. I didn't know how to put the horn together. It was not mine if I could not navigate that simple, treacherous obligation. I had wanted something and I had been given it, but I now appeared a fraud.

I thought the neck (the "curve," as I called it) was a permanent part of the instrument. It lay separate and mute alongside the detached mouthpiece and the ligature that held the reed—the reed mocking its own muteness, distant from any possibility of musical expression. What a lame collection of disassembled parts whose coordination existed in some empire of hipness to which I had no access. I confessed my ignorance. I had no idea how to put the instrument together. I was happy and also mortified. My mother had purchased the exact horn that I wanted, a tenor saxophone, even though I had been unable to even name what I had in mind. She had figured it out; she made it happen for me. I was the crazy, dumb, deviant, precocious kid who pointed vaguely toward Nirvana. Now I was both blessed and cursed by the fulfillment of my desire.

Of course, my proud and generous mother had no better idea than I did how to assemble the instrument lying before us in pieces, looking like a disheveled tinker toy. Luckily, she remembered that three blocks away, on Bouvier Street near where we once lived, Tony Mitchell played a saxophone. He could rescue us! Immediately we headed to his house, only four doors from where we used to live. Once more mother saved me. Tony showed me how to assemble my horn. The horn would now truly become *my* horn. He put the reed into the mouthpiece with the ligature, with the neck strap holding the horn securely to free my putatively artistic hands. Tony cradled the new instrument and advised me sweetly. I stood in the middle of Tony Mitchell's living room with my very own saxophone around my neck. If I looked impressive to anyone anywhere the universe, it was my own illusion.

Tony asked me to "play something." My first bleats sounded like an animal being slaughtered. It was awful. Mercifully, Tony put on a Duke Ellington recording of "Raincheck," and took my horn. He played my horn right along with Duke's band. He sounded fantastic. I had hardly known Tony before this happy occasion, but he suddenly appeared a hero. "My" horn was wonderful, my new best friend. I had a real tenor saxophone! Maybe there is hope, I thought. Inside, I was dancing. My heartbeat bounced off Tony's walls: *My saxophone! My very own saxophone!* Even now I cannot fully describe the elation and sense of blessing that I felt. I was embarking on an uncertain adventure, but the uncertainty did not matter. I was meant to travel this road, I could never turn back. I was resolved, compelled from that moment to master the instrument. I would become a saxophonist. Artistic desire surged within me. My course was set.

My mother purchased the saxophone downtown at Wurlitzer's, on Chestnut Street, one block behind the Earle Theater where I had seen Lionel Hampton's Orchestra. My life has included many moments of serendipity, surprises, unsuspected overlaps, and sympathetic deliria—signposts for the bizarre synchronic ride up ahead. Wurlitzer made jukeboxes and pianos. The company allowed us to pay a dollar down and a dollar a week in perpetuity or until the instrument was fully paid. Without such an open-ended payment plan, I would never have owned a saxophone—certainly not a new one. Wurlitzer also had a plan to pay for lessons. Ten lessons for $12.50 up front. Then for each half-hour lesson they deducted $1.25 from a prepaid account.

Now, once more, I hit pay dirt. Raymond Ziegler was my teacher, a strong professional player who had been on the road with Charlie Barnet's high-powered orchestra, which competed for Ivy League and elite gigs in New York, and against Basie's and Ellington's orchestras from the 1940s through the 1960s. Ziegler was a thorough, motivating teacher who taught me how to listen for, and create, an optimum sound from my horn. He taught me how to sight-read. I knew how to read music, but I badly needed to become familiar with the location of positions and notes on my horn. Ray Ziegler also taught me how to transpose, how to play cut time and 6/8 in 2, as well as how to articulate effectively. He did not—could not—teach me how to play a solo. That didn't bother me at the time. In 1943, I was learning what my instrument was all about. I was fourteen years old. Years later, after considerable work and experimentation, I would discover that the release of a note is just as important as its attack. That rudimentary truth was not taught by most teachers. Being able to execute such a fundamental part of the instrument's dynamic force is crucial to articulating the feeling that any sax player wants and needs to express.

After I received my saxophone, I began a long battle with sunsets. I didn't want to sleep because I was eager to learn everything possible on my horn. Every moment not dedicated to that goal seemed unproductive. Sleep shortened my day. Once lost to the land of Nod, I dreamed of the coming dawn, when I'd renew my musical advancement. From then until now, I have believed in *forward motion*, the willed possibility of commitment and hope undeterred by impediments.

I now listened to recordings of sax players with much greater awareness. After all, I actually *owned* a saxophone, and I was steadily becoming a sax player. Whatever it cost me, I was determined to be in sync with the heavyweight players. I viewed it as only a matter of time and hard work. When I found a jukebox, I invested a nickel to hear a sax solo. Soon I noticed something I had previously never noticed. I thought I understood the categories of music on jukeboxes: "popular," "folk," and some I can't remember. The one that grabbed me now was "race." Only black artists (including Coleman Hawkins) were listed under "race" music. That jive nomenclature stood proud and stupid before the emergence of the far more generous category, "rhythm and blues." Somehow blacks were not offended by this stark musical identity, "race." Like many black people, I was not disturbed by that in 1943 and 1944, a scant five years after Hawk made his legendary recording of "Body and Soul" in 1939.

The year I received my saxophone I was fourteen. Prejudicial labeling continued well into the 1950s, eventually phased out by the recording and jukebox industries themselves. What they wanted from the black community, what jukeboxes were designed to produce, was a constant flow of money from individual songs played in bars and cafeterias, hopefully leading, then, to even more sales from records. Only satisfied customers make ongoing sales possible. People hearing songs on the jukebox led to sales for the recording industry. Eventually, black America came to resent its derogatory categorical niche. Other resentments followed that, especially after thousands of black men returned from World War II, too often with no job prospects. Some young black men gave their lives for their country. Others were physically or psychologically maimed, and many more black men were unemployed and left to despair. Slowly, disillusionment, futility, and even rage set in. In our 'hood we heard a constant and ongoing refrain. *What did we fight for overseas? Have we come home to be rewarded with more injustice?*

America's social climate was changing as I went through my teenage years. "The land of the free and the home of the brave" did not include black people as equals. These issues, however, did not concern me at the time; I was consumed with my horn, trying to find my musical voice, with the help and permission of my instrument. My struggle to mature artistically left me oblivious to all else. I now lived in a musical world that I had never known existed. I was obsessed with everything related to jazz. Black and white glossy photographs of my musical heroes covered the walls of my small bedroom. I stared at them often. I lay in bed dreaming, projecting my own photograph side by side with theirs, imagining the day when I would be the artistic equal of my heroes.

CHAPTER 7

Welfare Days, Hard Times

URING THE POST-DEPRESSION YEARS, my neighborhood was poverty-stricken. The war ended the worst of the Great Depression, but that news was slow to trickle into the 'hood. Most people in our urban area were prisoners of scarcity and carried a heavy sense of confinement. Luckily, mother and I were poor in money but not in spirit. Growing up, I saw poverty devastate people whom I knew quite well. It dogged their lives from birth and sent them early to their graves. It robbed many of the most personal of freedoms: dignity, education, and health. Chronic poverty conspires with pain and deadly diseases, bringing woeful (though sadly sometimes welcome) endings to wretchedly damaged lives. Many Americans hold high humanitarian ideals and concern for others. But although I love my country, no one needs to travel far to witness conditions similar to those of the Third World. America's inner cities are hollowed out by despair and impossibility.

In my view, the three pillars of human society are politics, finance, and religion. Black neighborhoods in Philadelphia in the 1940s, however, were defined by lack of money, need for better nourishment, and the bare bones necessities of brute survival. Life was raw and harsh. Somehow, my mother and I escaped the worst, partly thanks to her caring, intelligence, and high spirits. But things were very hard for my mother. Jobs were scarce and she was forced to raise me without a father. Everyone in our neighborhood knew who was on welfare because the clothes we were given all looked exactly the same. I wonder if such state-sponsored generosity was also a way of branding us as down and out. Our uniforms said "Loser." The stiff and scratchy pants we received, marked with bold stripes, were appropriate for an undertaker's casket brigade. But they were free, along with cans of dried beans, butter, and corned beef bearing white labels with big black letters that warned NOT TO BE SOLD. We all knew that our "corned beef" was actually horsemeat. That's what I heard my mother say, though it never produced ill effects. We were glad to get it because we were hungry.

I was born the year the Great Depression began, in 1929. I grew up unaware that we were living through a nationwide economic crisis. Our neighborhood was *always* in an economic crisis, and people do not miss what they have never had. I was too young to understand or care. I had more important things on my mind. *Would Albert Connolly and I be allowed to go to the movies on Saturday? Would I track down an abandoned fish box to build my soapbox racer? Was it really impossible for people to fly like birds? Would I find the secret for human flight someday? Would spinach honestly make me strong like Popeye? And, damn, would I have to eat liver forever?*

To me, and every other kid in our neighborhood, difficult conditions were normal. Black parents who had jobs worked hard for little money. They had no choice. Dirty hands scratching out a living, for the sake of loved ones, come clean with soap and with the lava of integrity. Hard work was not automatically a way out of poverty, but it *was* a means of day-to-day survival. The profound integrity motivating my mother grew directly from my existence. She spared no inconvenience for my benefit, accomplishing wonderful and sometimes miraculous things. I now understand the heroism of her life more than ever, many years after she came to rest. Kids do not know life's grim truths, and would not understand their meaning if they were told. Only in looking back through the eyes of experience can we see the past accurately. My mother worked hard every day of my childhood. She was exhausted, spent, every evening, yet the next morning she was always recharged. Of course, I took her efforts for granted and expected genuinely difficult things with innocent anticipation. What did I know? I had a lot to learn about life. I believe the greatest gift childhood can offer is the space to experiment and mature, and my mother's efforts provided me with that opportunity

I remember one of the night jobs mother held. She worked as a waitress at Shwartz's Bar, three blocks from where we lived. During the day, she worked as a seamstress, at a government-sponsored job with the Work Projects Administration. Her salary was essentially an honorarium. It did little to help needy people. As a waitress she earned six dollars a week. That small amount was augmented by tips that paid our bills. Mother had a good personality. People liked her. That translated into good tips, which often surpassed her salary.

My shoes never seemed to last long; they were often in tatters in two weeks. Maybe I put unusually hard demands on them: I was a wild kid who showed up in the street as Tom Mix, cowboy extraordinaire, or Flash Gordon, or Buck Rogers of the twenty-fifth century. (Superman had not yet made an appearance in *Action Comics*.) Perhaps my shoes were just cheap, their material barely above the quality of cardboard. They cost two or three dollars a pair and I wore holes in both shoes at the same time. When this happened and we had no money, mother took cardboard inserts, of the type one finds in laundered shirts, and created soles shaped for my shoe size, which she tucked inside my shoes. The inserts kept my feet from directly touching the ground. In winter this was a real benefit, so I became an amateur cobbler myself, even better than she was. This padding was fine until it rained. Water quickly soaked through the flimsy cardboard and functioned as a splendid blotter. To minimize this, I developed a technique of walking on the outer edges of my soles, keeping the cardboard from the ground and, thus, relatively dry.

George Bernard Shaw noted that "money is indeed the most important thing in the world." If that is true, then poverty is a bane that destroys human progress. Poverty harms universal educational goals and relegates those who "have not" to lesser existences. In a capitalistic society, some have an embarrassment of wealth. Others have only embarrassment. In Philadelphia, as I grew up, I came to know that difference from the inside out.

Nonetheless, it is wonderful to see how children can make themselves content with whatever they have at hand. On sweltering summer nights, sleeping on the floor because it was cooler, with a wooden pallet covered with a blanket for a bed and only a sheet on top—this was an adventure, something out of the ordinary and, therefore, enjoyable. Reality is whatever a kid's Technicolor imagination makes it. Our tiny family unit didn't have much, but I didn't know that. I was happy, perhaps too happy. I did not like dressing nicely on Sundays. Also, Sundays meant collard greens on the dinner menu. Okay, I'm black, but I hate collard greens. And I wondered why kids couldn't just wear comfortable clothes all the time. Baths and dressing up wasted perfectly good time for play. Grown-ups didn't understand. I despised useless, fussy things.

In 1939 the World's Fair came to New York. Most of us wanted to go to the fair, because it was heavily advertised. One day, my mother announced we were making the trip. I was beside myself. She had been saving money so we could go. The fair was a spectacle. I remember being baffled by daringly designed "cars of the future" driven on platforms seemingly supported by nothing. The Savoy Ballroom in Harlem had an affiliated display, with black couples jitterbugging, girls thrown over the heads of their partners and then through their legs. They danced as if they were "plugged in" to an electrical force. I was fascinated by things that pointed to "tomorrow"—things that are now all but forgotten in the push for technological change. Back then, wow!

I remember coming home for lunch one day and finding mother washing clothes by hand, on a washboard in the bathtub. She was weeping quietly. I asked her why. "It's nothing," she said. Years later I found out that she had run out of washing soap and didn't have a nickel to buy another bar. One week when the piano teacher came to give me a lesson, mother asked to speak to him in another room. I found out years later that she took him aside to confess that she didn't have seventy-five cents to pay for my lesson. She was embarrassed and despondent. He told her not to worry because I was one of his best students and nothing should hinder my progress. He imagined, as I did, that I would become a concert pianist. A concert pianist, indeed! No one in the ghetto listened to anything but the low-down dirty blues. What a fantasy!

I routinely came home from school for lunch while mother was at work. My lunch would be waiting for me in the oven, with the heat on as low as possible to assure I'd have a warm meal. Before one lunchtime, after a night of rain, my Uncle Dewey's ferocious German shepherd, Sporty, jumped the backyard fence, frightened by the thunder and lightning. Worried that the dog might bite someone, my uncle put him in the cellar. He left for work in the morning without letting the dog back into the yard. When I entered the kitchen, I heard Sporty scratching at the cellar door.

I took my lunch from the oven. I was unusually hungry, but I wanted to pet Sporty. I opened the cellar door just a crack, putting my knee against it so I could rub his neck yet keep him contained on the other side. But the dog pushed through the door and headed right for the table and my lunch. I grabbed him around his neck. He was too powerful, and he scared me. I remembered how he would stop chewing if a stranger got too close while he ate and, motionless, give a nasty low growl. So I gave Sporty space, he leaped on my chair, and my lunch was gone in a few quick gulps. Sporty was king of beasts, devouring a small banquet. Afterwards he lovingly licked my face with sincere canine appreciation. He owed me that. I was still hungry.

I loved that dog and he loved me. I came to see that clearly over time. When my mother whipped me, Sporty ran wildly around the yard, eager to defend my carcass. Uncle Dewey told me often that, if Sporty ever got to her during one of those beatings, he would "eat her alive." Everyone in the neighborhood was afraid of Sporty, for good reason. I now see that he was far too dangerous for Uncle Dewey to own safely. But he was my friend, nevertheless. One day a playmate came to visit me. We went out to play in the yard, where my uncle was working. Sporty was told to stay in his doghouse. In one of our games, my friend grabbed me in jest, and Sporty, thinking I was truly in danger, sprang at Johnny in a fury. Teeth bared, mouth open, he tore viciously at Johnny's face, nearly severing his bottom lip. It was terrifying. Johnny tried to escape through the kitchen into our dining room, where the dog pounced on his back. Sporty tore the boy's back open before Uncle Dewey was able to lift him off, in his powerful arms. Johnny spent a long time in the hospital even after his lip was repaired, and he carried those scars until he died many years later, a hopeless alcoholic. I knew how dangerous Sporty was, and I felt certain he would never attack me, but I thank my good fortune he never did.

I was wise enough to conclude early on that girls were smarter than boys. They knew how to jump rope double-dutch with ease. Two girls, two ropes: facing one other about eight feet apart, ropes twirling in opposite directions. The ropes overlapped each other as they spun. That part wasn't hard to accomplish, but a third girl stood to one side and, rocking back and forth in a steady rhythm (like a metronome), she paced the timing of the ropes. Suddenly she sprang directly into the blur of swirling ropes and began jumping. Her legs moving up and down, alternating foot springs, she jumped confidently, barely missing the churning ropes as they came swiftly around again and again. Ropes flashed around her, head to foot, arms worked in rhythm with bouncing feet. The whole gymnastic exercise required (and honed) instinctive balance. The ropes whirled and the girls jumped ceaselessly, for inordinate periods of time. If the boys attempted this feat, we got completely tangled in the ropes and the girls promptly shooed us away, victorious. We were hopeless. They knew it and enjoyed our spastic failure. No matter how hard I tried, I never did understand the mystery of those ropes. To this day I'm sure it is a secret revealed only to girls.

Being poor was completely normal to me because I had never known any other life. In sum, we made do. We did the best we possibly could with our opportunities and resources. We did not feel sorry for ourselves. Our lot in life allowed us to enjoy each day in a variety of ways. I confess that I didn't enjoy my first T-bone steak until I was playing with Bull Moose Jackson's band in 1951 in Columbus, Ohio, when I was twenty-two years old. I couldn't believe how good that steak tasted. I ate a steak every day for a month after that. At home we could never have afforded such high-quality meat. Once my career got underway, it took me awhile to become accustomed to having more money in my pocket.

The truth is that, like other kids in my neighborhood, I was genuinely as happy as a kid could be in spite of hardship. None of us knew what "welfare" meant, other than the obvious fact that our parents had very little money and we received inferior, donated items. We knew nothing of the humiliation our parents and families underwent. For the most part, our parents seemed to satisfy our meager needs and desires. In retrospect, that was truly remarkable. Intuitively, we thought small. We could have felt depressed or victimized because our families could not afford luxuries, I suppose. But our ignorance was an emotional safety valve, a benign, unconscious form of self-protection. On the whole, I think the people in my neighborhood, as I grew up, longed only for things they knew to be within reach.

Surveying my childhood now, I see that we were joyful kids. We played with the most meager of things. For example, we created skateboards or derby racer boxes. We made skateboards from worn-out skates that, instead of throwing away, we nailed to the bottom of a flat board about two and a half feet long and four or five inches wide, just wide enough for a little foot. Each skate had two wheels on each end. A second plank was nailed perpendicularly to the one with the wheels. These nifty devices now resembled the letter "L." With the skate wheels on the bottom, our contraptions looked somewhat like scooters. Because the skates were worn, they made noise, which was partly why we liked them so much. Getting fancy, we could make a handlebar and add streamers at each end that waved in the breeze when we pedaled down the street. We made headlights by placing candles in tin cans, nailed to the front vertical plank. We covered the open end with a piece of celluloid after taking an ice pick and puncturing a few holes in the side of the can, facing upward so that the candle could get air and stay lit. Sometimes we enhanced our brilliant creations with bright colors, if we could scrape up enough money to buy paint.

To make a derby racer, we would first go to a fish store and snag a sturdy discarded box, large enough to sit in, that once contained shipments of fish packed in ice. These boxes were plentiful and fish merchants were glad to dispose of them. To make a derby racer we used two skates, unlike our skateboards. We attached two wheels to the back of the box. Then we turned the box over to nail a plank down the middle so that it stuck out about twenty inches over one end of the box. This was the front, of course. We cut another plank the width of the box and made a hole in each board, right where they crossed, and then secured these with a bolt and washers on each side. After screwing on the nut to keep both planks together, allowing them to turn, we fixed half a skate (two wheels) to each end of the perpendicular board. A rope extended to each end of that piece, so that it could swivel. Pulling hard to one side or the other made a derby boxcar turn this direction or that. We thus constructed steering wheels that enabled us to maneuver our direction with ropes.

Of course, we needed someone to push if we were not on a slope. Plunging downhill was the most fun of all, roaring onward with gravity's pull—independent movement, just like driving a car, except that our brakes were our own feet. We gave our parents fits. One shoe always wore out before the other. If we wanted to get fancy, we could attach a long, thick stick that could be manipulated like a lever on one side of the box. Pulled back, the stick scraped the ground or the wheel, serving as a kid-scale version of a sophisticated brake. Alas, this worked only if we weren't going too fast. The one real problem we had with the vehicles we built was the pungent fish smell, though for the most part we didn't care. In the end, we had our very own derby boxes. That made us as happy as anybody in the world could ever be. I look back and see how beautiful that was. Believe me, we were genuinely happy; we didn't know anything else. Nothing altered our simple pleasures.

When I was somewhat younger than that, I noticed that black people usually sat in the kitchen to converse and socialize. After a meal, no one withdrew to the living room, the way white people did. Black people remained at the table long after the meal was over, exchanging thoughts, jokes, lies, and imaginings, and dissecting current events, memories, and love triangles. The kitchen was *the* meeting place. "Living room" was a misnomer. We sat in the living room only on special occasions: when the doctor came, or when we entertained the preacher, or if an important stranger came to visit. Our house on Bouvier Street had a coal-burning stove in the kitchen, which furnished heat for the rear of the house on the first floor. A round hole in the ceiling above the stove also permitted heat to rise into my mother's room just above. In her room, that hole, covered with a grate, sat behind a chest of drawers. Grown-ups always insisted on having conversations that excluded kids. I was curious to know what the grown-ups were saying. While the grown-ups thought I was asleep, I would sneak behind my mother's chest of drawers, where not only heat drifted up but also conversations. I heard things I was never meant to hear. My immaturity, however, enjoyed a short duration.

PART III *Great People*

One of the greatest artists our country has is Benny Golson.
He is not only a great musician but also an original and
fabulous composer. He is inventive and creative, and his work
is loved the world over. Benny is a rare, creative genius. . . .
THREE CHEERS for Benny Golson!

—TONY BENNETT

CHAPTER 8

No One Else / BOBBIE HURD

PLAYING WITH ART BLAKEY and his band was special in many ways, but one aspect of my association with Art stands out above all others. The most profound event of my life occurred while I was with Art's group. The truly unforgettable moments in life are often unexpected. In April 1958, our band traveled to Washington, D.C., to play The Spotlight Club. One evening toward the end of our week's engagement, Bobby Timmons approached me during the intermission to tell me a slight problem had developed. He had invited a lady friend to hear us play that evening, and this friend brought another friend. But the second lady was not on management's "comp list," and they would not admit her. Only one of them, Bobby's lady friend, was penciled in for free admittance. Bobby asked me to go to the entrance with him and declare the second woman my guest. I did so, and both ladies were admitted. Standing in the dim light of the doorway, Bobby introduced me to Ann and her friend. We then went separate ways.

With intermission almost over, I returned to the bandstand first, as I always did, to signal to my colleagues that it was time to dig in again. I began noodling on my horn, jukebox strains underneath, my back to the audience. When I turned around, I looked directly at Bobby's friend Ann, who was sitting close to the bandstand, and then I looked to her left. My heart almost came to a halt. In front of me was the most adorable face I had ever seen. My eyes traveled shamelessly to the girl's legs, which she held together properly, in aristocratic fashion. Clearly, Auguste Rodin created the mold for those gorgeous legs. They were sculpted for eternal posterity. The enchanting goddess sitting before me was beautiful beyond belief, ethereal yet seductive, beyond my ability (then or now) to adequately describe. Elegant, regal yet unpretentious, powerfully athletic, her bearing calm, she stopped me cold just sitting there. I did not want to play another note that evening. I wanted to introduce myself and take my luck in hand. My saxophone had nothing to say that could be equal to this woman's wordless presence. If I had attempted to speak, I would have stammered. In truth, I was fortunate to be employed for the evening; playing the next set might give me time to regain the lost art of speech.

This lovely girl could have been named *Va Va Voom* or *Madame X of Enigmatic Allure*. She had that magical *je ne sais quoi*, and she had it without reservation or excess. Modest black horned-rimmed glasses complemented her chic coiffure. She was self-contained and explosively understated; she owned the lion's share of everything "female." She was all things that aroused me in a single unit. I felt a strange feeling I had never experienced before. My legs were rubber inner tubes. I'd heard of this phenomenon, "weak in the knees," and it was happening to me right now in public, unsuspecting and defenseless. I couldn't believe it. I'd been around the block a few times and thought nothing again could ever throw me for a loop this way.

In turmoil, I now had to remember to avoid F-sharp in the revised bridge to a song I didn't even want to play anymore. I leaned against the piano, my horn resting idly in my hands, to avoid losing my balance, which had now become questionable. I looked in her direction once again and felt another emotional jolt. This was *indeed* new for me. Could this beautiful, brown-skinned young woman actually slaughter me wordlessly, undefended in a public space, just like this?

I knew intuitively I could never hope to have such a fantastic woman as my own. She was an elusive dream, beyond the reach of mortal men. Hopelessness descended on me. All of these conflicting feelings swamped my mind and body in the space of a few seconds. I *had* been around a few blocks, but not this one!

By the time Bobby Timmons returned to the piano, I was a mess inside. I asked him who this dangerous woman was, since she was sitting with Ann. He laughed. "That's the girl you just brought in here as your guest. I introduced you to her when they let her in." What I missed in the dim light moments back was glowing brightly near the stage. When we finally began playing again, I found myself in a different musical space than I had ever before experienced. Physically I stood on the stage with my horn, but my soul was elsewhere, and my emotions careening. The stage, the club, my band mates, the music, all seemed enchanted but unreal. A floating quality suffused everything; nothing, not even my body, was solid. Yet there she was, very real, thoroughly enchanting and sitting directly in front of me, oblivious to my quandary. I was playing *for* her and *to* her, with no response at all. The music made her foot tap now and then—that was it. Her gorgeous, twinkling brown eyes said I didn't exist in her world. And yet, I was there only for her! I was ready to paint portraits of her, write songs for her, send our kids off to school with her. I was half demented for her, but she didn't know I was alive.

What would I do when the music finally ceased its annoying pulse? I had to be ready. What would I say? How would I act? What kind of impression would I make? I had no clue. I wanted to disappear. But I wanted to go on. I couldn't stay like this. I didn't know how to stop being the goofy dope I now was.

The most beautiful creature I had ever seen was making me crazy, though she had done nothing other than show up where I had a gig on an evening just like any other evening. Of all the jazz clubs in the universe, she had to drop in on this one … If I just sat on the stage after the set ended, she and her friend might just get up and go home. Maybe I'd wave to her slightly, or nod in her direction. Perhaps she would notice how cool I was, my restraint a sign of ferocious calm and authority. That's it. That would be my ploy—just sit there and don't move. Prepare for the last set as if something truly compelling was on my mind, as if I had hardly noticed her. This way I could cover for my torment and confusion. I was uncertain whether I could even stand, walk over and say hello without falling down, or without my voice cracking or maybe peeing in my breeches.

The set ended. I approached her table with Bobby, who went over to talk to Ann. I hadn't decided what to say. I had to play it by ear, not show my real feelings. I would be calm. I would be cool as ice. Was I about to make a complete fool of myself? That must be avoided at all costs. I wanted to do cartwheels. I wanted to show this divine presence my cheerful, resilient personality. Maybe I would do a cartwheel right in front of the bandstand? Or first a hand stand, then a double cartwheel? Nope, very difficult in such a confined space. I might land on a table or kick a waitress in the chin. No, stay calm, keep it lighthearted. So, I said simply, "Hello!"

I don't remember what she said in response, just that the sound of her voice matched her angelic physical command. I could not hear the words she spoke; I was seeing landscapes with exotic gardens, erotic flowers, amorous colors. Her voice was musical, her deep golden eyes were lakes where I might drown myself in ecstasy, if she would let me. Transported, I struggled to get back to the here and now. I was still standing, I think, not tilting or weaving, itching or bobbing. Good, I thought, very good. Going okay so far. Now if I could just make out precisely what she is saying. She smiled at me! Good work, Benny. I got that her name was Bobbie Hurd. I won't forget it, but how do I find her again? Does she want to be found? Have I let her know yet that I want to know her? Have I signaled that yet? I have been waiting for this woman all my life, even if I didn't know that until a few minutes ago. I gotta make sure she knows it, too. Perhaps she has been waiting for me for a long time, too?! Even if *she* didn't know that until now. Wait, what have I said to her so far? Did she understand it? Does she care?

I couldn't let this amazing person disappear, whom I've been wanting for so long, even though I never saw her before tonight. She probably thinks I'm just another hound dog, a typical jazz gangster, with base motives. I'm not a hound dog, though I feel like one right now, because I cannot let her get away, this impossible, angelic, amazing creature whom I cannot take my eyes off. *I want to be with her all the time.*

How can she know she has taken up residence in my heart? I have to tell her. What have I said to her so far? I've got to stay calm, act natural, be positive. I am suddenly certain this amazing girl is going to be my wife. Yes, definitely, yes!

How can anyone be nonchalant in a situation like this? I have to ask for her telephone number, but I can't be anxious. Ask off-hand, like it's occurred to me it might, more or less, be a good idea. Go ahead: just ask her.

So, I did it. Sheepishly, I asked her for her telephone number. Cool as a gentle breeze, almost indifferent (damn), she said: "Well, if you want my number, you can look in the telephone book under Frances Hurd, my mother." I saw that she was setting up hurdles for me. Do I really want to pursue this? I wondered. I am all messed up here. What do I do now?

The very next day, at dawn, I searched feverishly for a telephone directory at a nearby phone booth. I was staying at someone else's home and I didn't have a phone in my temporary room. I dialed. A male voice, Malcolm, her brother, answered. She had gone to school; she attended a dance school. So she dances, but what kind of dancing? Is she good? I was slightly annoyed because she had to know I was going to call. Why did she go out? Never mind. I decided to call again later. The next time I called, she had gone out to do the laundry. That's it! This girl was trying to make me jump through hoops. I didn't want to join a circus. I resolved not to call again.

I did call again, of course. This time, not only was she at home; she invited me to visit. When I arrived, I was inspected by her mother. From the other room, I heard her brother say, "Who's that nigger?" I ignored that; I knew he thought I was one of those traveling jazz jerks, and everybody knows you can't trust those guys.

After meeting the family, including her grandmother, I began a sustained and ambitious letter writing and telephone calling campaign from multiple destinations where the Blakey band earned its wages. I learned that Bobbie Hurd had been studying ballet for over ten years and was an extremely talented ballerina. However, she was black, which meant she was likely to thwarted or frustrated in her career. I wondered what hope of success she had. Was her talent enough to overcome the odds against her because of her heritage? Bobbie and Chita Rivera, also from Washington, D.C., studied at Jones-Haywood. I went one day and watched one of her classes from a small upstairs window overlooking the practice floor below. Her hair pulled back in a bun, she moved like a swan, and she was even more beautiful to me than ever. She moved effortlessly to Schubert's "Unfinished Symphony," her arms floating gracefully like beautiful wings. Weeks later, I went to Boston to see her perform. Bobbie Hurd was magnificent. In 1959, she moved to New York City to continue her dance studies. She had been there twice before: once with the New York Negro Ballet Company and later on scholarship with a major New York ballet company. Briefly, she studied on scholarship with the Washington Ballet Company, which was an all-white company. Bobbie was the first black person to study there. Then, perhaps even now, blacks (regardless of talent) were not fully accepted into white ballet companies. When her token participation had served its purpose, she was let go quickly and unexpectedly.

Although most of Bobbie's friends (though not her mother) told her to stay away from a jazz musician, somehow, she fell in love with me. Bobbie Hurd and I were married on March 28, 1959, almost one year from the day she first knocked me off my feet. I had been married once before. My three children were all boys. I had always wanted a daughter, but I had abandoned the idea. How I wanted to see my own little girl grow up wearing all the beautiful clothes girls wear. It seemed it would never happen. However, on June 12, 1961, Bobbie presented me with my little girl, Brielle. This adorable girl gave us no problems of any sort, and she grew up to be a talented, beautiful, and powerful woman. In 1993, Brielle moved to Germany. She was taught French from the time she was six years old, later Spanish and German, too. She studied for a time in Los Angeles, where our home is, then left for Germany and began teaching English at a college language school to BMW and Audi automobile engineers and other business professionals. I have had the profound good luck to affirm that, with the best wife possible, it is also possible to have a daughter who is truly daddy's girl.

One thing I regret looking back on our fifty years of marriage is that Bobbie stopped dancing. She wanted to be a complete wife and a loving mother to Brielle. She willingly gave her entire life over to me and Brielle, not as a sacrifice, but as a natural extension of her love. She essentially refuses to let me do anything for her in return. Therefore, I am responsible for the death of a fantastic dancing talent. Bobbie did come out of retirement in 1986 for a few performances as the partner of a dance company created by an extraordinary choreographer/dancer, Wayne Bascomb, in Los Angeles. That company, the Jazz Music Exchange, gave many performances during their five or six years of existence. After that brief return to the stage, Bobbie did not dance again. Her work with the Jones-Haywood school, her work in New York City, and her partnership with the Jazz Movement Exchange represent the extent of her career. Bobbie literally stopped her career when it had just begun, altruistically pouring her energy into my career instead over the years. I know she must wonder, as I do, just how far *she* might have gone had she not been dedicated to that unreliable jazz gangster, Benny Golson.

I'm sure I was selfish early in our marriage, in not preventing her from giving so much of herself away and, thus, eclipsing her own talent. Without question, Bobbie is as talented artistically as I am, if not more so. I have been an artist, but Bobbie is no less an artist. This realization carries for me a guilt that is immutable because of Bobbie's unremitting dedication to my work. I tried, in later years, to make up for this imbalance, but I cannot. Nothing can compensate for her loss. Time is one-directional, never backing up to assuage guilt or heal a broken heart.

Only after Brielle completed high school did Bobbie begin to travel the world with me. She became my wardrobe mistress, dresser, secretary, travel agent, and one-woman claque. She is a keen-eared specialist to ensure high-quality stage sound. She has also been my public relations representative. But best of all, she is an unmatched source of love and encouragement. No matter what I want to do, or where I want to go, her reply is always the same: "When do you want to do that?" or "When do we leave?" Such dedication is invaluable to any creative person. Resistance or neglect, failed support or opposition, can make a marriage agonizing. Friends who once advised Bobbie to have nothing to do me are now unfortunately mostly divorced or separated. I knew that special night in Washington, D.C., more than four decades ago—my brain scrambled and my legs turned to rubber—that Bobbie was the one for me. The only one. She still does deep and amazing things that are wonderful, unforgettable, and lasting. I often feel like writing a love letter to her all across the sky.

Sometimes, in the middle of night, I remain absolutely still and listen to Bobbie breathe in and breathe out. If I'm touching her, I also feel the smooth beating of her heart. I'm ecstatic that she is alive. And, if the light from outside is bright enough, I fix my gaze on her lovely face. I resist kissing her for fear I'll wake her from the sleep she deserves after devoting her waking hours to me and to our welfare.

At that point sometimes fear overcomes me. What if her breathing suddenly stopped? Or some terrible thing *made* it stop? She would be gone. I would be bereft, empty. I force the thought from my mind and continue looking and listening in quiet ecstasy. I always realize how fortunate I am that she is my wife. The reality is almost too good to be true. But it *is* true. What did I do to deserve Bobbie? It's as if God gave her to me out of infinite kindness. When I'm apart from Bobbie for an extended time, I find myself attempting to caress her beautiful face, which is not there. Until this day, I am taken aback when she is near or steps into my vision. Bobbie Jean Hurd, how I love you! I want to travel forever with you.

CHAPTER 9

Moose and Bostic

W HEN I STARTED my jazz career in Philadelphia with David "Bull Moose" Jackson's big band, my playing was awful—deadly, really. My practicing at home was a hardship for our neighbors. Everyone in David's band was a high school student, including him. Three weeks after I joined the band, we landed a gig at The Wharton Settlement, 22nd Street and Columbia Avenue, a public venue for basketball, dances, swimming, checkers (anything to keep kids from idleness on city streets). We were paid: too good to be true, but welcome. Jackson's band played stock arrangements that cost seventy-five cents each, most of them written by Spud Murphy or Van Alexander (who recently died at age one hundred) and other writers I have forgotten. Our repertoire included "Take the 'A' Train," "One O'Clock Jump," "Tuxedo Junction," "Jumpin' at the Woodside," "The 9:20 Special," "Stardust," "Down for Double," and a variety of other honorable standards. Sure enough, I received four dollars that night. It was months before I actually spent those precious few dollars, but I was on my way.

I didn't know where I was headed, but I strove constantly to achieve musical understanding and skill on my horn. Most of all, I pushed for knowledge, to escape the gauntlet of confusion and disappointment. Any form of enlightenment would eventually become wind in my sails. David's band was a genuine professional beginning for me. He was an alto sax player, only a couple of years older than I was. We became best friends and roommates at Howard University. David is gone now, but I cherish memories of our wonderful early days in Philly and in college.

Calvin Todd directed a local band that was much better than ours. His players were a bit older and more experienced. They traveled in and around Philadelphia in a school bus. Returning from a gig in Delaware one night, their bus broke down. They sat on the side of the road waiting for the driver to determine the problem. Luckily, the whole band had just disembarked when, out of the darkness, they heard a car bearing down on them at high speed. Headlights grew brighter and the roar of the engine more desperate. Moving well over a hundred miles an hour, the car plowed directly into the bus. Everyone dove into the bushes just in time. In the hopeless tangle of scalding metal, the drunk, sleeping driver was killed instantly, his foot pasted to the accelerator. His body was inseparable from the rubble. Who can imagine how those kids felt? They were surely traumatized for months or longer. The event still haunts my aging memory.

Bull Moose Jackson's band escaped such near-disasters, though we had our own close calls and dilemmas. Once, after playing a gig in San Antonio, Texas, we found ourselves with several days free, so we headed to Mexico, only a few miles away. The nearest town was Nuevo Laredo. We checked into a quaint hotel and had a great time. After hours of telling tall tales and trading enormous whoppers, we all went to bed. Tadd Dameron had consumed more than his share of tequila. He was feeling no pain. Not long after we retired, I was awoken by a chilling scream, which was followed by another as loud as the first, then two more unmerciful screams. It sounded like someone was being tortured. I did not get up to explore; in the morning, I learned none of us did. We all kept our doors locked. The town was unfamiliar, and most of us didn't speak a word of Spanish.

When we came down for breakfast in the morning, we saw the large bandage on Tadd's thigh. His pants leg was cut off. Tadd had been the one screaming so horribly. His voice had been unrecognizable, distorted by anguish. He had fallen asleep smoking. His bed covers were set alight, then burst into flames. As the fire spread, Tadd, anaesthetized, felt nothing. Even when he did wake, alcohol slowed his flight response. Fortunately, the hotel clerk had broken down the door and rescued Tadd, who by then was writhing on the floor in pain. His thigh was badly burned. The clerk wrestled with the flaming mattress, finally heaving it out the window. We stared at Tadd's leg; the scenario was hard to take in.

Tadd was a lucky man; he could well have died in those flames. When we checked out of the hotel the next morning, Tadd's ill-fated mattress was still smoldering in the street. The hotel would not let him leave until he paid for new bedding—a small price to pay for being alive. After the shock wore off, days later, we began teasing Tadd, calling him "Flame Thrower," "Mattress Man," and "Fireball." Tadd laughed with us, but he carried that horrible scar for the rest of his life.

When I joined Earl Bostic's group, years later, we always set out from New York in his Cadillac limousine, which carried most of the group. He drove like a demon. Our piano player, Stash O'Laughlin, rode in the accompanying station wagon, which carried instruments and baggage. A valet who did not perform with the group drove the station wagon. He, too, was a speedster behind the wheel. The two of them were, fortunately, excellent drivers. Otherwise no one would have gotten much sleep and we might have become road statistics.

George Tucker, our bass player, was a talented fellow from Palatka, Florida, a town so small you could drive completely through it holding your breath. George always called it the biggest little town in the United States. When we drove through Palatka months later, we saw that George was right; we all, including George, laughed for five minutes. He and I were inseparable during that period. After we both left Bostic's band, I recommended him to Art Blakey, who hired him to play with The Jazz Messengers. I was heartbroken when George Tucker passed away.

Blue Mitchell, one of our two trumpeters, was from Miami, Florida. He brought high spirits with him. He had a distinctive style and he always played the right notes in a chord. In truth, Blue Mitchell poured his heart into everything he played, even during rehearsals, which for most of us are more relaxed. Most musicians save their best stuff for live gigs. Not Blue— he had something to say musically, all the time. Years later I discovered that pianist Ellis Marsalis, father of a slew of talented jazz sons, had once played with Blue. All the guys in Earl's band got a chance to play, but of course, Earl featured his own hits. Our repertoire put Earl constantly in the spotlight. Elmon Wright, who played in Dizzy Gillespie's band, became our other trumpeter, and G. T. Hogan, from Lubbock, Texas, played drums. He had a nice groove.

Bostic's band played a lot of one-night gigs. To stave off boredom while we drove for hours, the guys frequently played cards. Blue often cheated, throwing cards he didn't want out the window of the speeding car. When we arrived at our destination, the deck was usually pretty thin. Catching him in the act was difficult, even though Mack, driving the station wagon behind us, often saw cards flying crazily from our limo. These guys were all upbeat and friendly. At the time, however, my first marriage was on the rocks, and in the throes of these emotional tribulations I would check into a separate hotel from the rest of the band. To show sincere friendship, the guys often offered me female companionship—girls they knew. I always refused. I found out later they were trying to figure out if I was gay.

Blue Mitchell left Earl Bostic's group. On my recommendation, Johnny Coles took his place, and he did not let us down. Johnny played with fire, soul, and lyrical purpose. He was one of the few musicians who knew how to make a wrong note a thing of beauty. I'm not exaggerating. Johnny had enormous feeling for melody and all the delicate emotion possible there. Tadd fell in love with his playing. Johnny Coles was a fantastic trumpet player who was not recorded as much as he should have been. Most musicians knew of his talent, but the world outside our ranks did not.

Stanley Turrentine once worked with Bostic and so did John Coltrane. Stan and I met in 1952 when Moose played the now defunct Roosevelt Theater in Pittsburgh, Stan's hometown. I met his brother, Tommy, in 1948 while I was at Howard University and he was in George Hudson's very popular band. George was from St. Louis and Ernie Wilkins wrote some of his arrangements. Earl Bostic was an anomaly. He made a strong, positive impression on John Coltrane, who told me about Bostic's technical ability. I recalled the snakes he played on the alto when I first heard him with Lionel Hampton at the Earle Theater. Discussion of anything deeply technical or sophisticated was lost on me at the time, but John was right. Earl Bostic remains the most astute saxophone technician I have ever heard. Technically, no one has touched him yet, not John Coltrane, Charlie Parker, or Marcel Mule. The only one who comes close is Al Galadoro, the master (with Paul Whiteman) of double and triple tonguing. Bostic could do it all: sight read marvelously; transpose on the fly, to and from any key; play effortlessly in any key; play wide guitar voicings (completely unnatural for any horn), one chord after the other; and play at length above and outside the range of his horn. Arthur Blythe reminds me of Earl in this regard. But Bostic was breathtaking, a prodigy at all of these specialized abilities. He employed circular breathing (when a player breathes air in through his nose while phrasing and playing notes), before I even knew what it was. The technique allows a player to execute extraordinarily long phrases without appearing to inhale. Baritone saxophonist Harry Carney, who played with Ellington's for decades, was also a master of circular breathing. It's a great skill that carries a touch of Muhammad Ali's deft caginess.

I asked Bostic how he became proficient at all this. He told me that as a teenager from Oklahoma, he longed to move to New York. To facilitate his dream, he developed an unusual regimen. He began practice at 8:00 A.M. every day, as if playing were his job. At noon, he took an hour for lunch, then resumed practicing. He finished promptly at 5:00 P.M. He took Sundays off. For years, he followed this routine tirelessly. He practiced every song he knew over and over *ad nauseam*. When he finally got to New York, he headed directly to Minton's Playhouse in Harlem, which soon became world famous. That first night at Minton's, he joined Don Byas, Coleman Hawkins, Charlie Parker, Joe Guy, and Thelonious Monk. His playing bedazzled everyone. Bostic did not report this to me, of course, but others corroborated for me the fact that everyone in the club stood back and listened intently. Apparently Bird shook his head in disbelief. I'm not describing Earl Bostic's style or his improvisational concepts; I'm reporting what I have been told about the man's purely technical ability. He was all over his horn in an incredible way.

I can attest that Earl appeared to know everything there was to know about a saxophone. He showed me fingerings I had never heard or thought of. Once I asked him how to make a certain note above the range of the horn. His response was simple: "What kind of horn is it?" I told him it was a Selmer. "On a *Selmer*," he said, demonstrating, "you make it this way." So I asked how you would do it on a Martin. "On a Martin, you'd do *this*," he replied. His knowledge was almost inhuman, and he was impossible to outdo technically

One day we played an afternoon jam session in Baltimore and chose tunes we had not played together before. It was a great pleasure. Bostic became carried away; he went to the dressing room and came back with his clarinet. I knew what he could do on the saxophone, but I had never heard him play the clarinet. He called "Cherokee," and proceeded to blow through it easily in every key. That clarinet must have been pleading for mercy. Earl was brilliant. It's a shame that those who knew him only for his hits missed this other talent of the "real" Earl Bostic. Success sometimes seems to demand that an artist hide his brightest light under a blanket.

About a year into my time with Bostic I began to become very bored. The band had many good musicians, but we weren't given much time to play. The group was Earl Bostic's aggregation. He was the star, always stage center. We played many tunes in which the rest of us played only the last chord, usually a triad, sometimes with a sixth added. I wanted no more of it. It had become, for me, Earl Bostic's aggravation.

We went south for a series of one-night gigs and our fearsome leader took his electric guitar with him. He played a few bits of funky blues on it that he figured pleased a crowd. He was right, but I hated standing there as a stage accessory, like a mannequin or a kid picking his nose. The dark side of me began to emerge. I regressed to the boy in Philly who once offered a beverage of cool toilet water to a guest of my mother's who said she was thirsty. Crazy ideas came to me. One night, the Mr. Hyde to my Dr. Jekyll made his debut. When we left the stage for intermission, I found Bostic's guitar resting in its stand, and when no one was looking I quickly tightened a few strings and loosened others. When we returned to the stage, as usual, the first tune featured his guitar. Not bothering to check whether the guitar was in tune, he kicked off the song. The moment he hit the first chord, every head in the dance hall turned to look at him. He was flummoxed. No one but me knew what I had done—which is what I wanted. Keeping a straight face was the hard part.

The next night I did the same thing. After intermission, Bostic picked up his guitar and it was *twang-twang clunk* all over again. Bostic was out of his mind. "What's wrong with this crazy guitar? I gotta have it checked." The guys muffled their hilarity, but by then they had guessed I was culprit, as I was the practical joker. When on the third night the out-of-tune guitar once again debuted after intermission, this time the guys all looked right at me. I stood innocent faced. Bostic didn't have a clue, but the fact that I was the only one not laughing soon gave me away. Bostic was known to become violent on occasion; fortunately, he merely asked me not to do it again. I got the message. I knew something very unpleasant would happen otherwise.

Mr. Hyde did not disappear so easily, however. This feeling I had wouldn't let go. One night in Kansas City, while Bostic was deep into his self-indulgent solo, I remembered something I once saw Illinois Jacquet do. I walked to the back of the stage, took my saxophone from its hook behind where the drummer sat, and ran toward the front of the stage waving my horn over my head as if I were going to throw it into the audience. When the audience saw me charging at them, Bostic completely lost their attention. At the edge of the stage I stopped abruptly, dipped the horn behind me, then swung it forward as if to hurl it into their midst. Everyone ducked, then laughed when they realized I was only pretending. By now no one was listening to our star, who watched my antics from the corner of his eye. Later, he told me I could do whatever I wanted on my solo, but not to interrupt his. Mr. Hyde struck again.

Not long after that, we were playing a gig in Seattle. A tenor saxophonist friend, Walter Benton, who was playing local gigs got in touch with me. He asked me whether Bostic ever let anyone sit in with his group. Oh, yes, I assured Walter, probably it would be fine—though I knew it would *not* be fine with Bostic. I told Walter to take his horn out back stage, and just follow Bostic when he finished his solo. As Bostic finished his glorious solo that evening and stepped away from the microphone, Benton, who happened to be a very large fellow, swooped in out of nowhere, zeroing in on the mike. Bostic looked around in bewilderment. "Who the hell is this guy!?" I admitted he was a friend of mine. "Did you tell him he could play?" Bostic asked. I told him the truth. At the end of the night, he paid me and let me go. He couldn't take any more of my shenanigans. Mr. Hyde got me fired. I happily flew to New York the next day. I had no other gigs in sight, but I felt as if I had just been released from prison. I was particularly pleased that Bostic gave me plane fare, which he would not have done had I quit rather than being fired.

The very next morning I got a call from Quincy Jones. He wanted to know if I was free to join Dizzy Gillespie's band, as Ernie Wilkins was leaving. Do sharks still poop in the ocean? I asked when I could start. "Tomorrow at the Howard Theater in D.C." How brilliant the mischievous Mr. Hyde truly is.

Strangely, Earl Bostic and I did not find our friendship ruined by my hijinks. Years later he asked me to join his group again, probably thinking I had matured. He offered me an extremely juicy salary, much better than I earned during my first stint with his group, not only to play but also to serve as the group's musical director. I turned him down, with appreciation. I had, in the intervening years, become addicted to the kind of music I love so much—strictly jazz, nothing but the best.

CHAPTER 10

Art Blakey's Neophytes and
Tadd Dameron's Luck

CRAZY THINGS HAPPENED in each iteration of Blakey's Messengers band. Two in particular amused me. One night, during the period when Terence Blanchard, Donald Harrison, Mulgrew Miller, and Essiet Essiet were members, the band played an engagement and everyone expected to be paid at the end of the gig, as usual. True to form, Art told the guys they would be paid all fees outstanding when they recorded their next album, which would not be long. Satisfied, everyone plowed forward until the record date arrived. After the album was finished Art was asked once again about money he owed the band. They reminded him of his promise. One of the guys said to Art, "This is the record date! We need our bread." Art looked at him like he had two heads, as though he didn't have the intelligence to understand the real situation. With the seriousness of a night court judge, Art responded emphatically, "Not *this* record date!" Such shuck and jive slipperiness pretty much sums up Art Blakey's collegial business strategy. Bait and switch. Promise and temporize. Art perfected the artistry of a three-card monte dealer.

All of this is long behind them now, and these men laugh about Art's (shall we say) proclivities. Another time, Art was trying to find a replacement for a departing pianist. Several players showed up where his group was playing for a couple of nights. Art tried them out right on the gig. No rehearsals, just jump in and see if you survive. One fellow seemed as though he might be the choice; he showed up every night, Art seemed to like him, and there was no competition. Art said nothing negative about him. Occasionally he'd exclaim encouragingly, "Okay, yeah! My man!" So this guy figured he got the job. He played his heart out all week. At the end of the engagement, while everyone was being paid, he patiently waited his turn. It never came. Befuddled, he asked Art about his money. Feigning surprise, Art responded bluntly, "Money? I thought you were sittin' in with us, man!"

Sometimes new fellows in The Messengers played inordinately long solos. Art tolerated this sometimes, but when he got bored or annoyed, he'd say something like, "Hey, you can play it all in two choruses." When a player really got on his nerves, he'd snap, "The audience applauded because they're glad you stopped." Despite all else, Art's sarcastic hyperbole was often right on the money.

Before my years with Blakey, when I traveled with Bull Moose Jackson, we often toured the South. One day, on the way to Daytona Beach, Florida, Tadd Dameron was driving pretty fast. He loved speed. It was extremely hot and the windows were rolled down. The wind was blowing fiercely so that we heard very few sounds outside the car. This reinforced a problem we soon encountered. We apparently roared right by a state trooper, hidden from view. Before we knew it, he was on our bumper. We were going so fast that he had to gun his patrol car to catch us. The sound of his siren was completely muffled in the wind and excessive speed. We suspected nothing.

Tadd was in the habit of checking his rear view mirror, but that day he drove as if he were in the lead at the Indianapolis 500. The siren blared behind us unheard. The sun was shining so intensely, Tadd did not at first see the blinking red lights atop the car behind us. By then it was too late to cop a plea. We were traveling way over the speed limit, racing along like gangsters escaping a heist. Tadd brought the car to a stop on the shoulder.

In the back seat, Jymie Merritt, our bassist, was in the habit of scribbling in a little notebook he carried all the time. None of us knew what he wrote in it. Today, Jymie was jotting notes in his book as usual, except that he had pulled a blanket over his legs and chest to protect his pages from the angry wind.

The trooper appeared at Tadd's open window, extolling the virtues of observing the Florida speed limit. As he lectured Tadd, I noticed that the officer had become uneasy. Suddenly he stopped and looked right at Jymie.

His hand was on his gun. He was obviously displeased about something. Finally he made it clear: "If you don't stop fumblin' under dem blankets, I'm gonna give ya a third eye." (What he really said was "thud eye.") Jymie froze as if paralyzed. That seemed to do the trick; the cop didn't give Tadd the ticket he surely deserved. Call it good luck or fantastic karma. I call it slipping through the horns of a dilemma.

CHAPTER 11

Further Adventures with Tadd and an Evening with Louis Armstrong

NOT MANY vaguely aware of the infamous name "Golson," of youthful Philadelphia mischief, covertly aspiring to Red Rodney's inimitable trouble-making at Fort Knox and back home in the Philadelphia mint, realize that the still unheralded rhythm-and-blues group led by the unlikely but honorable Bull Moose Jackson launched Benny Golson's career. Imagine Golson's joy and surprise on discovering that the pianist in that group was Tadd Dameron, his idol. Tadd and Bull Moose (known early on as Ben Jackson) went to school together. One day in Harlem, they bumped into each other. Tadd wasn't working. His pal had a band. The rest was designed for the improbable future good fortune of Mr. Golson.

So much for semiobjective-seeming third-person references. As a saxophone plebe in Philly in the mid-1940s, I listened to everyone and everything, arrangers no less than composers, instrumental wizards and lyricists—anyone whose energy and raw talent appeared in view. Tadd Dameron demanded my attention because of his penchant for writing seductive melodies. His compositions were always memorable. They linger after one hears them just as exquisite meals, Hawaiian sunsets, vintage Barolo, and private evenings with your most intimate companion define life's best pleasures.

For good reasons, some think of Tadd Dameron as a composer, while others consider him primarily an arranger. He was both. Those talents were entwined. My friend Jim Merod suggests that Tadd was among the definitive "quantum enigmas" in the jazz universe because (like Billy Strayhorn and Oliver Nelson) he escapes reduction to one artistic or musical role. That may be a useful way to consider Tadd's amazing talent and rich accomplishments. He was a fine pianist, a strong songwriter, and a remarkably creative arranger. His musical "identity" was mercurial and iconoclastic. He played an "arranger's piano" with less than complete facility, and yet, even when he was arranging, he was composing because he was always aware of the flow of melody in subthemes that support primary song material. Tadd's background lines were memorably melodic. That is rare.

Tadd Dameron was and is a "melody master." He was my idol. No wonder I developed a tenacious affinity for all things melodic. To this day, I saturate myself in pursuit of melody. Songful integrity is a composer's first responsibility. I listened to Tadd's recordings with amazement. He gave enormous sonic body and texture to any small group voicing. His arrangements were sensational because they carried harmonic fullness and passionate, unabbreviated lyric feeling. Nothing in the world of instrumental music ever sounded like his melodic offerings. From exotic chords, Tadd built genuine small-ensemble masterpieces. Few "mini-orchestras" have ever approached such tonal complexity and beauty. Think of it like this. Cruising Venice's large and small canals, have you ever encountered light with greater majesty and grandeur? Tadd's big band arrangements are no less superb because they seem illuminated from within. Dameron was in a class by himself. When I joined Bull Moose's crew, I knew I had to really get to know Tadd Dameron.

The first night Tadd heard me play, he told me at intermission that he wanted me to join him on his next European trip. "Maybe we can record," he added. I was more than pleased by this. Perhaps I had arrived; I knew Tadd used only great players on his recordings. I first heard Fats Navarro on one of Tadd's recordings. Tadd could get anyone he wanted, and he wanted me. It was hard for me to believe then, but we became the best of friends, and remained close until he passed in 1965. Tadd taught me everything he knew about composition. I owe enormous respect and gratitude to Tadd Dameron.

Tadd was a good and gentle mentor. Sometimes, hearing chords I had chosen, Tadd would frown and suggest instead, "How about like this?" Then he played what was in *his* creative grasp. I learned a great deal from those instructive gestures. They changed the way I thought and helped to shape me as a composer and writer. I still carry vestiges of them within me.

Tadd took me under his wing and gave me a loving "shove" in the right direction. I will never forget his help and his care and candor.

After I had been playing with Bull Moose's group for a few months, under Tadd's tutelage, my writing underwent a significant transformation. I had been so influenced by Tadd that people sometimes approached him after hearing the band play a set that included some of my songs to tell him how much they enjoyed hearing his writing, which, they said, was so distinct. Eventually, he told me that he found it "a real drag" that people mistook my writing for his. He was extremely proud that I grasped so completely what he had taught me, but it must have felt strange for someone else's work to sound so much like his. Later, my song writing changed as I embraced new ideas and incorporated them into my own unique style and lyric voice. When I hear a certain segment of Puccini's "Or tutto èchiaro," from *Tosca*, I become tearful. It sounds just like Tadd's writing and recalls to me all our wonderful times together as well as the beauty of his writing. How privileged I was to have Tadd's friendship.

Not long after we left Bull Moose, Tadd called me and some of the other guys who had played in that band. He had a record date with Bob Weinstock's Prestige label. He would write and play the piano arrangements, and he chose Clifford Brown and Idrees Sulieman on trumpets, Gigi Gryce on alto, me on tenor, Oscar Estelle on baritone sax, Herb Mullins on trombone, Percy Heath on bass, and on drums Philadelphia's own Joe Jones, whose name Tadd changed to Philly Joe Jones for the album (*A Study in Dameronia*, June 1953). The recording studio was the smallest I had ever seen except when making demos. Nine musicians plus a grand piano and a set of drums were crammed into a thimble-sized room. Clifford sat behind me. When he stood up to play, his microphone was just in front of me to my left. As he played, his horn was slightly above my left shoulder and directly adjacent to my ear. He created so many deep emotional moments musically that he almost drove me nuts. It felt as if he were playing for me only. Take after take, I heard his trumpet like I had never heard it before. Whenever I hear that album now, I think to myself, "Clifford Brown solos for Benny." After the first session, I told Clifford that I knew everything about him, down to his very breath. He laughed as he always did. After we completed four songs for the ten-inch album, I headed back to Philly to join my family.

That same year, not long before the tourist season began in Atlantic City, New Jersey, Tadd called from New York. Clarence Robinson, a successful black producer of variety shows that included chorus girls and a bevy of acts, had asked him to write music for a summer show at Atlantic City's Paradise Club. Clarence also wanted Tadd to organize and lead the house band. Our group featured Johnny Coles, Clifford Brown, and Idrees Sulieman on trumpet and Gigi Gryce, Cecil Payne, and me on saxes. We had a trombonist, whose name I cannot remember, alongside Philly Joe on drums and Jymie Merritt on bass. Tadd Dameron, pianist and leader, composed music for the show. This band was much like the Dameronia format we had with Bob Weinstock. There was a wrinkle, however. Atlantic City was still more than a little bit racist. In 1953, segregation reigned unabated there. We all had to find single rooms in black homes. The discomfort was complete. When black folks went to the beach in Atlantic City, we were limited to an area several blocks away from the water. The surf coast—miles of it—was reserved for whites only.

Having Clifford Brown with us was interesting because it hadn't been long since his release from the hospital after he survived a terrible automobile accident. The driver of the car had plowed their vehicle into a bridge abutment. Though he had broken a leg and suffered internal injuries, he returned to the scene after a lengthy recuperation in Wilmington, Delaware, near his home. In the hospital he practiced constantly, with his leg hoisted in a sling. Although he had almost died, he never talked about the accident. The horrible irony of his death years later, under *identical* circumstances in a second accident, still haunts me. Clifford's first brush with mortality left him with a stiff leg, but the experience never interfered with the brilliance that emerged from his horn. I once teased him, as he hobbled upstairs to our dressing room on his bad leg. "You could pass for Peg Leg Bates," a funky one-legged performer on the Chitlin' Circuit, I told him. He laughed genially. Clifford never seemed to be offended by anything. He carried happiness liked a parakeet on his shoulder. How we all loved him and his gorgeous trumpet. From the first notes he played, Clifford cast a spell on anyone who listened.

After a week of rehearsals, we were ready for the show's grand opening. This show had it all: Bob Bailey, master of ceremonies and singer; Little Buck, tap dancer; Gloria Howard, an interpretive dancer from Chicago who used the stage name La Bommie; Iron Jaws Jackson, who clasped incredible loads of tables and chairs in his teeth as he danced, holding his burden tightly clenched; a comedy team, Stump and Stumpy; a young singer named Betty "Be-Bop" Carter, who had recently toured with Lionel

Hampton's band; Haitian dancers called Princess Tondelayo and Bobby Lopez; and us, Tadd Dameron's unknown "all stars." What we had to do as a part of Tadd's band was a complete anomaly. We were jazz musicians who played almost no jazz at all. The band had great players but, for the most part, we played only show and dance music. We played the entire summer season. Incredible! We received *one hundred dollars* for seven days' work, without a single day off. Saturday night, we first played a 9:00 P.M. show, and we did not leave until 8:00 A.M. because, after the last show was finished around 2:00 A.M., a breakfast show kicked in at 4:00 A.M. What a grind. Sunday morning's early light was nearly detestable. I suppose we all stayed through the entire season because none of us (with the exception of Tadd) had yet established a reputation as a famous or notable jazz artist. Our show was in direct competition with a well-established annual event at Club Harlem, whose director was the highly regarded Larry Steele. His line-up was much like ours. However, Club Harlem was the center of black night life. We were on the outer edge, just off the commercial mainstream; nonetheless, we were successful. We were the new kids on the block, and people wanted to see who we were and what we sounded like.

One night just before we kicked off, Louis Armstrong came in to the club. Many celebrities frequented the show, and Pops seemed not to be an exception. His horn was elsewhere; apparently, the great man was out on the town having a good time. We were all delighted to see him. Some of us knew him. Others knew only his reputation. This night, Pops displayed extraordinarily good spirits, so Tadd urged him to play a couple of numbers with us. The great man declined; he didn't have his horn with him. Johnny Coles offered his, and Pops relented.

Armstrong came from the era preceding Dizzy Gillespie, Miles Davis, Donald Byrd, and Freddie Hubbard. He was a terrific soloist in his own right and matched the giants who came later. His style was different, but his talent and ability were unmatched. Clifford Brown, a youthful dynamo, was at that time featured within our circle, and he played at a virtually unsurpassed height. Here we were at an incidental occasion, on an otherwise forgettable gig—before Louis Armstrong added his glory. Now we had a voice from the past as well as one from the present. Tadd wanted to set up a battle of sorts between Clifford and Louis, but with love and admiration: no cutting session, no strain, no embarrassment.

Louis didn't know bebop tunes such as "Confirmation," so "Sweet Georgia Brown" was called. The band had fun on the opening chorus, but after that the evening was all Clifford and Pops. Each displayed his chops, while drawing from his own era's traditions. It was a gorgeous uproar. The spontaneous beauty touched all our hearts. No one there had ever experienced this conjunction of forces. I wasn't sure if Pops played like a man working to survive, or if he was exuberant with lyric freedom, but the duo soared above our pedestrian vantage.

A strong admiration and friendship was evident in their shared ferocity. They attacked one another as if laughing joyously through their horns. They both hit that shrill, upper-register bleat of erotic triumph like a celebration of uncontainable life. Their creative energy was mesmerizing. Where did this kind of playing come from? How did they find these previously unheard notes and phrases? I'm sure that none of us cared. We were caught up in something large and undecipherable as the universe.

Pops was always known for his big smile and his white teeth, and for holding a rumpled white handkerchief while he played. That night we saw none of this. Louis Armstrong was seriously searching for everything that had ever been available to his horn—and more than that. The eruptive moment contained no room for showmanship. On occasion, narrow-minded black musicians put down Pops as an "Uncle Tom," as if he had emerged from the shuck and jive world of minstrels—black entertainers who pandered to what they thought the white man wanted to see and hear. But this great man was never a minstrel or a minstrel sympathizer. Louis Armstrong was a volcanically happy trumpet player who wanted to share his jubilant talent with everybody on the globe. That cheer landed him many parts in major Hollywood films with big-name stars such as Bing Crosby who, at the time, was the undisputed king of musical success.

Clifford Brown, for his part, played that night like an urgent traveler stepping on the gas pedal in a convertible speeding downhill. Both men played low as well as mid-range and high notes with abandon and bravura. On that memorable evening in Atlantic City, there seemed no limitations or restrictions between them. Eyes closed tightly, they executed unscripted passages as if contemplating lost secrets. You could almost hear their thoughts: "Where do I go from here?" "What do I want to do now?" Listeners breathed in short, astonished gasps.

On that unparalleled night, Clifford Brown and Louis Armstrong launched mind-boggling solos in cascading succession. Tadd Dameron was provocative and brilliant as well. How much, I wonder, would a decent recording of that event be worth today? Most of all, I see that Clifford, with his kind and loving attitude, had no desire to embarrass his elegant partner, who (uncharacteristically) played like a Mafioso hit man. This moment, though it was never to be repeated, did not transpire in musical heaven. It was even more sublime. As they finished, I rubbed my eyes and recomposed myself on stage. The maelstrom ceased as if a monsoon had passed, leaving no trace.

He didn't have his trumpet with him, so he played Johnny Coles's horn. After Pops was done, Johnny held the trumpet at arms' length in both hands. He stared at it fixedly; Louie had put something heavy on it. Like Cootie Williams and Roy Eldridge, Armstrong was a power player. One could almost reach out and touch the notes he pushed through the bell of Johnny's trumpet. Of course, his style was his own, different from Johnny's. Louis Armstrong was the John Coltrane of the trumpet and of his expressive style. He was unbelievable. What ideas and power that man had. Louis Armstrong must never be overlooked when great trumpet players are counted. He was the first and set the standard for everyone who followed.

CHAPTER 12

The Duel / CLIFFORD BROWN
AND FATS NAVARRO

CLIFFORD BROWN was beginning to make his mark in and around Philly in 1948. I was home from Howard University that summer and went to a Sunday concert featuring our homeboy Clifford with Fats Navarro, an established guest trumpeter from New York. The idea was to increase the intensity by adding an out-of-town star to the local talent. Those evenings were successful because people enjoy what they perceive to be a battle. Norman Granz's jam sessions around the United States in the 1940s created high-profile all-star competitions between heavyweight players like Lester Young, Coleman Hawkins, Charlie Parker, and Illinois Jacquet, alongside Roy Eldridge, Red Allen, and Dizzy Gillespie. Such events were musical gladiatorial matches. No blood, but jazz fans savor instrumental combat.

This was my first chance to see and hear Fats. Both he and Clifford were extraordinary trumpet players. Brownie hadn't yet recorded as a jazz artist, only with Chris Powell and The Five Blue Flames. Brownie was an aberration in such a group. He was above their level, and he kicked up a lot of dust. Clifford had a unique style and was so gifted that even those who sought a simpler form of musical entertainment found him immensely exciting. Most people had no idea what he was up to, and yet they sensed he was brilliant. Because of him, more and more people paid to hear that otherwise parochial group. Clifford Brown was astounding.

The concert started late because Fats was delayed on his way from New York. Eventually the music began without him. Brownie came roaring out of the starting block. He was playing so much amazing stuff that I wondered what would be left for his guest when he arrived. Fats Navarro was already a recording star; Clifford was merely on the verge of becoming one. Even though the majority of the crowd came to hear Fats, no one was disappointed by the soft-spoken local fellow who turned out to be a raging tiger on the trumpet and later became the predictably lovable Clifford Brown.

The concert well underway, Fats appeared at the rear of the auditorium, aware he was late and hurrying toward the stage by the aisle next to the wall. Clifford was in full stride on stage. As he took in what Clifford was playing, Fats slowed his steps, finally stopping to lean against the wall to listen with absorption. His face told the story. "What's going on up there?" He was obviously thoroughly delighted and surprised by such meaningful lyric power. Clifford finished his solo. Fats climbed the steps to the stage and disappeared through the side curtain. I found out later that the first thing he asked was directly to the point: "Who is this guy?" After the tune was over, Clifford and Fats came together on stage. The *real* meeting was about to take place.

One clearly heard Fats's influence on Clifford's playing in the early days before Brownie started recording, traveling with Sonny Rollins and working countless gigs. He must have been extremely pleased to meet Fats. As I observed all this, I remember thinking, "What a great way to meet your idol, *mano a mano*." John Joyner, a good alto saxophonist, played the concert, too. He was more melodically inclined than wired into bop. History stood in the wings, preparing its entrance. Fats called something up-tempo; the entire auditorium leaned forward with anticipation. I don't remember the tune, but Joyner was "singing" the melody with his horn, sailing happily along. The entire band sounded great. Their tonal complexity meshed beautifully. Fats took the first solo. He played as if it were his last solo ever. He called upon everything he was capable of sharing. Desire and talent told a deep, affirmative story. Could it get any better than this? Fats played five or six choruses, then reluctantly backed away from the microphone, trailing off into the next chorus as if asking himself if he'd said enough.

Brownie moved toward the mic, snagging vestiges of sound and thought Fats had left behind. As he added his terrifying energy to the room, the audience was taken captive. The crowd was enraptured, exultant. Fats made a statement. Clifford compounded its volatility. Detonation grew close. Before welcoming Joyner back into their circle, Clifford and Fats embarked upon an excursion of mind-bending fours. Their friendly ripostes were quick and devastating. A daredevil, Clifford then shifted gears. It was almost too much to endure. When I thought they had gone as far as possible, they went further. Then they did it all again. It was almost supernatural. I heard things the magnitude and extent of which neither I nor anyone present was prepared for emotionally. We had seats on Mount Olympus and the gods on stage played despite our devastation.

Joyner played extremely well before their inhuman opening *tête-à-tête*. He was completely intimidated afterward. From that point on, when he took a solo he played the melody straight, with no improvisation. It must have been embarrassing to do that, but discretion is the soul of valor. Joyner played melodically unadorned for the remainder of the concert. If I attempted to describe more of what I heard and saw that astonishing day, I would grapple with the limits of representation. Seldom have I witnessed such Promethean force and endurance in a live performance. I have no choice but to repeat an often incontestable truth: *It should have been recorded for posterity*. Clifford more than proved his mettle that glorious afternoon in 1948. Any glimmer of doubt that remained about Clifford's ability to perform under extreme pressure was obliterated. Like Homer's Achilles, Clifford Brown was blessed by godlike talent and given too little time to enjoy it.

CHAPTER 13

Wonder and Beauty / BETTY CARTER AND ART FARMER

WHILE I PLAYED with Tadd Dameron in Atlantic City in the summer of 1953, I worked with Betty Carter. She was a member of our show's eclectic cast. She was a master at the complex and inevitably self-defined art of freely improvised "scat singing." Betty's instrument-inflected vocal pyrotechnics were as good as, perhaps better than, many accomplished instrumentalists. She had rare stage presence and vocal command. When Betty was on a bandstand, she was as consequential as any saxophonist or trumpet player. She was at the top of the female vocal profession. The years only made her better. Betty Carter was genuinely a "wonder woman."

Thinking of her among the guys in Tadd's troupe, I have to laugh. Betty's pulchritude, her figure, was exceptional. She could have become Miss America, had that been possible for a black woman in the early 1950s. She had it all. After a week of rehearsals in baggy leisure clothes, on opening night when we all stepped onto the stage in Atlantic City, none of the guys could believe our eyes. Betty was a glorious apparition. None of us had a clue. We were unprepared for her startling beauty. Thus, on stage, we were so focused on her dazzling good looks that our sheet music was, at best, the second object of our individual and collective interest. All our preparations in rehearsal fell apart, and as a result Betty's rock solid instrumental support wobbled. Clunkers here—dissonance there—harmonic and melodic precision in the tank. On opening night, Tadd's aspiring all-star ensemble created all sorts of strange sounds. Betty made the best of it that night. What was the solution? Hilariously, we all memorized her music, so that we could look at her uninterrupted on stage.

Over the years, Betty and I laughed about our nutty opening night in Atlantic City. In 1995, I was hanging out at a jazz club, a casual listener, when unexpectedly Betty showed up. The band asked her to sit in. Her vocal presence made it seem as if the group had added another horn. Betty added a brilliant and arresting dimension, articulating what the musicians were reaching for. When she was done, the set completed, I headed to the bandstand, only a foot or so high, and lifted her onto the floor. I put my arms around her and squeezed. "I love it," I enthused, and kissed her in great admiration of what she had just accomplished and all that she had always been. Both of us were delighted, two aging jazz veterans who went "all the way back."

In 1992 I was preparing a jingle for a Coca Cola television commercial in New York City with my partner, Roy Eaton. I told him Betty would be perfect for what we had in mind. He called her. When she heard the music, she exclaimed that it was not jazz and refused our offer. The money, which was extremely good, didn't matter to her. Betty Carter was a purist devoted to her art at the highest level. Her refusal caused no bad feelings between us. I understood. What she couldn't know was that I loved her even more for her dedication to artistic purity. She was my girl, a pal and a complete professional buddy.

Betty was ambitious in her singing career, and a teacher as well. Most musicians that she hired were just beginning their careers. Her acute sense of timing, dynamics, intervals, and choice of material, in addition to her expansive experience, were passed to them. Like Art Blakey, she was a natural teacher, to the benefit of those fortunate enough to perform with her. Betty left us in September 1998, but she left a coterie of talented musicians whom she had tutored, who continue to sustain and enrich the incalculable art called jazz.

In 1953 I joined Lionel Hampton's band. One of the first musicians of whom I took special notice in the band was Art Farmer. Art had a beautiful style, lyrically delicate and sonically mellow. Art's music was gorgeous. He was a quiet romantic, philosophical, often silently taking into account everything going on around him. Art lived with a cultivated habit of calm scrutiny. When he said anything at all, it was discerning and consequential. His "voice" meant even more when he picked up his trumpet. I had never heard a sound or a style quite like his. Over the course of his long years of artistic development, he developed an absolute understanding of what he once called "the value of a single note." When Art played, he cocked his head to the side and offered passionate love from his horn to his listeners. In turn, he often received sincere and effusive expressions of gratitude and appreciation for his gentle musical intelligence. Art's affection for his instrument (mere brass, shaped and beaten into the shape of a trumpet) had few rivals. Its mouthpiece rested against his expressive mouth and lips, obediently awaiting instruction. One heard a truly creative mind giving direction to subtle ideas and phrases. Art reached out meaningfully and touched his listeners' hearts. When I met him in 1953, I perceived that he was a young master in the early stages of what would be a singular artistic trajectory. After more than four decades of knowing him and playing alongside him on countless occasions, I can say I was not wrong. Art Farmer was a master of the highest magnitude. It is said that a romantic disposition deprecates logic and reason. Art disproved that every time he pushed air through his horn with forceful spiritual precision.

Though he could play every possible tempo and execute any time signature with elusive gradations of pace and feeling, more than any trumpeter I have ever heard or played with, Art Farmer owned the art of the ballad. Ben Webster often insisted that a jazz musician's worth could be assessed accurately only by the way a player handled the depth of thought and feeling in strong ballads such as "Body and Soul" and "Chelsea Bridge." When Art picked up his horn, he was always conscious of the interior intervallic structure of songs. He was conscientious in crafting a framework for melodic emotion, regardless of genre or meter. One can almost hear unwritten lyrics in his solos. We once recorded a series of Bach's Brandenburg Concertos. I found it difficult at moments to tell where Bach's notations ended and Art's improvisation began. His predilection for melody and the underlying lyric logic that carries meaningful song structures forward was profound. He had a preternatural instinct for tonal rightness and expressive touch, an intimate awareness of the most sensitive sonic shadings and dynamic punctuations.

Art's preference for live performances over studio recording work may not have been fully appreciated across the professional world we shared. Art's private nature dictated that he kept many issues of personal choice and discretion completely to himself. But the truth was that he was at his best and most open playing for audiences. I think he felt most himself on stage with his horn in hand, expressing unfathomable depths of feeling where he could see and feel the flesh-and-blood souls who came to share his love of sonic beauty. He enjoyed an audience's affirmation. He often heard astonished or encouraging feedback. "Yes! Yes! Yes!" Art confessed that he intended to give his complete best to his audience each night since, as he put it tersely, "You never know when the person in front of you will only hear you that one night and will remember you just that way forever, good or bad."

In all the years I knew him, Art worked diligently to compress a unique form of poetic thought into his resistant trumpet or flugelhorn. A sense of the need to overcome artistic limitations and physical resistances was with him constantly. The need to achieve compliance from an instrument may account for the enthusiasm that he developed in the last decade or so of his life for a hybrid horn that he had constructed. The *flumpet* was a combination flugel and trumpet, with two bells and protrusions emerging from a single traditional valved housing. Without changing instruments, Art achieved the warmth of a flugel's sound and the force of a trumpet in a single horn.

Fire as much as sweetness was a staple of Art's repertoire. When he turned the heat up on stage, there was usually a kind of low boil at work. I was amused that younger trumpet players sometimes viewed him as old fashioned. If a young player had the surprising good luck to occupy a bandstand with Art, they might be startled to find they got skinned up a bit—a rough but inevitable way to learn who Art Farmer was and what he brought to his performances each night. Art's way of playing the horn was impossible to emulate and not obvious to follow, owing to his enormous sympathy for sudden impulses and odd ideas. Art's mind sometimes carried him in unpredictable directions, making it difficult to anticipate where he was leading musically. He could come out of left field, a total stranger, only to soon reveal himself as your best possible artistic friend. He did that for so long that it became second nature to him, part of his inexplicable artistic allure.

In 1994, Art was honored with a tribute concert at Lincoln Center. The all-star group that night included Gerry Mulligan, Wynton Marsalis, Slide Hampton, Jerome Richardson, Geoffrey Keezer, Ron Carter, Lewis Nash, and me. Humans are hopelessly imperfect creatures, but when he played that night Art Farmer was close to perfect. I never heard him sound so strong and confident. He was absolutely magnificent. As the evening concluded, his scintillating performance provoked a marathon ovation. That night Art was king. What wonderful and merciful musical gifts he gave us. Art Farmer's playing is virtually unmatched anywhere. I love him and always will.

CHAPTER 14

Genius Squared / JIMMY AND PERCY HEATH

URING THE YEARS the young and aspiring musicians in my cohort in Philadelphia were apprenticed to the future, formulating plans for tomorrow, Jimmy Heath's older brother, Percy, served as a pilot in the U.S. Army Air Corps. It was not yet called The U.S. Air Force, but Percy was in a special unit of black men whose academic skills qualified them to join an experimental group formed in Alabama at the Tuskegee Institute. Many political and commercial bigwigs had no confidence in them. They thought these men would fall flat on their faces, embarrassing those who suggested the idea. Failure was not an option for these men. Too much was riding on their performance. The all knew they represented both the United States and their racial counterparts everywhere. They were closely scrutinized and they passed with flying colors.

Percy learned to fly with this unit and did quite well for himself in a professional formation that accomplished a number of remarkable goals and outcomes that many government administrators considered impossible, especially from black airmen. Pressure to dissolve the unit faded with its success. White bomber pilots testified that they depended on this unit's skill in escort duty to enhance the safety of their missions. Percy's escort group never lost a bomber.

Back home, Jimmy Heath was extremely proud of his older brother. He carried Percy's photo in his wallet, a handsome young man dressed in his

Air Corps uniform. At every opportunity, Jimmy produced that photograph and declared emphatically, "This is my brother!" He repeated that routine so often, we laughed not at Jimmy, but at his undeviating script. Percy had no intention of making a career of flying. When the war ended, he took his discharge and returned to Philly as a local hero. Percy was one of a kind. Fortunately, Percy took notice of what Jimmy and the rest of us were up to. He decided to be a part of it, so he took bass lessons at the Granoff School of Music, with assistance from the G.I. Bill. Incredibly, in less than a year, he became the bassist with The Hollis Hoppers, led by pianist Bill Hollis. I was astounded the first time I heard Percy play with the group. He made it all seem easy while I was struggling uphill as if my life were on the line. A year or so later, Percy moved to New York, where he displaced Nelson Boyd as the most sought-after bassist on the scene. Percy was soon recording with Coleman Hawkins and notable others. I could not comprehend how a pilot turned on the proverbial dime and almost instantly morphed into a jazz bassist extraordinaire. There's no script to match that story. The man was a phenomenon on his way, while I hadn't even gotten past the city limits.

Many years later, after I established myself, Percy came down to the Five Spot to hear me play with Curtis Fuller. At the end of the night, he talked to our bass player and was soon playing bass at the foot of the bandstand. My horn was packed away, but his playing sounded so good that I "scat sang" chorus after chorus with him. He played so many interesting licks that night, genuinely fresh ideas and unusual riffs, that I never forgot what he did (though I suspect he did). After Percy joined The Modern Jazz Quartet, he had time to pursue one of his deepest pleasures, deep-sea fishing from the deck of his own boat. Percy Heath was a man for all seasons. I doubt anyone ever made such quick progress on an instrument as Percy did. But the astonishing part of his success was how far his art developed after such a late start in music, which at no point revealed anything except profound and enduring good taste.

By 1946, after three years of earnest commitment to my horn, I had met and played with everyone who made up the cohort of my generation's jazz musicians in Philly: John Coltrane, Philly Joe Jones, Tommy and Ray Bryant, Red Rodney, Coatesville Harris, Butch Ballard, and Jimmy and Percy Heath. There were others that only local musicians of my generation would recall. From the outset, Jimmy Heath wanted to grasp everything Diz and Bird were creating. He had exalted ideas about the way to accomplish that. Jimmy was always deep inside the music of our recorded heroes, gleaning new things from their playing. But, for us, Jimmy was a hero, too. When I was seventeen years old, I heard that he was organizing a big band. I was sure Jimmy would make that happen. He had enough knowledge. He had drive and ambition. And the music was going to be hip. If only I were good enough to play in that band, I thought. I was resigned to wait for something of that magnitude to appear when I was ready. After all, I had been dismissed from Jimmy Johnson's band just the year before because I wasn't up to par. It seemed that heartbreak and disappointment were part of the vetting process to become a professional musician. The burning question for me was who would play in Jimmy Heath's new band?

A few days later Jimmy called. He wanted me in his band! I couldn't believe it—me, in that hip, exploratory big band? Had he asked, I would have run from North Philly all the way to Jimmy's house in South Philly at that very moment. He said I would be fourth tenor. "Sax" Young would be second tenor and would take most of the solos. (Sax Young had a son whom he named Lester, after his famous predecessor on the tenor sax, Lester Young.) He was a better saxophone player than I was then, no question. But no matter: I was in the band. Wowie-zowie! I felt as if I had just been asked to join Dizzy Gillespie or Charlie Parker, Jimmy's offer was honestly that meaningful to me. I would not let him down.

Already the local jazz community was abuzz about this band. Every chair in the band was highly coveted. Everyone who aspired to be a significant jazz musician wanted to be in that band. Jimmy asked John Coltrane to play third alto. That meant Jimmy, who played alto then, would take most of the alto solos, which was reasonable because it was his band. John Joyner was first chair alto. His playing had a singing quality which made him a natural for that spot.

Since Jimmy knew so many musicians in New York, the word spread there, too. A trumpet player and arranger named Johnny Acea, a Philly expatriate, wrote several arrangements for our band. Therefore, soon I would no longer have to play cheap stock arrangements. We were all moving up. Leroy Lovett, a successful Philadelphia writer who had written songs for Nat Cole, also wrote for us. Tadd Dameron was supposed to craft something, too, but I don't remember him doing so. Jimmy Heath was an excellent writer, so he wrote many of the songs we played. This was absolutely certain: no other big band would sound like this one. We rehearsed often to sound as strong and polished as possible. And, man, we did sound good. We rehearsed at Jimmy's house. His parents were our champions.

Their house wasn't large, and in order to fit the band into the limited space, we had to move furniture around drastically. Jimmy's little brother, Tootie, was always running through the house in his short pants, appearing important to other little kids who climbed up to peek through the windows. Great commotion and furniture swapping invaded little Tootie's house. By extension that conferred importance on him. He'd run inside and then back out to shoot marbles with his buddies. There was no way to know that, eventually, we would wait for him to be our drummer.

Soon we were ready for the band's inaugural appearance. We were the new band in town, kids with talent, ambition, and hope. Jimmy bought a new suit and someone straightened his hair. On opening night he looked the part, bandleader par excellence. How proud I was of him. This totally great guy knew what to do. He was truly our leader. We opened at The Elite Ballroom in South Philly, often used as a skating rink, where I had heard Dizzy's big band a year before. We were greeted by a room jammed with people. We gave everything we had and we were a smash success. It was glorious! I must confess that this performance was one of the happiest, most rewarding moments of my early life as a musician. I was privileged to be a part of something grand. Even bringing back the memory now, those feelings course through me all over again.

Like John Coltrane and Ray Bryant, I met Jimmy Heath when we were teenagers. Jimmy's youthful knowledge of the saxophone and of musical structures and concepts made things accessible to him that most of us struggled slowly to understand. He seemed genuinely comfortable with everything he played. No one is born with such knowledge. Musical accomplishment comes hard. Everyone has to listen, practice, study, analyze, conjecture, and progress by trial and error. But Jimmy's capacious mind quickly absorbed the necessary things that, early on, advanced his career. He always "danced" through chord changes like spilled quicksilver. With all that in his grasp, he gave us something to shoot for.

In 1998, Jimmy had been a professor at Lincoln Center, Queens College, for a decade. He was given a retirement bash, and friends, including me, came to share the honor bestowed on him. Along with others, he played that evening in his always engaging, flawless way. Before he went on stage, he sat with a gang of musicians backstage. Sitting on a high stool that bassists sometimes use, he listened attentively to the performance out front. His saxophone rested in his lap. Almost involuntarily, he put the horn in his mouth and quietly played with the group performing on stage as they took up Dizzy Gillespie's "Con Alma." That song is not easy to execute if your goal is to make it really mean something. It's a thinking man's song. Backstage, Jimmy began quietly, masterfully gliding through its complex changes. His *sotto voce* rendition was magnificent. I was so moved as I listened that I felt like jumping up with praise. When he stopped, I said simply, "See what I mean?" He looked at me, puzzled. I was, of course, referring to what I had told him many times: he really knows chords. He never plays them wrong. Jimmy always dismisses such praise. That's the way he is, much like John Coltrane and Clifford Brown. I don't think anybody in the world knows more about chords than Jimmy Heath. The man is absolutely remarkable. He is the boss.

Thank you, boss—how can I ever say "thank you" to the once and always fantastic Jimmy Heath?

CHAPTER 15

Unrivaled Aces / SARAH VAUGHAN
AND BILL EVANS

I N 1952 I had been playing with Bull Moose Jackson's band for almost a year when we took an engagement at the famed Apollo Theater in Harlem. I was excited because the venue was famous and I felt that such appearances helped me move forward. Even though the band's music was not what I wanted to pursue, when you're starting out as a nobody, you take advantage of any opportunity in reach. You always hope for the best. The day before we opened, Tadd Dameron and I walked past the Theresa Hotel at 125th Street and Seventh Avenue, just a block down the street from the Apollo, still in its heyday. Tadd told me that he always kept a suite at the Theresa no matter where he went. I later discovered that that wasn't true, but I laughed to myself when I realized that he wanted to impress me. Tadd took a liking to me. He knew that he was my idol and so he wanted to be a worldly mentor. I think he amused himself when he told a whopper. He promised to take me to Europe and give me an appropriate introduction to the European public. Tadd went to Europe before I met him, but he never returned. I was always impressed by his visions of glory until they went belly up.

The Apollo featured Pigmeat Markham, a comedian, on the bill with us. I had heard of Pigmeat, and after seeing his act I understood why he was popular in the black community. His comic style was vaudevillian, inspired by a time long past. He worked with a straight man, who would set up his pranks perfectly, in much the way Bud Abbott made Lou Costello the butt of his jokes. Those two white comedians rode Pigmeat's old-fashioned style right into Hollywood films.

The week at the Apollo was especially significant because I met Sarah Vaughan, who was also featured on the program. When I began playing sax, I became aware that she sang with Billy Eckstine's band. What really brought her to my attention was the recording (a two-sided seventy-eight-rpm disc) she made with Tadd for the Craft Music label. Sarah was featured on both sides: "My Kinda Love" and "I Could Make You Love Me," where Freddie Webster, a friend of Tadd's from Cleveland who was known for his beautiful sound (as well as his influence on the early Miles Davis), played a gorgeous trumpet introduction. On "My Kinda Love," Leo Parker played a terrific baritone sax solo. That record knocked me out. I almost wore it out. I fell in love with the songs and with Tadd's arrangements, along with the soloists and, of course, Sassy's voice. How I loved her voice. I think every jazz musician did. Sarah's voice was a bold yet infinitely refined musical instrument with its own authority and autonomy.

In later life, Sarah became heavy, but during the week we played at the Apollo, she weighed all of a hundred and ten pounds. The band rehearsed her music for the show, and soon after that Tadd introduced us to one another. I was thrilled. What a lovely human being and what a stunning artist and woman. Even though she was gaining commercial recognition and wide popular acceptance, Sarah was relaxed and clearly unaffected by her growing stature. She was grounded by her calm good humor and self-confidence.

Tadd had just purchased a new car, a Kaiser, and wanted to take us for a ride in it. Between shows that week, Sarah and I climbed into Tadd's new vehicle with him at the wheel. From the Apollo's backstage behind 126th Street, we headed for Central Park and took a brief summer ride around the park—once around the park only. We were, indeed, impressed with Tadd's sparkling new Kaiser. He squired us along Manhattan streets and byways, beaming. I think it was the first new car he ever owned. The three of us bubbled with conversation. Sarah was ebullient like a schoolgirl. She was honest, funny, and completely free of hang-ups. At one point, moving through the park, Tadd hit the brakes pretty hard. Startled, Sarah broke out cheerfully, "Lawdy!"

That car ride was the beginning of a friendship that lasted until Sarah's death, which came much too early, a week after her sixty-sixth birthday, in

1990. Joe Henderson and I recorded with her once, in a big band setting. On occasion, she would show up where I was playing. If I asked her to sit in for a number or two, as I did with Dinah Washington, Sarah always agreed. Once in Los Angeles she came up to sing "The Man I Love." My piano player was young and didn't know the song. She sat down and accompanied herself on keyboard as we played it together. Sarah, like Carmen MacRae, was an excellent pianist.

About six years after I met her, I was performing at Birdland on 52nd Street with Dizzy Gillespie. Sassy came in during intermission. I was standing near the bar talking to Gigi Gryce. It was clear she had had a few drinks. I was about to greet her with a hug when she began to cuss me out loudly. I was dumfounded and a little hurt. Strangely, she never told me what had angered her. As Gigi and I walked away, he told me that he felt she "had eyes" for me and probably was angry because I had never "given her a tumble." I didn't believe him, but I also had no clue what triggered her diatribe. The next time I saw her I braced for the worst, but she acted as if nothing strange had ever happened. We hugged one another and exchanged pleasant greetings. Maybe she didn't remember the incident at Birdland. Maybe she had had more than a little to drink that perplexing night. She never said anything about our weird interlude, nor did I. Everything was normal once again. All's well as such.

Sarah often starred at the Blue Note in Tokyo. She had an enormous fan base and appeared there for the last time only ten days before she died. Evidence of several kinds suggests that her last concert, backed by a hundred-piece orchestra and her Los Angeles pianist, George Gaffney, was as powerful and artistically moving as any she ever gave in her long career. She was already booked for a return engagement to the club not long after. Ironically, after she passed away, the club called to ask me to stand in as her replacement. It was a deeply bittersweet engagement. I was glad to play there, but the circumstances were painfully personal for me. Only a few months before, I had composed a new ballad, "Sad to Say." I played it every night during that gig in Tokyo, dedicating it to Sarah. I had lost a very dear friend. All of us lost an artist without equal.

In 1952, in Philly, I received a call from Skeets Marsh, a drummer who had once worked with me and Jimmy Preston. He was traveling with Herbie Fields, a tenor and soprano player who was the only white member in that band. Herbie used to laugh because everyone thought he was black since he was playing with spades. On our trips down south, that assumption resulted in his repeated inability to get rooms in white hotels. Herbie loved the bigots' mistake. He wouldn't stay separately in lily-white accommodations anyway. He was that kind of guy, but he enjoyed innocent fun with common human foibles. At one point he left Lionel Hampton's band (which paid notoriously low wages) to form his own group. As luck had it, Herbie recorded a big hit, "Dardanella," which kept him going strong for quite a while.

Skeets recommended my twenty-two-year old savvy for a spot in Herbie's band. His group was usually small, but from time to time he enlarged it when he went on a tour consisting of engagements at four predominantly black theaters. When I joined the group, I met an unknown piano player who looked and played like a country hick. He bore no resemblance whatsoever to any talented jazz pianist I had ever known. He looked like a college student majoring, perhaps, in archeology or advanced botany. Although it pains me to admit this, he was a classic nerd. His name was Bill Evans. He later became *the* Bill Evans. When we first met, however, he was far from being the path-breaking, transformational piano shaman whom everyone came to respect and adore. His playing was corny and stiff, with spastic movements augmenting his cornpone squareness. This version of Bill Evans sat rigidly straight, bouncing up and down when he became engaged in the music. His sound was reminiscent of Milt Buckner, a long-time pianist and organ player with Hamp, though he lacked Milt's residual drive and swing. This early incarnation of Bill Evans had an absurd way of patting his feet. Notice I said *feet*. While he played, he would lock his feet together and roll or wobble their knotted unity back and forth from beat-to-beat—heels then toes, over and over, again and again, creating a kind of rocking-chair gait with both feet clamped together like a vise. I have never understood how he did that. I assure you, he had a performance persona so estranged from any jazz posture or attitude or, for that matter, from any musical self-presentation that I encountered before or since that I truly cannot fathom how the great musician he became could have originated from that.

I was enthralled by his entire demeanor. If one can accurately assert that profound perplexity is able to frame aesthetic engagement, then Bill Evans's performance on that occasion constitutes the single instance in my life when I enjoyed a live musical event that, bizarrely, tempted me equally toward laughter and astonishment. Mostly I scratched my head that night. I never could find a way to comprehend such awkward and frankly dorky unself-consciousness. Let me come right out and say it. This aberrational version of "Bill Evans" was a cornball. I could tell he had talent, but he exploited it in an oddly lonely, yet nonetheless sincerely sweet way.

I left that band after a very short stay. The next time my path intersected with Bill's was at least three years later. In fact, on that occasion I heard Bill play before I spoke with him. Unbelievably, the Bill Evans I had briefly encountered years earlier had disappeared. Someone with the same name took his place, an utterly different Bill Evans. What I heard across those ear-opening moments left me breathless. This former "cornball" played some of the most beautiful chords and voicings I had ever heard. That night he touched my heart again and again: amazing tonal complexity, unearthly lyric beauty. I listened flabbergasted. How could this be? Not only were Bill's chord choices enchanting; his pace and time sense were otherworldly. He knew when and how to suggest dark and light shades, holding overt dynamic contrast in reserve. He had a knack for jumping ahead to compress or elaborate his melodic narrative. His playing kept me riveted and off guard. I did not know what to expect at any moment. I was overwhelmed with admiration. This was musical genius.

When the set was over, I went over and asked Bill, "What happened?" A stupid question. I had just heard what happened. Bill was courteous and replied quietly. "Sometimes we have to make changes." He added that he now heard other things in his head and was trying to bring them into his technique. I wasn't at all sure what he was hearing, but what I heard was more than impressive. His delicate passion touched my heart. What a delightful, memorable evening the "real" Bill Evans gave me.

Several years later I ran into Bill on a Manhattan sidewalk. I asked him how things were going. I knew he had formed a stable trio with Scott LaFaro and Paul Motian on bass and percussion. Bill said he was not happy. Scott was driving him crazy. I wasn't familiar with Scott's playing but I knew he was very good. Simply enough, Bill wanted Scott to "walk" (maintaining a strolling, deliberate pace on the bass) more frequently. Apparently Scott was doing very little of that. Instead, he was creating subthemes and spontaneous motifs, not with quarter notes in a walking style, but with syncopated figures that came spontaneously forward with determined emphasis. Scott's approach was eccentric and Bill had not yet absorbed its possibilities. As we know, Bill soon came to love Scott's style, and their partnership was about to change jazz history. Eventually, the two of them developed a profound, unscripted interplay, both as a tandem and within their trio setting. Their Village Vanguard recordings from July 1961 set a permanent benchmark for empathetic trio interaction, a standard of nearly telepathic musical communication. When Scott departed from his drifting, aleatoric inclinations and began "walking" underneath Bill's figures, the differentiation in pace and attack accentuated (perhaps intensified) the metrical value and undercarriage of the walking bass line. Even the sound of clinking glasses, as can be heard on Bill's live recordings at the Vanguard from 1961, couldn't diminish the deep integrity of his transcendentally meditative music. His vision and internal focus overcame distraction. Tragically, Scott LaFaro was killed in an automobile accident shortly after those inimitable live sets were captured. For me, it is more than merely unfortunate that I never got to know this very special bassist.

Bill Evans overcame many problems across the span of his career. Perhaps guitarist Mundell Lowe, who first recognized Bill's unrivaled genius and alerted Orrin Keepnews at Riverside Records, saw the strength and artistic resolve in Bill that (despite his self-destructive heavy drug use) carried him to success. During an interim within the long odyssey of Bill's personal and artistic metamorphosis, we ran into each other in Stockholm. I was there on a special summer project when Bill's trio came to Sweden for a week to play at a club called the Golden Circle. I had not seen Bill in years, but as I approached him he pulled out a hundred dollar bill and said, "This is what I owe you. Sorry it took so long." If he owed me money I had completely forgotten, but he hadn't. He had reclaimed his life and looked better for gaining some weight, which he carried gracefully. The frail, sickly guy was gone. His son had recently been born, an event that seemed to inspire Bill toward even greater musical seriousness and intensity. Later still, at the Monterey Jazz Festival in California, I asked him what he had named his son. "Evan Evans," he said. I asked how he could do such a thing to his own kid. We both laughed and that was the last time I saw Bill.

I also recall a visit he made to my James Towers penthouse in New York sometime in the 1960s, I think. He came to wish me well and to find out what I was up to. He spoke of his home in Plainfield, New Jersey—not far from New York in miles, but by then so very far spiritually and existentially for him. Bill had come a long way, but not as far as he wished. Scott LaFaro's death had troubled him immensely. His work with Scott, a brief but ineradicable advance upon previous trio conceptions, surely constitutes Bill Evans's most permanent legacy. He knew that once again, he had to move on. But how? In the 1950s, Miles Davis had tapped him, and he brought exotic delicate feeling to Miles's late 1950s classic sextet, perhaps Miles's most glorious ensemble. The legendary *Kind of Blue* sessions in the spring of 1959 emerged from an improbable group of six highly individualistic men, each an artist of distinction. There was a time in my life when I wondered what might have transpired if, in some counterintuitive but angelic way, Philly Joe had recommended me instead of my dear pal John for Miles's quintet. I am deeply, ironically aware that despite the world's absurdity and evil, most of the important events that define reality are shaped with rare tact and surprising finesse.

In my estimation, Bill Evans's transformation in the mid-1950s was a miracle. I was so fascinated by it that I began to think about the ramifications of changing my approach to the horn. I'm not sure how many people are aware of what such a transformation entails. Consider this. Some musicians span more than one artistic and cultural generation. A few who straddle two eras in this way are able to successfully leave stylistic habits and expectations behind, or to enhance and refine a former approach, as Bill Evans did. Such adventurers embrace a *newer* style. For all intents and purposes, they are heroic. Such a complete artistic change is akin to revolutionizing the way you think and act, the way you walk, laugh, and speak. In the head of a performer who has remade himself in this way, two entirely different expressive and stylistic personalities vie for predominance. Perhaps he chooses to explore the new style or approach most of the time, but at times the older artistic persona steps up again, demanding acknowledgment. Self-transformation is extremely difficult. Ask Sonny Rollins, George Coleman, or Clark Terry about this daunting challenge.

Every now and then I slip into yesterday, as I'm told others from my era sometimes do, too. George Coleman, who used to play with B.B. King, is able to do wonderful things on his horn when he ransacks his earlier expressive techniques. It is wonderful to hear him play like Lester Young, holding his horn high in the air, making even George laugh. When I do similar things, my musical colleagues stare at me and crack up. I must confess, sometimes I enjoy such foolishness. There are moments when the music and the occasion dictate it, not often, never permanently. I don't live my life as a musician according to the rigidity of a calendar, and I don't permit age to stop me from exploring what I want to pursue creatively. A curiosity-seeking, ambitious kid still lives inside me. I let him prowl about musically and influence what I play and write as much as possible.

CHAPTER 16

Four "Brothers" | MULGREW MILLER,
WOODY HERMAN,
HENRY BRANT, AND
GEORGE RUSSELL

FIRST HEARD pianist Mulgrew Miller during his appearance with The Messengers in Los Angeles. Mulgrew's playing is always daring. I call his approach "sandwich playing" because it combines related and unrelated things seamlessly within unfolding musical structures. The ability to fuse extraordinary ideas and licks with ordinary riffs and conventional phrases made Mulgrew's imaginings unique. His technique aroused both attention and emotion. When Mulgrew played piano in my quartet, along with Peter Washington and Tony Reedus, some nights he played with such intensity it seemed as if his existence were at stake. One night, on a European tour, Mulgrew became so lost in the upsurge of his playing that he leaned so far across the upper key range that he almost fell off the bench. He quickly regained his balance and dug in even more ferociously. He was clearly in an altered state of consciousness, his hands flying left and right. His musical poetry was superb.

I wish Mulgrew had been recorded that night. Though he was a quiet man, much like Clifford Brown, when Mulgrew Miller began playing, he was transformed into another creature, a passionate lover or a raging tiger. Like all great musicians, he threw himself completely into his art to the point that, in a sense, he *became* what he played. It often seems that we best express our innermost energy when we are liberated from intrinsic structures. When Mulgrew Miller played, I felt his heart and soul as much as I heard what he was playing.

There were sides to Mulgrew Miller that few people knew. He could go to sleep as fast as a gunslinger in the old Wild West could draw on an enemy. When we traveled together, I often saw Mulgrew drop into sleep instantly. Peter Washington told me about a plane flight the two of them took together. Mulgrew fell asleep before everyone had even boarded the plane. As the plane began rolling down the runway for takeoff, Mulgrew woke up and asked, "Are we there?"

Once, in Japan, our group piled into a car heading for Yokohama. Our driver got lost on the way. Mulgrew, of course, had nodded off within minutes of departure. We were lost for two *horrible* hours. We passed the same places three or four times, our moods darkening. Finally we arrived at our hotel tired, disgusted, and frustrated. We opened the doors of the car in triumph. Here we were at last! Either the cessation of movement or the opening of the taxi's doors awakened Mulgrew, for he roused himself right then and exclaimed happily, "Wow, that was quick!"

Mulgrew Miller always accomplished the unexpected. Anticipation prevailed when he played. His band mates knew something rare was about to occur. His musical groove, the inspiration he radiated toward others, his calm urgency to move in sync with the whole ensemble, elevated those who played with him. It was impossible not to take inspiration from Mulgrew Miller. I appreciated his unique uplift. Nonetheless, Mulgrew felt that his talent was not unique. The truly great players are often self-deprecating. Inferior players often compensate by acting as if they are underacclaimed. Mulgrew's outlook, however, motived his constant self-improvement.

When I think of great and special people, I remember the night I spent with Woody Herman soon after he dissolved his big band, to everyone's dismay, and formed a sextet. He chose Nat Adderley as his trumpet player. Nat was a strong asset. That small group sounded very good. One day Nat called to ask me to join Woody's gang as a sub at the popular but now defunct Metropole, downtown on Seventh Avenue. The unusual thing about that celebrated venue was its openness to the street. People routinely stood on the sidewalk and enjoyed performances on the high stage near the front door. I suppose this served as a musical tease, since people often walked in seemingly impulsively. The Metropole's bill of fare was usually

Dixieland, though sometimes the management diversified their offerings. Henry "Red" Allen was a fixture, so Woody's sextet was just visiting.

I headed over that night without any knowledge of what would happen. The only thing I clearly remember playing was "Moonglow." I had heard the tune many times but had never played it. I made my ears as big as an elephant's all evening. When the gig was over, Woody thanked me and said he liked my playing. But, then, I grew up with "Woodchopper's Ball." Woody was a legendary musician whom I deeply respected. His approval was good for my self-respect. One is not always totally sure about one's art. A venerable musician such as Maestro Herman giving one kudos was wonderful personal reinforcement.

About this time, I became interested in composing film scores. I realized how much extra life music can bring to a film's story lines and cinematography, even if they are vivid already. Tom McIntosh, a former trombonist with The Jazztet, and a fine arranger, told me that trumpeter Jimmy Owens had been attending a class put together by aspiring musicians interested in learning advanced techniques of orchestration. A formidable orchestrator, Henry Brant (1913–2008), taught them once a week and they shared the cost of his fee. This arrangement sounded like exactly what I'd been looking for, so Tom and I explored working with the group. Unfortunately the class ended not long after that, so we missed our chance. I approached Mr. Brant to ask if I could be his student, and he accepted me. Over our time together, I learned a great deal.

Brant was teaching at Bennington College in Vermont and returned home to Brooklyn every weekend. My appointment with him was at ten o'clock each Sunday morning at his house. I had never met him before my first class. I was surprised when I first encountered him. He was maybe five feet tall and wore horn-rimmed glasses, cloth-covered, crepe-soled shoes, and a baseball cap. The legendary Henry Brant looked like a guy who owns the corner newspaper stand, completely unlike my expectation of the brilliant composer and master orchestrator he truly was.

My first lesson with Henry Brant in Brooklyn was almost as exciting as the time John Coltrane and I went to hear Charlie Parker for the first time in Philly. Epiphanies emerged from all directions. I began an apprenticeship toward my fullest artistic maturity. I soon learned that Brant was the orchestrator for the Hollywood composer extraordinaire, Alex North. Brant orchestrated scores for *Cleopatra*, *Spartacus*, and *Kings Go Forth*, outstanding films with remarkable music brilliantly orchestrated. My new mentor let me copy sections of the score to *Cleopatra,* and I was immediately dazzled by his work. As we sat at his piano each week, he often demonstrated the techniques he used to write complicated, beautiful music. He composed as easily as I would write a note to myself or to my wife. Henry Brant opened one technical door after another for me, all of them creating lyrical beauty or intrigue or grandeur. He introduced me to pandiatonic (free) composing, symmetrical chords, binary and trinary chords, mirror writing, and antiphonal writing, and he taught me how to craft notes for one instrument alone with messages implied for the remaining elements in a symphonic configuration. He showed me how to create musical messages for all symphonic instruments ("chance music") as well as how to employ multiple time signatures, polyrhythm, and double and triple twelve-tone writing.

After a number of weeks absorbing these powerful lessons, I was asked to write the score for a European film. I dug into that assignment using everything Henry Brant had taught me. Eventually, I brought a tape of the score to him, thinking he would be interested because I had taken full advantage of his creative tutelage. Although I had executed some complicated new techniques, the, maestro was most interested in the "chance music" I had sketched out, involving no written notes.

That choice gave me pause. Brant was a perfectionist. Every note transcribed had to be precise and accurate. Absolute order and discipline were necessary. Of course, Henry Brant was right. That lesson made all the difference for me when I began working full time in movie studios. Notating legibly saves time. Time saved is money earned or, at least, not squandered. Studio copyists never once had problems of any sort with my work, thanks to Henry Brant's didactic expectations. I now teach with the same aim and outlook. Brant also worked strictly by the clock. When we began our one-hour session each Sunday morning, he would set his clock on the piano. When the hour was up, he stopped whatever we were doing, even if it meant halting at the end of a sentence (his or mine). The session was over, no more discussion about anything. Not a minute extra. That was fine with me, because the information I took in during that one hour was nearly overwhelming.

I am left with an ineradicable memory of my time with Henry Brant. During one session, I listened to a large orchestral work that Brant had composed. It was fantastic. He played just enough for me to get the sense of what he had done. "How many parts do you think I actually wrote?"

he asked me. I had no idea. Surprisingly, he had written only the flute part, the lead voice. The rest of the orchestra had messages written out for them, directions that indicated what to do. It was chance music, of course, but that did not mean it was music under the sway of raw chance. Brant gave directions to inspire (in fact, to prompt) precisely those sounds I had just heard. I think of that music as the invention of "best possible chances." There is nothing obvious about such composing. An ineffable form of imagination and a profound musical intelligence are at work in such writing. Henry Brant taught me extremely well. He gave me an education for the whole of my future, but that future was completely up to me to carry out in practice. As I think back, I suppose learning always comes to this: What should we do with what we have learned and how should we do it?

When George Russell (1923–2009) moved to New York, it was not with an instrument under his arm, but with a pen in his hand. A redoubtable pen that was, too, a pen without fear. George Russell's compositions probed for things never before encountered. George Russell was not inclined to follow the well-worn paths of those who preceded him. For a composer, adventurousness is an instant liability. Anyone who creates something that deviates from traditional frameworks finds the going rough. The utterly new is always marginalized or rejected. A far easier route is to pursue new ways of approaching the same old thing. But George Russell had a special compositional magic. His avoidance of the predictable and his aversion to every form of musical cliché produced consequential and meaningful music. Such brave self-disregard is undertaken only by a master.

I remember George working with great élan, always undaunted by setbacks or uncertainty. He was not arrogant, however. He had only one agenda, to find refreshing new approaches to music. He wanted to expand the jazz heritage. In particular, I remember one massive project he undertook, an album for Columbia Records. He called it *New York, New York*. Jon Hendricks wrote the lyrics, and John Coltrane was also involved. John was brilliant, of course. This project was the first and only time John and I ever recorded anything *together*, though we were inseparable early in our maturing careers. I worked on that album while I was playing at the Five Spot with Curtis Fuller over a span of eighteen months. I looked up one night and saw George Russell, sitting in the audience silent and attentive. After the set was over, he asked me if I would like to join the group recording his new album. I jumped at the opportunity. After all, this was "Mr. Russell." I still chuckle to myself about the brute fact that he had come to make sure I had what he was looking for. Had he not liked what he heard, I would not have the memories of those sessions that I cherish.

Years later, the world has still not caught up with George Russell's artistic mind. Like most creative people, he lived with one foot in the present and the other planted firmly in the future. Thank goodness for a mind like George Russell's. If some opportunities did not come his way, it was because of *fools in high places.* In every profession, "important" people with closed minds and full bank accounts hold power over genuinely innovative people whose dedication to expressive or conceptual difference unnerves them.

Too many friends are now gone—special people and sometimes great people. Old age is a failing battle with flesh. Those who survive a long span of years find themselves engaged with a hopeless task. Dwelling on that finale obscures each day's joy. Composers and musicians look ahead, as does anyone who has made a long journey. Each day is an opportunity to improve. The goal is to keep trying sincerely for as long as possible, and we love it. I have been deeply blessed by association with many wonderful and amazing people. Among them is George Russell. Those who studied with Russell were very fortunate and should always feel privileged. From one composer to another, I proudly salute this rare man, George Allen Russell.

PART IV *Hollywood*

The Grand Maestro di Maestri Benny Golson is, and throughout my lifetime will always be, a guiding light and inspiration for me. We all are blessed to be in his audience. Saluti, Mr. Golson!

   —JOE LOVANO

CHAPTER 17

Starting Over

REAKING INTO the major leagues of cinema is exhausting and discouraging. At least, that was how I encountered it. I constantly ran into brick walls. I was firmly established in New York, but I left "The City" and headed west. Hollywood was immensely disappointing. I wanted no limitations on what and how I wrote, and I refused to be typecast. I wanted to write jazz and everything else.

However, in Hollywood everyone operates within well-defined niches and under known labels. I resisted stereotyping; I did not want to be branded as a "jazz guy." I refused local club gigs for fear my reputation would lock me in. I took refuge in my self-assured uniqueness as an enlightened product of Charlie Parker and Henry Brant. Who else could claim such elite company? I succeeded, in a way, at resisting being labeled a jazz guy. After a year or so, I no longer received calls asking me to play clubs or festivals. I had burned old bridges. But that left me no obvious way to return to safety in sight. Now it was all or nothing.

I put my saxophone in its case, intending never to take it out again. Maybe I was nuts. Or perhaps, I thought, I had said all I could say on the instrument. But although I wanted to move on musically, I did not know where, or how to get there. Not long after arriving in Smogville, frustration began to devour me. I was worried about my self-imposed plight. My good old saxophone days were gone forever, but what was next?

My old friend tenor sax titan Eddie "Lockjaw" Davis came out west in 1970 for a gig at an L.A. club. Bobbie and I went to hear him play. Before the break, Lockjaw suddenly unfastened his neck strap and came over to where we sat. The rhythm section was still digging in. He put his horn in my hands. I had no desire to play, but we would both be embarrassed if I refused.

I found myself in an awkward spot, unrehearsed on the horn and distracted by my search for another life. I played, as requested—sort of. It was impossible not to hear how different I sounded. Recognizing that was not fun for me. I was not the same player I once was. I put that compromising moment out of my mind for the duration of my four years of jazz exile. The horn ceased to exist for me as I became a successful Hollywood composer. Then, out of nowhere, in 1974 I received an offer from Cobi Narita of the Universal Jazz Coalition summoning me to New York. Although I had previously turned down Cobi's many offers to feature me in a Town Hall concert, somehow this time the occasion seemed right. My old itch to play was returning.

That invitation began a long voyage back that I had previously shunned without regret. When I took out my saxophone, it felt foreign, like a piece of lead plumbing. Everything I had previously possessed was gone: concepts, comfort, embouchure, and repertoire. Even the corn on the thumb that had supported my horn had disappeared. It felt like I was recuperating from a stroke. In truth, my playing at that concert was a pale image of how I had played before my hiatus. I embarrassed myself. The audience surely expected more of me. At my back on stage, Frank Foster, a tremendous tenor saxophonist, sat front and center of the big band, supporting my humble efforts, but that was not enough to salvage it. Moves that took me no effort previously were difficult or worse.

I continued to struggle for years afterward, performing publically only at summer festivals. Each fall, I was harnessed again to Hollywood scoring stages. All of this created a different crisis than before. I was sadly lacking as a "saxophonist." At best I was a "former jazz" guy. It took ten agonizing years before I felt comfortable playing the horn again. That long, bleak interlude from my instrument did tremendous damage to my confidence and execution. Had I known coming back would be so difficult, the ease and joy I had once taken confidently for granted now so elusive, I might not have tried to do it.

Hollywood's moguls were more than fair to me. Surprisingly, at the outset those who hired me to compose for film and television did not seem concerned about my inexperience with the rather tricky film-creation timing process. In retrospect, I am amazed that I got away with such ignorance. Early on, I was often asked, casually but confidently, questions such as, "You *do* know about timing and click tracks, don't you?" My "Yes" was an outright lie. Since I had to learn quickly, I asked another film writer for help, and he directed me to a useful book and told me where to get it. That book saved my Hollywood career. When I did my first show, I was dealing with higher mathematics. I had never been a great math student. With this book, all I had to do was establish a desired tempo, find the right page, and track where each beat of that tempo sat in real time. Everyone assumed I could handle various orchestras, large and small. Fortunately, that was true, so I never had a problem there.

When I was spotting my first show at Universal (looking at the film without music, to decide where adding music would be appropriate), during the viewing I saw that the setting was in a French city. The narrow streets and European cars gave it away, I thought. I casually told Stanley Wilson that the film was shot in Europe, probably in France. He chuckled and said no, that it was shot on the back lot of the studio right there. I was flabbergasted. The whole scene looked authentic. I went back to take a look at the set, and I understood then that the crew could make a set look like any place. The sculpting of physical space is a genuine art that draws upon mysteries of human perception and visual illusion. I encountered the same believable unreality at Twentieth Century–Fox. I touched the Batmobile and probed inside. It is not in the least what anyone would expect. Hollywood creates belief without an ounce of truth to support it; it's a world of convincing illusions. No wonder our media, which tell us who and what we should trust, possess the power to manipulate billions of people.

Hollywood success did not arrive quickly or all at once for me. In fact, it came so slowly that I feared it would never arrive at all. Living in Los Angeles during those first months away from New York, I struggled to get established. It was excruciating and often felt both futile and foolish. The transition to new professional expectations, to tasks and forms of music that were still strange to me, demanded intense focus. I had to grow a fresh pair of ears. Back east, I had had plenty of work. Here my bank account plunged like a free-falling elevator. I made regular trips to pawn shops. My cameras and photographic equipment went first. Then my instruments: clarinets, flutes, and saxophones. Unloading such useful items was horrible. It didn't stop. I had bought many special pieces of jewelry for Bobbie. She gave them up willingly. After that, we sold her furs. Bobbie never complained. I didn't have the money for her to buy new clothes, but she never reproached me. Since our top priority was to keep Brielle in her private school, our financial pressure became almost unbearable.

During that period Bobbie became the "coordinator of all sartorial coordinators," talented at mixing and matching her wardrobe. I felt humiliated. If she felt bad, she never showed it. As we approached the two-year anniversary of our West Coast destitution, our plight became grim, but that was when our fortunes changed. When it finally happened, I truly caught fire. I became busier with work than I could possibly have expected. I retrieved our gear and wardrobe from the pawnshop; we were done making hopeless interest payments. Those long, threatening days made me appreciate deeply every success that has blessed our lives since that traumatic time. Even now, I do not take success for granted.

Bobby Helfer was the contractor for Universal Pictures. He and Ben Barrett were probably the two biggest contractors of film work in Los Angeles. Bobby contracted both for Universal and for jobs off site from studio lots. He hosted a party at his house welcoming me officially to Hollywood. It was a delayed greeting, but we hugely appreciated it. He hired a chamber group to play, musicians whom he kept semi-permanently employed. Clarinetist Dominic Fera was outstanding. Brielle was enrolled in the same school as his nephew, and I soon employed Dominic and Russ Cheever, at Twentieth Century–Fox, whenever possible. Best of all, I met Jerry Goldsmith at that party. He was working on a symphony, solely for himself. Soon he recommended me to write for a television pilot called *Pomeroy's People*. I was grateful and sincerely impressed by his help. I badly needed it.

Bobby Helfer was demanding on scoring and recording stages; in fact, he was hard to deal with sometimes. Every year at Christmas, however, he drove to composers' and musicians' homes all over Los Angeles. He personally delivered gifts to a very large contingent, including me. His effort took several days of driving and delivery time. Bobby was demanding but fair and always supportive. In some ways, he was selfless. No one was prepared for his suicide. It shocked everyone within his extended world. Sandy, his secretary, somehow kept his work going after he was gone.

When Twentieth Century–Fox offered me a private room on its lot so I could work close to the action, I declined because I prefer composing at home. When ideas pop up at any moment, I like to be able to catch them immediately. Sometimes I get up in the morning without showering, don my bathrobe, and set to work. By day's end I might be someone to avoid. Nevertheless, hindering the flow of ideas blocks my groove, and a good groove is necessary to do the best work. In fact, I cannot "concoct" anything until the groove finds me.

CHAPTER 18

Gettin' My Mojo Workin'

SOMETIMES I WORK in my underwear all day, which would obviously be impossible on a studio lot. I wear my robe when I write, unless hot weather dictates otherwise. One old robe I was particularly fond of; there was a period when I could not work if I didn't have that robe. I literally wore it out. It now hangs useless in my closet in Los Angeles, a relic of former creative agonies. I can't bring myself to throw it away.

Months after Bobby Helfer's party, Bobbie and I were invited to the home of Lou Sher, a film producer I had only recently met. Five of us were there: Lou and his wife, Bobbie and me, and Mario Puzo. His book *The Godfather* had just been made into the first of three movies starring Al Pacino and Marlon Brando. I remember Puzo wondering if that initial film would be a success. *The Godfather* debuted in 1972 and became the number one film in the nation, grossing eighty million dollars, at that point the highest-earning film ever. What if I had written the music for that film, I mused. That was settled long before I met Mario. Since the picture was about "take no prisoners" Italians, the studio opted for an Italian composer, the fabulous Nino Rota. It worked like a charm. Everyone associated with that project made out like a lucky mobster. I am not sure Mario would have remembered me, since we spent only one very nice evening together at Lou Sher's hacienda. But I recall the camaraderie of that scene as if, for a moment, I were a Sicilian paisan.

Studio work was going well for me, but promoters and club owners on the West Coast were still calling to invite me to do jazz gigs. I refused; I had steady work in the movie industry, and I could not bust my cover. It would reduce my range of assignments. I had wanted to write other kinds of music, and I was finally doing it. Henry Brant's uncanny brilliance helped me acquire broad compositional skills. Before long, calls for jazz gigs stopped. Since I thought I would never play again, I sold one of my tenor saxophones as well as a soprano saxophone and a clarinet. I gave away my two flutes.

Nonetheless, "Benny Golson, jazz cat" was not completely dead. Doc Severinsen, who fronted Johnny Carson's *Tonight Show* orchestra for twenty-five years, began playing "Killer Joe" every night when the show paused for commercials. He played it constantly for studio audiences. Musicians in the band told me he loved it inordinately, maniacally. In accordance with the licensing rules promulgated by the American Society of Composers, Authors and Publishers (ASCAP) and Broadcast Music, Inc. (BMI), every time he played it, I earned a hundred dollars in royalty fees, whether the tune played for ten seconds or sixty. The abundance of Johnny Carson Production checks was a financial boost to me as a working composer. I made thousands of dollars in a few years for absolutely nothing—just the way things happen. My luck held until Johnny retired. Henry Mancini wrote a great song called "Mr. Lucky" that could have been inspired by my great fortune. Before that I saw Doc at a party, thanked him, and offered to write anything he needed as appreciation. He never took me up on the offer, but eventually moved to a gorgeous artist's colony in San Miguel de Allende, Mexico. Some people are talented. A few are completely unselfish. Doc is both.

Years earlier, I was about to write my first film music in Hollywood. Dave Grusin had just completed the theme for a television series called *It Takes a Thief,* starring Robert Wagner. Before the second show in the series, I was asked to write a score based on that theme. My old pal Quincy Jones was responsible for my takeoff. He does such things somewhat mysteriously, but he gave me enormous support. He's a genuine friend. I love him dearly. My work progressed so well that the producer, Stanley Wilson, asked me to do the next episode. I did, and the work continued onward. I was launched and soon received assignments for other shows from other studios.

My luck increased when the singular Peter Faith brought me to Twentieth Century–Fox to meet Lionel Newman, the legendary head of its music department. Lionel's brother was the world famous film composer and conductor Alfred Newman, whose accomplished nephew is Randy Newman. Their new show, *Room 222*, was just starting, with a theme written by Jerry Goldsmith, in my estimation the greatest film composer in Hollywood. I began composing for that show, and not long after that the job became mine. At Twentieth Century–Fox I experienced the elegant, old-fashioned treatment that was at one time afforded film composers, before the modern era's balkanized production values took hold—the one-job-at-a-time, gun-for-hire mentality driven by disposable relationships and endless disloyalty. A baton always sat on my conducting stand, which I never used but enjoyed symbolically; a sterling silver pitcher of cold water stood nearby, with a fluffy, fresh white towel at hand for comfort. Two people sat behind me with copies of my timing notes. One reset the clock each time I halted our progress. The other plotted (called "slating") the reel numbers and the number of each queue, instantly ready with any timing information I needed.

No other studio I was aware of supported its composers like that. It was expensive. At Columbia, for example, composers recorded their music for television (it worked differently for full-length films) without the benefit of viewing footage as they recorded. That gave them no margin for error. They recorded strictly by the clock, an abstract activity, at best. If a composer made a mistake in timing, a severe problem ensued that had to be corrected on the spot, without hesitation. Such pressure on creative and recording work was tremendous. Any composer strives for mistake-free recordings, because repeated corrections run costs well over budget. The Columbia model risked considerable amounts, at the expense of musicians and composers, in a self-defeating pursuit of false savings.

The need for precise timing between audio and video tracks called upon a technology called "click tracks" to ensure that video was in sync with audio no matter how many takes were recorded. Conductors and musicians heard the click tracks in their headphones, an unrelenting metronomic beat that could be set for any tempo. That technique was valuable, but at Twentieth Century I relied on the clock alone. I used streamers and punches, inserted on film footage by editors, to guide my work. A streamer is a line made directly onto film with a grease pencil as the entire footage moves forward on an editor's Moviola (a remarkable and indispensable machine that displays film on a small editing screen). As the film runs through the projector onto the screen, streamers travel left to right on the screen. When they reach the far right, you're at the exact point where the music needs to accomplish something special: to reinforce a dramatic moment, perhaps to register a gunshot or adumbrate a car crash, frame a passionate kiss, or punctuate with a unique note or chord a glance or look exchanged by the characters, or even the blink of an eye.

An editor makes a punch directly on the film at the precise spot needed, just as a train conductor punches tickets. It leaves a hole through which the projector's light makes a brilliant round flash. This visual notation is called the "punch" and each flash is a notation that says "Do something right here." Two streamers (one six feet and one three feet) alert one to a punch approaching. That trick allows time to speed or slow the music, to give it feeling without needless mechanical intrusions. I found a way to craft a warm enhancement of underscored feeling by speeding up or slowing down slightly as I followed the visual narrative in lieu of the metronomic click track. An alteration of musical tempo creates an increased emotional response to what the viewer sees on the screen. When the music speeds up or slows down, emotional response heightens or lowers. After a year or so, I no longer used click tracks at all. The crew on the lot was impressed by my bravura and spontaneity. Apparently my procedure reinvented the way the film composing masters once did it in the good old days. Working on the fly succeeded because I was not conducting large, lush orchestras, but the smaller ensembles appropriate for television shows. Creating delicate feeling or emotional nuance does not depend on the size of the orchestra. The work delighted me.

My work proceeded nicely at Twentieth Century–Fox. After my first year, I was promoted to write for an extremely successful show: *M*A*S*H*. The legendary Johnny Mandel wrote its unforgettable theme song, "Suicide Is Painless." On occasion, Johnny and I had dinner with our mutual pal Emile Charlap, New York's biggest music contractor. Johnny never changes persona socially or interpersonally. He's steady and stable, relaxed and amiable, as if success had never touched him. One evening when the three of us met for dinner, names, dates, and places came up that Emile and I couldn't remember. Johnny remembered everything with ease and lucidity. Johnny acts like a regular guy, though he could easily live regally for several lifetimes merely on the royalties he has earned from "The Shadow of Your Smile." I love Johnny Mandel's song writing. Who doesn't?

For three years, I was blessed to have the opportunity to build on Johnny's great theme to create the music for the television version of *M*A*S*H.* Infectiously lyrical, the song provided a solid foundation from which more music was continually born. In a million years I would never have believed that *M*A*S*H* would become "my show" to augment musically. Life is strange. Johnny's theme song, "Suicide Is Painless," suggests precisely that with preponderant mordant irony.

CHAPTER 19

M*A*S*H

I MADE THE ACQUAINTANCE of Alan Alda, the star of *M*A*S*H* and a great fellow. One day he let me come onto the set with my photographer, to get publicity shots for a brochure. Photographers are always unwelcome on live television and movie sets, but there I was, hoping to get a quick photo. The bell rang. Cameras rolled and Alan began his dialogue. Suddenly he stopped. Turning to Wayne Rogers, his co-star, he exclaimed, "We forgot to take photos with Benny!" Everything came to a dead halt. The crew looked daggers at me. We took photos right in front of the set's famous operating table. Alan returned to his lines, and I left, pronto.

Another time, I called Alan at his mother's house in New Jersey. I had an idea. I was a member of a promotional group called Tentmakers. We realized that many artists who were not really singers at all were recording as if they were truly "singers." Rock Hudson was a case in point. I asked Alan how he would feel about recording such an album. Tentmakers would produce it. Alan laughed and replied, "That would be a rip off. I can't sing a note."

During this period, I also worked at Screen Gems with the *Partridge Family* series. Only a few bits of music were called for, three or four seconds here and there, but whatever I wrote had to be no less precise than much longer musical passages. This miniature patchwork was extremely time-consuming. It drove me crazy. Nonetheless, the job was do-able because the music was not recorded while the video was shot.

I was subvented, too, by BMI, an organization that collects money all over the world for the use of (as well as performances of) songs. This arrangement brought me a sizable advance each year against royalties collected from the use of my compositions. This income helped Bobbie's and my improving prospects. Subpublishers throughout the world began to call. Increasingly, my name was circulating and my songs were being recorded internationally. With legal help, I crafted separate royalty fee agreements in Japan, England, Germany, Scandinavia, Italy, Switzerland, and other countries. It was much easier to keep track of a complicated royalty stream that way. We had no agreements with Russia or any of the Eastern bloc countries back then. They were behind a wall of otherness, now becoming normalized to capitalist logic.

In short, life was improving steadily for Bobbie and me. "Five Spot after Dark," my jaunty semi-noir spook theme, was extremely popular in Japan. ("Five Spot" referred to the famous jazz club in the Village.) The tune was used regularly by a Japanese advertising agency for a major product. The Japanese subpublisher called with the good news, soon followed by the first check. The next year I gave a lecture there, and a Japanese girl told me that her mother liked my song a lot. Her mother was not a jazz fan, but took a liking to the piece after hearing it repeatedly on that commercial. A guy takes his victories wherever he can.

M*A*S*H was one of the most popular television comedy series of all time. Everyone involved with the show was given a commemorative plaque when it won best comedy. Mine still hangs on the wall in my New York studio. That same year Quincy Jones was chosen to be the musical conductor for the Academy Awards ceremony. He asked me to write something for the event—specifically, to write an orchestration of the theme for M*A*S*H, which would be played, to a worldwide audience, each time the show was mentioned in competition with other comedy shows. I did so and it received a first-place honor.

M*A*S*H was a fantastic show. It was filmed at Malibu Creek State Park. A rusted Jeep still marks the location. The show ran for eleven years and won fourteen Emmys and a Golden Globe award, as well as numerous other nominations and awards for acting, technical execution, and dialogue. Gene Reynolds was the show's producer. Many mornings I found myself near his office to do spotting. I dropped by to chat sometimes. He had been a child movie star and understood the Hollywood scene completely. One morning I asked how his team unfailingly came up with such great dialogue. He looked at me for a few seconds, then said simply, "The same way you keep making new music." Only then did I get it: writing is writing.

On the cast of *Room 222*, Karen Valentine became so popular that she eventually received a show of her own, *The Karen Valentine Show*. I was asked to write music for the pilot and for the episodes to follow. The show lasted only one season, but I also created several more pilots for Fox. Not long after that, I began working for Lorimer Productions on the Warner Brothers lot in Burbank. They created a black version of a highly popular show, *The Waltons*, which they called *Pomeroy's People*. It featured Brock Peters. Writing for *Pomeroy's People* was the break I had hoped for when Jerry Goldsmith landed that work for me with the pilot. The show never launched, unfortunately; Madison Avenue backers scuttled it for reasons that were unspecified but not hard to deduce. The Lorimer group was undaunted: before long, their hit show *Dallas* put them squarely on the pop culture map. By then, however, I had left television work. I returned to my first and deepest love, jazz. My music was patient with me, a wayward ephebe.

In retrospect, I see clearly the pros and the cons of those rigorous years of studio work on the West Coast. On the one hand, writing film and television soundtracks never allowed a single definitive, lastingly satisfying composition to emerge from my labors. The demand was for episodic music, to enhance the meaning and emotion of an unfolding plot line. My work was constrained by a multitude of structural and sonic techniques that underscored visual development, and supported the requirements of drama, plot, action, and intrigue. Some occasions called for strong melodies; *Doctor Zhivago* was a cinematic instance. Such rare openings gave me enormous pleasure, but on the whole my work was defined by the studio mantra to get in and get out quickly and stay within budget. The prevailing ideal was containing costs to increase revenues. If I wanted sixty musicians for a piece, I was always asked if thirty would suffice. When I requested thirty, the response was that maybe fifteen could work just fine. I soon came to understand the game: if I wanted thirty musicians, I asked for sixty.

Music required for full-length films was inevitably more extravagant and cost-intensive than television scores. Cinema work allowed access to large ensembles and orchestras as well as more time to generate and refine ideas. Film scores are recorded on a grand scale, while television scores derive from sheer expedience. Keep costs down but make it adequate. A producer once summed it up: "There's good TV and bad TV, only that." This cynicism defined the industry's outlook. In short, what works is what sells; forget about "art."

On the other hand, I very much appreciated the latitude I was often given to do my best work under pressured circumstances. I still appreciate that I was allowed to write exactly what I wanted to write. No one ever second-guessed me, or altered or censored my creative output. I suppose you might say I smuggled my art through the front door in broad daylight. To use a racetrack motif, the suits "gave me my head." Once I did something outlandish. In one hyperdramatic scene for a TV show, I decided to draw upon my early composition, "Stablemates," recorded first by Miles Davis and John Coltrane in 1955. I disguised the melody by changing note values and meters as well as inserting eccentric chords. The only musician who caught on, when we recorded it, was jazz saxophonist Tom Scott. He knew the song's eccentric structure. When he heard the displacement and the subsequent structural estrangements laid over it, he identified it right away. The pooh-bahs in charge had no clue about that private joke and they had no reason to care. This was "artist stuff," nothing they would ever discuss sipping their dry martinis over lunch.

On occasion I employed mixed meters, symmetrical chords, and serial writing, though rarely antiphonal writing. I also used mirror writing. All of these techniques derived from my study under Henry Brant. I explored pandiatonic techniques as well, which draw upon the diatonic (as opposed to the chromatic) scale without regard to boundaries of tonal expectation. Stravinsky, Aaron Copland, Henryk Górecki, and Eric Dolphy have all used this device. Sometimes I would drop happy music into a sad scene, or set gloomy strains against an upbeat moment in the plot. My objective was to play with viewers' emotional responses and to keep them alert and engaged: strictly expedient artistic fascism.

Thus in writing for studios in Hollywood and Burbank, I actually enjoyed much more freedom than I ever experienced when performing in traditional jazz contexts. Jazz draws from and speaks to a variety of expectations on the part of both players and listeners, and sometimes that anticipation and the courtesy musicians grant it restrict artistic imagination and instinct. Creativity is perverse, an aspect of music that often eludes the music-loving public. Paradoxically, I was often able to truly go "out there" when I underscored films. In composing for film and television I learned a great deal about my talent, my instincts, and my own evolving lyric inclinations. While the jazz world is far more rewarding to my soul than Hollywood could ever be, I still marvel that I was allowed such compositional freedom when working in capitalist enterprises. Was Hollywood everything I imagined? Maybe more and maybe less.

CHAPTER 20

Movie Stars Like Jazz, Too

I DID CONTRACT WORK on the West Coast, too, lining up performers for clubs, work that I did not particularly enjoy. I once hired O.C. Smith, a popular Columbia recording artist, to perform at The Forum in Los Angeles. O.C. was riding high with his hit, "Little Green Apples." Headed to the show that evening, he stopped by my house to change clothes. He owned a German shepherd, born and raised in hell, who was dutifully waiting for him in the car. I did not know about the dog's nasty disposition. I love animals so I approached his car unconcerned. O.C. told me to be careful, his pooch was "a bit aggressive." I had always had a way with dogs, going back to Sporty, my childhood pet who once stole my lunch. I took O.C.'s warning lightly.

O.C. was ten steps or so behind me when I arrived at his car. The cagey dog sat absolutely still in the front seat on the passenger's side. I thought I knew how to charm dogs. I talked to him in a soothing voice, my head tilted to the side, palms up. I used a voice in the upper register. Evidently none of his canine pals had told him about me. My murmurings meant nothing to him. As I moved closer to the door, he remained completely still, tail not happily wagging. Stupid me. When I put my face near the window he went berserk, slamming himself against the window so violently that the vent and window glass nearly shattered. This beast wanted me for lunch. I broke out all over my body in bumps the size of the warts on massive kosher pickles. If I hadn't taken care of business before we left the house, involuntary evacuation would have added to the moment's bleak comedy. I was terrified the car windows wouldn't hold him. Fortunately, O.C.'s arrival alleviated the monster's wrath, and he subsided like an innocent puppy— not a second too soon.

We arrived at The Forum before it filled up. Fifteen minutes before show time, I heard someone to my rear say, "Excuse me." I turned to find myself face to face with Edward G. Robinson, who (redundantly) told me who he was. "Do you think it's possible for me to meet Mr. Smith?" I was flummoxed. I called over to O.C., who was equally amazed that this elegant man wanted to meet him to snag an autograph. Even the biggest Big Shot craves good music. We are all suckers for the proximity of social grease.

One night I was in a Hollywood jazz club where Bill Henderson was appearing. The house was full that evening. When the set was over and the lights came up, again a voice from behind. (I've since solved stealth greetings: a sign on the back of my jackets now reads "Off Duty"!) This portentous night it was Marty Feldman, the rather off-kilter comic actor. "I'll be darned," he said. "I'll be darned, myself," I agreed.

Marty was a well-regarded actor whose one "wandering eye" always seemed to gaze vaguely toward a comically irrelevant distance. He was accompanied by his wife, Lauretta. "You're Benny Golson!" he reminded me. I've never discovered why I need help remembering it so often, but he was right. He confessed that he loved "I Remember Clifford." Our chat was brief but on target. Parenthetically here, I must admit that being in Marty Feldman's innately zany company animates my life-long inclination for mischief (I'm convinced that the only other person I have known who is similarly inclined is my collaborator on this narrative).

Marty invited Bobbie and me to visit him at home the following week-end. "Bring your horn, please. Other musicians will be there," he chortled. Indeed, pianist Victor Feldman (no relation to Marty), who played gloriously with Cannonball Adderley, was at Marty's that night, with the all-star bassist Leroy Vinnegar, the saxophonist Jerome Richardson, and several others. The guests' welcoming table was a gourmet feast fit for Falstaff. A bell rang and James Coburn sauntered in. I had enjoyed his acting in the film, *In like Flint*. Leroy knew him and asked him to help carry in his heavy bass amp. The star complied. Coburn was a totally regular guy. Dick Van Dyke arrived with Lee Marvin's recently (in)famous ex-common-law wife,

Michelle Triola Marvin, on his arm. Her palimony suit was spread across L.A. newspapers and TV news. I had no clue why she was with Dick, but they seemed happy.

Everybody at Marty's that night was a bebop fan. The entire well-chosen contingent—"the fortunate few" (to quote Stendhal)—sincerely loved jazz. Everyone heartily indulged. I asked Maestro Coburn about acting. He compared it to playing a jazz instrument. His explanations were fun and made sense. The successful actors at Marty's that night enjoyed the good things most highly successful people enjoy: exquisite food and drink, entertaining repartee, the gratification of a collective buzz, and the self-confirming romance of inclusion in elite circles. As Nick Carraway, narrator of *The Great Gatsby*, affirms, "The rich are not like you and me."

For that evening of great music and good company, I was momentarily part of Gatsby's world. Afterward, James Coburn and I ran into each other at other soirées. He is an impressive man—a truly hip person, as he appears on-screen.

Sometimes I wonder if my life has been a dream. I became friends with George Rand, who was with the Ogilvy-Mather Ad Agency, which advertises Mattel Toys. George invited me to his home in Pacific Palisades. I don't remember the occasion, but he had a full house that night. Tom McIntosh went along. We arrived as the party was warming up, and I sat down next to a fellow who looked familiar. He was Lloyd Bochner, a popular character actor I had seen in many films. The joint was jumping. Tom and I milled around and eventually settled ourselves on a couch. We began discussing some of Tom's ideas for screenplays, as we often did, and eventually became aware that a fellow standing nearby had been listening to our conversation with intense interest. Perhaps he became self-conscious, or his curiosity demanded confessional give and take, and he introduced himself. He was Rod Serling, star of *The Twilight Zone* television series. He was intrigued by Tom's enthusiasm. He asked us if he could replenish our drinks, and returned in a few minutes to reclaim his seat on the floor in front of us. Our conversation continued and it was clear how acute Rod was, almost professorial. We enjoyed our banter for some time.

George Rand later cautioned Tom to be careful about casual revelations of scripts—or ideas for scripts—in the presence of people he did not know and might not trust. Although this advice had nothing to do with Rod, the brutal fact is that eager writers and unethical aspirants sometimes steal ideas. It's the oldest trick in Hollywood: Change a few textual details, give the script a new name, and offer it to someone with the clout and the funds to produce it. Voila! You've scored. You're famous, free of charge. There is little accountability or risk of prosecution. Years later, Tom suffered this himself at the hands of a well-respected Hollywood director who should have been above thievery. Legally, manuscript and conceptual rip-offs are difficult to establish definitively, unless the plagiarist is so naïve that he doesn't bother to change the details of the story line in any way. In Hollywood, crooks are Ivy League sophisticates. George Rand, an expert on precaution, wanted Tom to understand that he was now in Hollywood, the land of Darwin's law, survival of the fittest (and most cautious). Loose lips sink ships, and loose fingers pilfer scripts. Paranoid mantras are useful in dangerous territory. All of our mothers taught us to take nothing from strangers. L.A. is the Land of Glamor and cutthroat competition. If you squander your intellectual chips, you may be throwing away wealth you could have collected.

In 1986, as if to prove George Rand right on slightly different terrain, I received a letter in New York from Orion Pictures. They informed me they had used my tune, "Killer Joe," as the theme music throughout a film called *52 Pick-Up*, whose production was nearing completion. Clarence Williams III played the part of a psychopathic killer. Every time he killed someone, he whistled "Killer Joe." Orion offered a ridiculously small payment for use of my song, and they approached me *after* they made the film. To say I was surprised is an understatement. Mostly, I was amused. Looking back, it is clear why a major shake-up ensued afterward. They couldn't reshoot the entire picture so Clarence could whistle another tune. And their letter admitted that they had not taken care of business properly. Rules are rules. Orion knew the money wasn't right and they needed to know what I wanted.

When the film opened in New York, Bobbie and I were there with a stopwatch. I wanted to quantify the exact number of minutes that my melody was heard in the film. We clocked it carefully. Looking back, I could have demanded a completely unreasonable fee. I had Orion over a barrel and they knew it. Their negligence was unconscionable. But I wanted to be fair even though Orion had not been fair to me or my interests. I have been told once or twice by people whom I respect deeply that I may be too inclined toward "fairness" unreciprocated.

The character of Clarence in *52 Pick-Up* is a psychopathic killer. He whistles "Killer Joe" as he murders his victims. My song was optimistic and innocent, inspired by sweet, derelict but fundamentally decent people: New York hipsters, my uptown neighbors, good folks motivated at times by need, opportunity, or perplexed urges—but never by murder.

Along with honest lawyers, doctors, teachers, and scientists, artists also care about human integrity. We went home after the movie and I wrote Orion a letter. I gave them a reasonable figure for the use of my comical song about a "killer" whose only mayhem results from the way ladies are attracted to his persona. Orion agreed with my request, of course. They got a break.

In the last analysis, my song distingué, "Killer Joe," made it to Hollywood. Not bad, even if he arrived indirectly. Over the years, "Killer" has gone everywhere on the globe. Joe's travels still underwrite my vacations. Strange, isn't it, how one's creations live beyond one's grasp. Perhaps I sold my old pal too cheap. No matter—I'm grateful for his generosity and thankful to the hipsters who appreciate his suave *je ne sais quoi.*

PHOTO ALBUM

Benny and his friend Josephine, both three years old, in Philadelphia's Fairmount Park in 1932. (Photo by Celedia Golson.)

Benny and his mother, Celedia Golson, in 1942. Benny is thirteen here, the year before his mother bought him his first saxophone. Celedia was an enormous supporter of both Benny and his pal John Coltrane.

FACING PAGE: *Benny and his saxophone. He had been playing for one year at the time of this photo.*

Benny at age seventeen, in 1946. Benny had met John Coltrane the year before, when he was sixteen and John was eighteen. Soon after this photo was taken, John and Benny joined a big band, Jimmy Johnson and His Ambassadors. Not long after they joined, Jimmy cut them from the band and replaced them with more experienced musicians.

Jimmy Johnson and His Ambassadors in 1946. Benny is seated in the front row at the left, next to the vocalist, who is standing. Johnson is the drummer. This photo was taken before Coltrane joined the band.

Benny with the Mickey Collins Orchestra. Benny is seventeen here. He is back row, center, with his saxophone; Ray Bryant, who was then fifteen, is on piano. Benny, who was in the band for two years, played with the group every Sunday at a venue called O. V. Catto's at 16th and Fitzwater Streets in Philadelphia.

The band Benny played in at Benjamin Franklin High School, in 1946. Benny is in the front row, on the right.

The band Benny played in at Howard University, pictured here in the university's old law building. Benny is in the front row, on the far left. Bass player Ed Jones went on to play with Count Basie. Rick Henderson, seated next to Benny, later played with Duke Ellington. Morris Ellis (trombone player; top row) still has a society band in Chicago. Oscar Gamby (trumpet player; top row, far right) taught music at several universities.

Benny and Philly Joe Jones at a gig at Café Society at 13th and Columbia Streets in Philadelphia in 1949. Benny, age twenty, was home from college for the summer.

Benny in Bull Moose Jackson's Band in St. Louis in 1952. Left to right: Philly Joe Jones (drums), Theodore "Snooky" Hulbert (alto; road manager), Bull Moose (tenor saxophone), Benny (saxophone), Johnny Coles (trumpet), and Jymie Merritt (bass). Tadd Dameron (not visible) was on the piano.

ABOVE: *The Earl Bostic Band in 1954. Left to right: Elmon Wright (trumpet), Johnny Coles (trumpet), George Tucker (bass), Earl Bostic (alto sax), and Benny (saxophone). G. T. Hogan, the drummer, and Stanley "Stash" O'Laughlin, the piano player, are not pictured.*

LEFT: *Benny and Dizzy Gillespie at a club gig in 1957*

FACING PAGE, BOTTOM: *Several members of the Dizzy Gillespie Big Band at the Blue Note Club in Chicago in 1957. Left to right: Paul West (bass), Ernie Henry (alto sax), Benny (saxophone), Charlie Persip (drums), and Lee Morgan (trumpet).*

The Dizzy Gillespie Big Band at Birdland in 1956. Diz, the leader, is in the foreground. Back row: Lee Morgan and Al Stewart (both on trumpet) and Charlie Persip (on drums; peeking over the cymbal). Front row: Wynton Kelly (piano; back view of head), Phil Woods (alto sax; next to Diz), Bill Elton (trombone), Jimmy Powell (alto sax), Rod Levitt (trombone), and Benny (saxophone; far right).

Benny and his wife, Bobbie Hurd, on their wedding day, March 28, 1959.

FACING PAGE:

TOP: *The Jazz Messengers at the Blue Note Club in Chicago in 1968.* Left to right: *Art Blakey (drums), Benny (saxophone), Bobby Timmons (piano), Lee Morgan (trumpet), and Jymie Merritt (bass).*

BOTTOM: *Lee Morgan and Benny at a recording session for Blue Note Records at Rudy Van Gelder's studio in 1957.* (Francis Wolff © Mosaic Images, LLC.)

Benny with Alan Alda (left) and Wayne Rogers (right) on the set of M*A*S*H.
Benny wrote the hit TV show's music at Twentieth Century–Fox for three years.

FACING PAGE:

TOP: *The Jazztet at a recording session for Argo Records in 1960.* Left to right: *Art Farmer (trumpet), McCoy Tyner (piano), Benny (saxophone), and Curtis Fuller (trombone).* (© Chuck Stewart.)

BOTTOM: *The Jazztet on stage at Sweet Basil in New York City in 1960.* Left to right: *Benny (saxophone), Addison Farmer (bass), and McCoy Tyner (piano). Art Farmer (not visible) was on the trumpet.*

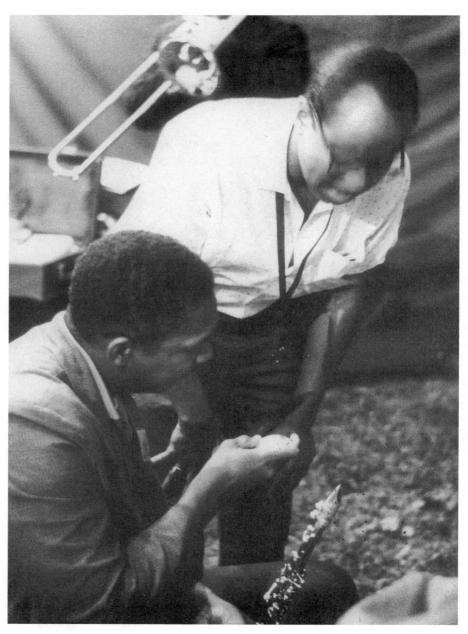

John Coltrane and Benny, backstage in the tent at the Newport Jazz Festival in 1957. Coltrane is looking for a reed and Benny is warming up. This is the only known shot of the boyhood pals, who became lifelong friends and colleagues. (Joe Alper, courtesy of Jackie Alper and Yasuhiro Fujioka.)

Benny with Dinah Washington, collaborating on an arrangement for a big band recording featuring Dinah's vocals in 1962.

Benny with Peggy Lee at her home, collaborating on arrangements for her next album in 1976.

Milt Jackson (vibraphone), Benny (saxophone), and Art Farmer (flugelhorn) on stage at the Baltic Jazz Festival in Kiel, Germany, in 1998. (Photo by Rolf Kissling.)

Benny delivering the graduation speech at William Paterson University, in Wayne, New Jersey, in 2002. Benny's honorary doctorate was conferred that day.

Benny with violinist Itzhak Perlman after a Lincoln Center rehearsal of Benny's violin piece written for Perlman and performed by the violinist and a youth orchestra.

Benny with Tito Puente.

Benny with Steven Spielberg on location in New York City, shooting The Terminal, *in 2007.*

Benny with Quincy Jones at the Jazz Bakery in Culver City, California, in 2009. The two had been roommates when they traveled with Dizzy Gillespie's Big Band.

Left to right: *Kenny Barron, Billy Taylor, and Benny at the Kennedy Center in Washington, D.C., for Benny's eightieth birthday tribute in 2009.* (Photo by Valerie Russell/Russellvisual for the Mid Atlantic Arts Foundation.)

President Barack Obama shaking hands with Bobbie Golson, Benny's wife, at the White House in 2011.

PART V *Amazing Friendships*

I met Benny Golson in 1953, when I suggested that he become a member of the Lionel Hampton band, of which I was a member. Time passed, and later we both became members of Dizzy Gillespie's band. . . . Benny and I were roommates. We became as close as brothers, and we admired each other's creativity. Benny is endowed with talent that has pushed him successfully forward into the awaiting arms of the future. He can proficiently handle any assignment. These many years have built up a trust that will challenge the very nature of immutable time. . . . It seems we're destined to be friends forever.

—QUINCY JONES

CHAPTER 21

Quincy Jones

I MET QUINCY JONES in Atlantic City in 1953 when I was playing with Tadd Dameron at the Paradise Club. The show boasted such talent that little room was left for the band to stretch out. Quincy was working with Lionel Hampton's band. They had two days off each week, I think. Not all bands suffered temporary indentured servitude in Atlantic City, as ours did. Perhaps because the cats in Hamp's band knew Clifford Brown, Gigi Gryce, Philly Joe Jones, Jymie Merritt, Tadd, and yours truly, Q and some bandmates came to check us out. No doubt they expected more *blowing* from us. But they heard enough to tell Gates (Lionel Hampton) about Clifford, Gigi, and me. Quincy recommended the three of us for that band, which was about to undergo significant changes. We were wanted over there immediately. However, a problem had to be resolved. First, Tadd needed a week's leave because of illness. Second, the management refused to release us because we had signed contracts for the show's duration. With Tadd's unavoidable absence, our departure would jeopardize the entire show. The producer was right. One way to resolve the problem, I thought, might satisfy everybody. I asked the producer to let Clifford and Gigi leave immediately. I would stay until their replacements learned the music completely. That idea was agreeable to him and to Hamp. So, Gigi and Clifford left soon after their replacements arrived from New York. Three weeks later, I joined Hamp's band in Greenville, South Carolina. I arrived early and had to wait all day on the steps of the hall where we were playing that evening.

Hamp's band was exciting. After the debacle in Atlantic City, I was pumped up. I would have a chance to let loose, even if it was within Lionel Hampton's fairly controlled musical scheme. It was great to be a jazz player—to just *blow*. Clifford Brown, Art Farmer, Jimmy Cleveland, Gigi Gryce, Monk Montgomery, along with drummer Alan Dawson, made it all a complete gas, and Quincy's writing was terrific. Hamp's set-up was not quite what I wanted, but we were moving in the right direction. I was getting a chance to meet talented musicians outside of Philadelphia, and to hear Art Farmer and Clifford Brown hook up every night was powerful. Gates pitted one guy against the other, which created excitement for everyone, especially when both players had real talent. Art and Clifford tore it up every night.

Quincy was ambitious and very talented. He was not a featured soloist but a "section man" with the trumpets. His strength was in composing and arranging, for which even in the early days he had a genuine penchant. He and I frequently shared our songs and compositions with each other. We used any available piano in any town where we were playing. We were young and full of enthusiasm. What a wonderful world we had access to: no competition, just love for music and for each other's abilities. Quincy's writing was always fresh and clean. His choice of chords expressed his own sense of sonic voicing, reaching not just the ear but the heart as well. I loved his writing. His musical concepts were unlike anyone else's. Quincy's aspirations were rooted in tomorrow. He sought expansive artistic openness and he wanted to celebrate what others were creating. I became so familiar with his unique sound that I could identify anything to which Quincy had put his pen. Quincy was beautiful.

I went to Seattle, Washington, and met his entire family. I fell in love with his sister, but she was not aware I existed. Such is life, but far less tolerable is the breaking of professional agreements. When I joined Lionel Hampton's band, I had no idea how long I would play with that group, but I found out sooner than I would have imagined. At the outset, I was promised twenty-two dollars a night for each single-night gig we played. George Hart, Hamp's road manager, made the agreement, and I thought no more of it and concentrated on playing my best. Two weeks later, Gladys Hampton, Lionel's wife and head of business operations, met the band in Columbia, South Carolina. My verbal contract for twenty-two dollars a night was torched. The road manager's word meant nothing to Gladys. We were treated like urchins out of Charles Dickens. Gladys had thought of a way to save money and that was all that counted. I was angry and appalled. I considered myself a person who lived a principled life. With me things have to be straight up. Two days later the band pulled into Washington, D.C., for an outdoor concert. When we arrived in Washington, I caught a train to Philadelphia. That was it. I would not be treated as a flunky or a vassal.

The day after I split, before the outdoor concert in D.C., Hamp's band opened a two-week stay at the Band Box, immediately next door to Birdland in midtown Manhattan. I regretted missing that gig, right in the city. After that, the band went to Europe. I had never been to Europe. I got a card from Quincy a few weeks later. He reported that the guys were making significant money recording on the side, without Gates's knowing of it. In fact, that trip was when the band made all those interesting recordings overseas, with Clifford, Quincy, Gigi, and Art Farmer. Quincy wrote a lot of the music, some of which they recorded with European and Scandinavian musicians. "We sure wish you had come with us," he concluded. I was now somewhat dubious about my "principles." Boy, am I a dope or what?

Long after these events, I was living on West 92nd Street in the same building Quincy lived in. He lived on the sixth floor, and we lived on the fourth. My son Reggie was fourteen years old then, in junior high school, and he liked Quincy's daughter, Jolie, who was a bit younger. Puppy love, no doubt, but Reggie asked me if he could invite her to dinner one evening—not an unreasonable request. However, when he asked my wife, Bobbie, his stepmother, if she would serve them dinner alone by candlelight, with soft romantic music, that was the end of the courtship. We all laughed hard about it years later.

That building was unique. It contained a cross-section not of America in miniature, but of underground New York City hipness and slick deviance: pimps, prostitutes, well-bedecked drug dealers, merchants of "hot" goods, a fantastic seamstress whose clients came from the well-to-do Upper East Side, gay couples of both sexes, straight folks, and two jazz musicians—Quincy and me. I composed many songs while living there, including "Killer Joe," inspired by that cultural ambience. Everyone knew everyone else. There were never any problems. It was a six-storey microcosm that mirrored a complex metropolitan mix of styles and outlooks.

Prior to this congenial era, Quincy and I were members of Dizzy Gillespie's band. Quincy directed the band as well as wrote for it. I con-

tributed to the songbook later, too. The band went on two State Department tours. I went to South America on the band's second overseas tour.
Quincy and I were roommates. He had so much energy that it was often
difficult to keep up with him. Quincy even walked fast, very fast. During
that trip we met Astor Piazzolla, a great composer/arranger from Buenos
Aires, who also brilliantly played the bandoneon, an instrument somewhat
like a small octagonal accordion. Its sound reminds you of French films.
Astor was a virtuoso. We also spent an afternoon with Villalobos, the composer. Although he was by then quite advanced in years, he was like one of
the boys, showing us his scores and the new ballet he had just written for
Margot Fonteyn, the famed London ballerina. Quincy and I shared things
that we composed. Those were great times, and I still have the autographed
photograph he gave me.

Quincy was beginning to get meaningful assignments with varying
styles. He did a session with Frank Sinatra and others with Peggy Lee,
Count Basie's Orchestra, and Ray Charles. He also did a special project for
Walt Disney. He worked with an organization that made television commercials and brought me to their attention. I cranked out some projects for
them. Quincy was really in gear, but he never lost the sound that made the
music uniquely his. I know that some people think that he sold out, that he
junked his jazz origins for commercial success. Look closer at that preju-
dice and you will see that a person with an eclectic talent such as Quincy's
has no need to stick with one creative mode. Quincy did not erode or
squander his talent. Instead, his talent took on broader parameters. His
business savvy led him to areas of music production so enormous that they
require the majority of his time. That is one of the definitions of success.
I have enjoyed watching Quincy accomplish the dreams I saw take shape
years ago. His success never changed his personality or the open way he
deals with people. He's the same guy now that I've known for almost sixty
years, ol' jailhouse Quincy, even though he has gone so far ahead of the rest
of us. In retrospect, it's evident that he had a vision all along. He didn't sit
down and wait for good things to happen to him. This man possessed the
know-how to *make* it all happen, season by season, victory upon victory. His
reputation is so redoubtable that if he calls, people respond as if they have
been summoned by royalty.

I once heard a saying that pertains directly to my dear friend of nearly
six decades. There are only three kinds of people: those who *make* things

happen; those who *wait* for things to happen; and those who ask, "What happened?" Quincy Jones has been in the first of those groups for his whole life.

To my distress, one night Quincy called me, his voice sounding very strange. He was deeply serious. He was about to undergo brain surgery, he said, the first of two procedures. He was not at all sure how the operations would turn out. He was calling to say good-bye "just in case." My heart sank with his sober words. The thought of his demise was devastating. He did not know how it made me feel because I made it my job to encourage him. Medical technology has advanced greatly. Brain surgery has become almost routine, and he would have the best doctors possible. I tried to muster some credible optimism, though I myself was not sure of anything. It wasn't until I heard that both operations were successful that I breathed easier.

I doubt he knows how much my life has been enriched by his. We still call each other "Tack," an inside tag from our days with Diz. Whenever we telephone each other, our conversation always begins with that personal code. Quincy is a man who cannot be summarized. His extraordinary talent, astute business acumen, grace, and dignity gave many of us concrete models of achievement to pursue our own dreams. Thank goodness I still have my dear pal Quincy Jones!

CHAPTER 22

Sweets and Diz

W AY BACK IN 1944, a sophisticated jazz film came to black urban theaters, *Jammin' the Blues*. *Everybody* in my neighborhood, including my mother, loved the low-down, dirty blues that Lil Green, Big Bill Broonzy, and Lonnie Johnson sang. Jazz had not yet arrived in the 'hood. I have a happy memory of going with my mother to see this cinematic jewel. There was something about this elegant film that people in our modest world identified with. Was it because most of the musicians were black? I had no idea, since I was thirteen years old, a piano student who had not yet begun to play the saxophone. However, I was intrigued to learn of this artistic universe—film—that I had never known existed. I'm sure few of us recognize the influence the cinema has had on our lives.

I had no clue who the musicians were, but it made no difference. Many were smoking or holding cigarettes. One or two held a lit cigarette between their fingers as they played. I've never been attracted to smoking, but these guys were cool. I found their musical cosmos relaxed and beguiling.

I now have a copy of that film that I first saw almost seventy years ago. It still looks good. Illinois Jacquet is featured, along with Jo Jones, Coleman Hawkins, Lester Young, and Harry "Sweets" Edison, who was twenty-nine years old. He had traveled to New York from Columbus, Ohio, while still a teenager seeking his fortune, like so many others who hoped to escape the burdens of the long economic depression. The youthful Harry Edison owned a raucously delicate, uniquely penetrating sound, a rapier quick thrust that said, "Here's Sweets Edison, no one else!"

After I became a professional musician, it took me awhile to discover that no one has to play a barrage of notes, unless he wants to, to make his mark. Lester Young was a minimalist. So was Monk. Both were extremely clever, shaping each note so that it "said something." Understatement has many virtues. A Prez (Young's nickname) solo always "tasted" good. And Sweets showed that no one is compelled to blast volcanic solos. Sweets played from his heart and in turn touched the hearts and souls of his listeners. His example of reserve makes me wonder sometimes about the overabundance of my own musical statements.

I knew about Sweets before I met him. His playing is uncanny. He seems to measure each note before releasing it. Of the incalculable possibilities dependent on song structure, lyrical mood, and tempo, Sweets always chooses the most consequential notes and phrases. He does more with a single repeated note than anyone in the history of music. Articulate repetition is not an easy concept to execute persuasively. Nonetheless, that iconoclastic trait is essential to Sweets Edison's stylistic repertoire.

Sweets once told me that he had just recorded with Freddie Hubbard and other young trumpeters. Genuinely concerned, he told me, "I don't know why I was there." I looked him straight in the eye and told him that he was there "because of who you are, what you do, and the way you do it." I insisted that he recognize how special his playing was. "Your style is unique; nobody else plays like you," I added. He reflected for a moment without responding, but I think he understood. What a deep man Harry Edison was, my hero!

Sweets maintained balance and decorum throughout his career. His inclination was always to underestimate or (to his own amusement) deprecate his talent and achievement, as if he were merely a wide-eyed country boy. Thankfully, he did what he did, year after year, to the delight of people such as Frank Sinatra and Billie Holiday, who employed him for important recordings as well as high-profile performances in New York, Los Angeles, and Las Vegas. Harry Edison's instinct for modesty and understatement made him a deeply lovable man whose profound humor, especially on display when he worked on tour, was tinged with wisdom.

I guess most people who are not prudes enjoy a degree of scatological comedy. Sweets perfected that art. He was infamous for breaking wind on a bus full of musicians barreling down a highway. Suddenly he would have rows of seats all to himself, while he sat straight-faced, oblivious, innocent. To the end Sweets never admitted to this ruse, which made it even more hilarious. Sweets Edison's special qualities were rare and fragile. Sweets was a delicate impressionist, a watercolor guru in a world of neon-lit bombast. His music had the disarming subtlety and savvy precision of a Swiss watch. His kind of gentle, lyrical soulfulness is all but lost today, as new technologies make constant distraction the cultural norm. Nevertheless, Harry Edison's recordings will please listeners for generations (those hip enough to understand). Sweets was an icon. There will not soon be another like him.

Every musician knows that Dizzy Gillespie brought radically new ideas to the jazz scene in the mid-1940s. Along with band mate Charlie Parker, John Birks Gillespie ("Diz") became bigger than life to many of us who aspired to greatness in jazz. Diz soared high without a safety net, taking enormous chances motivated by his indefatigable curiosity and his desire to abandon tradition. His ability to manifest new ideas in his playing was startling. Diz played his modified, up-tilted trumpet with such verve and power that his music seemed to be generated by an extremely fine-tuned lyrical engine, a musical Porsche or Lamborghini. Art Farmer often noted that there were three jazz players whom no one should ever "confront" musically on stage: Lionel Hampton, Buddy Rich, and Dizzy Gillespie. Each of these three could meet any competitor head on.

Diz had an almost inhuman ability to invent brilliant musical ideas instantaneously. There is a danger of taking Diz for granted; his innovations now seem so inevitable. Dizzy reinvented the jazz vocabulary and with it the possibilities of expressing joy and longing, hope and love and grief in musical terms. Almost two decades after his passing, it seems as if the world of jazz could not exist without his history-altering melodic and harmonic bravura. How could there not be a pugnacious Diz? How could Yosemite's Half Dome and Yellowstone's geysers not exist? As the decades passed, Diz became a patriarch of jazz, only making his human frailty seem less likely. I suppose I am concerned that Dizzy might come to be viewed with less consequentiality than his life and career deserve. I loved Dizzy Gillespie the flesh-and-blood man, but I also loved him for freeing my generation of jazz musicians from predictability and for giving us the courage to boldly explore the unknown. I never felt about Diz as some did: that his playing diminished with age, making him less relevant. Sometimes ability does depreciate with age, but in other cases it only *seems* to do so.

Dizzy's talent did not erode, nor did his music become irrelevant, even when the culture of jazz evolved in other directions.

People fall under the sway of new things; psychologically, this is known as the *transference of affect.* Earlier, the same occurred with Louis Armstrong when Dizzy came on the scene. It was nothing personal, merely the evolution of artistic styles, creating new perspectives and judgments. Diz's greatest impact was in his conceptual innovations. For example, the minor seventh chord had been employed for years, but Diz added the flat five, which gave it an entirely different color and character. Also, look at the turn back, going from one chorus into another (the 1–6-2-5 then commonly used, instead of merely 5, the dominant). That was his invention. There's also Dizzy's 2–5-1 progression, which was unknown before he brought it forward. All of these innovations became part of a standard jazz repertoire, single-handedly Dizzy's legacy.

Although Diz did lose some of his youthful fire, he never ceased exploring the deepest aspects of music. Who is not slowed a bit by age? Picasso was a different artist in his last years. Shakespeare retired shortly before his end. Dizzy played at his artistic limit until his final note.

One day in 1985 he invited me out to his house in Corona, New York, a suburb of New York City. I had never been to his house and considered it an honor. His wife, Lorraine, made us comfortable in the living room, and we talked for a long while, mainly about music. We became so involved that he took me downstairs to his basement studio. The first thing I saw was his trumpet, out of its case, lying on the couch as though waiting for its master. Diz did not play it right away. He was still making a point when, *boom*, he suddenly stopped and said, "Like this!" He played something on top of the simplest possible chords. I am sure my mouth fell open. What he played was so logical and direct that I wondered why I had never thought of it, too. I felt exactly as I did when I first began—the intense thrill of learning something new, on an extremely deep level. This lesson with the master showed me not only how he did what he did but also the thought process and the technical procedures from which he drew. After all my years on the scene, I felt like I was living a fantasy that day in Dizzy's basement. Our afternoon was capped off when Diz gave me a private audition of the familiar but rather undistinguished tune, "I Found a Million Dollar Baby (in a Five and Ten Cent Store)." I knew the song's structure but I had never played it. Dizzy chose a corny old song in order to show me its hidden possibilities, applying unusual moves as he stated the theme. Diz opened my mind. His point was that you can derive intriguing musical possibilities from anything, if you know how. That trip to Corona was more than a mere social visit. It was a loving and generous revelation from a master who gave me one epiphany after another. Diz was always immersed in the limitless power of "now."

A few months before his death, we played together at The Blue Note in Manhattan. The club was honoring him for an entire month in many different formats, including his big band. The night I was there, David Sánchez played with us. I visited Dizzy's dressing room before the first set. Since I had my horn, I ran down some things I knew he would call on the bandstand. When I got to "Woody 'n You" and reached the bridge, I played it just as I had done for years. Three or four bars into the song, he stopped me. "Everybody plays it that way," I said. "I know," he replied, "but it's wrong. It should go like this." Like Santa sliding down a chimney, he swooped in and showed me how it should go. He explained his reasoning and it made all the sense in the world. I wanted him to run through it once more before we headed out to the stage, but there wasn't time. I would have to telephone him to get it straight. Such fragile hope! I waited too long. Dizzy left us, and I'll never play that part of his brilliant song correctly. That bothers me immensely. Playing a song that you love and respect demands accuracy. My ignorance is disturbing. I take consolation from my enormous good fortune that the transcendent jazz guru Dizzy Gillespie shared so many ideas and techniques with me, across our long years together. I will cherish what he taught me to my very last note.

CHAPTER 23

Philly Joe Jones

FIRST SAW Philadelphia drummer Joe Jones play in Beryl Booker's trio in 1944, when I was fifteen years old. That was about a year after I started to play the sax. He was already a local celebrity. Beryl Booker was a good pianist and a celebrity in her own right. I don't remember the bass player, but she and Philly stood out. I thought I could never achieve their talent. Soon I found other heroes, but at the beginning Philly Joe was number one. Also on the scene were Jimmy Oliver, a soulful tenor player; Bill Barron, a tenor saxophonist (Kenny's older brother) who was a very good writer; Jerome "Bass" Ashford, an alto saxophonist; Fats Waller, an older pianist who taught me many songs; Nelson Boyd, a bassist; Jimmy Heath, on alto sax, who sounded a lot like Bird; Red Garland, a marvelous pianist; Ziggy Vines, a tall tenor player who became a legend in Philly (Bird liked him). There was also Johnny Lynch, a trumpeter who worked with Diz, and Coatesville Harris, a drummer who once played in Louis Armstrong's band. Somehow for me Philly Joe was always brilliant and out front. He was hip, slick, unpredictable, exciting, and unorthodox. And he could really swing!

I used to dream of playing with Philly Joe. He played with all my recorded heroes when they came to town: Coleman Hawkins, Ben Webster, Roy Eldridge, Charlie Parker, Dizzy Gillespie, and Eddie Heywood. I came home from my first year in college, in 1948, and "Bass" Ashford, a mainstay on the local scene, asked me to join his quartet for the entire summer season at Café Society, at 13th Street and Columbia Avenue. Café Society was a very popular jazz spot in North Philly, not far from where I lived and only three blocks from John Coltrane's house. John often popped in while the group played there. I showed up for the first rehearsal to find that Philly Joe would be our percussionist! I almost fainted. I acted as if nothing were unusual, but I was flying.

Our pianist was a fellow called Hen Gates (James Forman). He could play wonderfully despite the fact that he was severely crippled. His right arm and the upper part of his chest were strong from bearing the weight of his entire body with the use of a cane. The rest of him was underdeveloped. As a result, he had little control of his left hand. Undeterred, Henderson used a popsicle stick between his left fingers, which allowed him to play fifths and sometimes sevenths, depending on how he placed the stick. His style and execution were both hip and inspiring. I always wondered why he never went to New York. Some musicians, for personal reasons, are content to remain where they are comfortable. In Philly, Henderson was well accepted and always had work.

Philly Joe was outrageous and perfect. I soon discovered that his ears were unaccountable. He was one of the most sensitive and attentive drummers I have ever worked with. He inspired us every set and every night. When I took a breath, Philly was there, setting me up for my next idea or phrase: a rough accent here, a flam tap there, a rim shot out of nowhere, swinging as if under siege.

After that wonderful summer, Philly Joe and I worked together in many different situations with various musicians. One of them, Red Garland, was a former boxer, a real character. He was late for every gig. When he finally arrived, he would psych everyone out with pretend excitement and agitated hand claps. Red was the last guy there, but he donned the role of cheerleader as if he were right on time, ready to lead from the rear. "Come on, let's go! Here we go!" as if we couldn't have done it without his coaching moxie. We played along with the hilarity because Red was, in truth, a special player and a stupendous ally. Philly worked with rhythm-and-blues groups over a very long period. He thoroughly understood rhythm-and-blues, believe it or not. Few realized that aspect of his musical identity. Once I saw Philly Joe with Joe Morris's rhythm-and-blues group. Morris played trumpet with Lionel Hampton when Johnny Griffin was in the band. As a result, around 1950, Johnny and pianist Elmo Hope joined Morris's rhythm-and-blues quintet. That was when I first met Elmo and Johnny. Playing with that group, Philly was uniquely capable of driving the music into a shuffle back-beat groove, emotional and dazzling. He had an intuitive knack for setting and holding any rhythm needed by any band.

That was why I recommended Philly Joe for the drum slot with Bull Moose Jackson's group soon after I joined, and that was how Tadd Dameron came to know Philly. In fact, Tadd changed Philly's name from Joe Jones to Philly Joe Jones to avoid confusion with Jo Jones, Count Basie's legendary drummer—whom many astute jazz aficionados consider *the* jazz drum maestro. I'll not enter that debate, but I do attest here to the majestic rhythmic perfection of my friend and unmatched colleague, Philadelphia's son, Joe Jones.

Philly and I recorded the very special *Dameronia* album with Tadd. Clifford Brown was with us. Because it was Philly's recording debut, Tadd wanted to make sure there was no confusion between the younger Joe Jones and the older Jo Jones. "Philadelphia Joe Jones" was a ponderous moniker. Philly Joe it was. I think he loved it. His name was distinctive and he added distinction to it over time. With Ashford's 1948 group, Philly sang now and then. His voice was decent, especially when he sang ballads. Ashford played bass left handed. Surprisingly, Philly played bass right handed quite well. He played piano, too, and was also competent at arranging.

Philly had a way of accomplishing things that was sometimes unorthodox. Once, when I was not in the band, he and Joe Morris rolled their van on the way to Florida. The van and its two passengers were banged up and Philly's drums were destroyed. They arrived in Miami, roughed up, but headed directly to the Harlem Square Club in Miami's "black belt." They were ready to play—sort of. The venue was not really a club, but a dance hall, a huge empty square floor. Twenty-five percent of the floor—one corner—was occupied by a liquor store seven days a week.

Remarkably I was in Miami with Bull Moose and I had the night off. I headed over to the Harlem Square Club and heard what happened. Philly had one arm in a sling. He played the gig with two telephone books sitting on two chairs in front of him. In lieu of a bass drum, Philly stomped the heel of one shoe loudly on the wooden stage, which was hollow underneath. Ridiculous, imaginative, wild. Nonetheless, Philly kept the band swinging the whole night. My ear (every ear in the club) adjusted to the sound of his sticks on telephone books, the heel of one foot and the toe of another pounding a four-foot-high bandstand. The evening gave a new meaning to the notion of percussion. Life is defined, then rewritten, by desperation and surprise.

Long before that, soon after the huge 1944 Philadelphia riot protesting unequal opportunities for black people, the Philadelphia Transportation Company began hiring black motormen to operate streetcars and drive buses. Philly Joe was hired as a trolley operator, one of eight black men given those initial positions. Reporting for work the first day, they found that white strikers had shut down the entire intercity transport system. The racial situation was so tense that an armed military guard was placed on every streetcar so that blacks would not attack white operators traveling through black neighborhoods and vice versa. I remember this hateful chapter of my teenage years. It was terrible, but seventy years later I wonder if the world has changed all that much.

Philly Joe's route, number twenty-three, was the longest route in the city. It traversed the lower part of South Philadelphia and continued into North Philadelphia and into Germantown. That trolley journey took Philly Joe right past the Downbeat Club on 11th Street, where he often played with high-profile musicians. Max Roach was his close friend and sometimes rode the entire trolley route, end to end, when Joe was driving, talking about drumming, drummers, and jazz. That's who Max Roach was always—serious and gregarious. One night driving his route, Philly Joe came up 11th Street. Adjacent to the club, mid-block, he stopped, opened the doors, and quickly ran up to the club on the second floor. He enjoyed the sounds awhile. His passengers were outraged. When he returned, everyone was in an uproar. Streetcars were lined up behind his, their schedules compromised along with his own. The scene was mass confusion. Without a word, Philly climbed back in the driver's seat, closed the doors, and resumed his route north, as if all were normal. We'll never know how many nonpaying passengers had come onboard during his unauthorized visit to the Downbeat.

Philly Joe Jones was unpredictable on gigs, and everywhere else. He was frequently dubbed a "jailhouse" guy for certain covert and questionable acts. We teased, or admonished, him that if he had not become a musician, he might have found permanent residence at Alcatraz. One night Philly Joe took a cab home from a club and told the driver to take him to West Philly. He had no intention of paying for the ride, so he gave the driver a bogus address close to where he lived. When they arrived, the driver turned the meter off. Philly Joe was already out of the cab running down the dark street. Our hero had no idea the taxi driver had been a college track star only a few years before. He was young and fast. He caught Philly Joe from behind, and the outcome was unpleasant. Philly Joe confessed that he hurt for a long while after that unhappy ride.

Dick Katz was a very good pianist who recorded and played with dozens of groups after landing in Manhattan. He told me about an incident that occurred during the first week he worked with Philly Joe's group. The band finished a full week's engagement. After the other band members had been paid, Dick had received not a single word, nor any bread. Thinking he had been forgotten, Dick Katz asked Philly why he had been overlooked. His redoubtable leader looked at him with indignation: "Do you realize who you've been playing with? Philly Joe Jones, whose valuable experience you just absorbed. *You* should pay *me!*" Flabbergasted, Dick demanded his money. When Dick told me this story, we laughed like veterans who had negotiated the same war terrain. If Philly Joe had been with us, he would have laughed harder than we did.

After joining the Dameronia band put together by trumpeter Don Sickler, our perverse hero moved back to Philly. I had not seen Philly Joe for many years when he sent word to me, by a mutual friend: "Your drummer is waiting to hear from you." With luck, we would have played together once again. From my perspective, no one could resist his percussive art. To my regret, he died before that finale could occur. Philly Joe Jones was an unforgettable character. Born on July 15, 1923, he died in his sleep of a heart attack on August 30, 1985. I fondly remember him, his improbable perfect touch, and our great times together.

CHAPTER 24

Monk, Max, and Dinah

WITHOUT OPPORTUNITY, talent is moot and an artist may toil in obscurity. I am annoyed when I think about the way opportunities often elude talented musicians. A case in point is Thelonious Monk, whose brilliance went undiscovered and unrewarded for far too long. Though his music was played and recorded while he was alive, he was never accepted as the genius he is considered today. For two decades, at the heart of his artistic maturity, Monk was regarded mostly as "the guy who writes and plays weird stuff." But seemingly weird things can become the standard by which even stranger things later emerge and succeed. A couple of years before he died, Monk played on a Norman Granz tour called "The Giants of Jazz." The tour included Dizzy Gillespie, Sonny Stitt, Art Blakey, Al McKibbon, and, of course, Monk. It was the last consequential gig Monk ever played.

While I was living in Los Angeles, I visited Harry Colomby's home in Beverly Hills. Harry was Monk's manager. During my visit, Monk's name came up. Harry said that the label with whom Monk had signed a recording deal had just given him $10,000 to make his final album for them. They didn't care if he played solo piano or with a quartet or a big band. Ten grand had to cover it—no more money after that. It was clear they had no interest in Monk or his talent. They just wanted to complete the contract.

I was angry hearing this egregious example of a phenomenon that has occurred in jazz too often. If an artist doesn't make enough money for the company in a given period of time, he or she is dropped. A promotional campaign could have solved the problem, as the record companies usually organized for rock musicians in that golden era (and today more than ever, they still manufacture "stars" from stupidity and bombast). Jazz has faced a limited fan base ever since the "British invasion," fronted by the Beatles, in the 1960s, and small record companies do not have the income to do extensive promotional work. Deals for jazz albums are now usually made on a scaled-down basis. Jazz success, therefore, requires in effect a cult following. Predictably now, after a once-marginalized artist is gone, we hear what a genius he or she was. The best we can hope for is to protect what is left of the artist's legacy. Mary Lou Williams fell into this category. For several decades now, musicians have treated Monk's compositions as if they bear previously unexcavated veins of gold. They do, in fact; but his posthumous triumph is not a result of record companies suddenly getting hip. Monk's legacy was restored through the efforts of musicians, mostly younger, who possessed a keener sense of his genius than did his contemporaries. Musicians can miss the truth of genius in their midst no less than executives counting beans. Monk influenced Sonny Rollins and John Coltrane immensely, and inspired many others with his Zen-like teachings. But during his lifetime many respectable musicians found only eccentricities in Monk's work. I witnessed Monk's neglect over a long time span and I remember it well. Monk once (with considerable nobility) took a rap for his student prodigy and close friend, Bud Powell. After his arrest his cabaret card was voided, which prevented him from performing in Manhattan for several crucial years in his prime, a terrible blow to his career.

Later, Thelonious Monk institutes sprung up across the United States. Thelonious Monk competitions abound, which award substantial amounts of money to the winners. These events are prestigious, and ironically, record contracts are frequently offered to those who gain recognition in these events. Thanks to myopic executives and record producers (along with not a few ultra-square journalists and critics), Thelonious Monk had the sad fortune to become a genius deferred. Late in his career, Orrin Keepnews signed him to the Riverside label, and that led Columbia to cash in on Monk's refurbished identity. And yet, there is one more dilemma here. We musicians who *did* know who and what this man was should have proclaimed the truth loudly and often. We might have awakened others, much earlier, to Monk's benefit and to our own. Most of the listening public did not have "ears" sufficiently acute to discern his joyful singularity.

The norm is that people wait for critics and record companies to tell them what is hip. That reality is lamentably evident today. Clearly, I, too, should have done more. I confess that I bitterly resent his mistreatment by all as a result of our indifference.

Thelonious Monk was abused and neglected as a result of the outright ignorance that permeated nearly every sector of the jazz community. It was even worse outside that circle, where both his name and his avant-garde energy were frequently mocked and stigmatized. Even the great comedian, Sid Caesar, who was himself an accomplished professional baritone saxophonist, gibed at jazz sophistication in his funny but profoundly misguided skit about "Cool McCool," in which Carl Reiner interviews a way-too-far-out horn player. The skit was funny, but pandered to the worst in this country's anti-intellectual parochialism.

Somehow Monk survived against the odds, with moral and spiritual assistance from Baroness Nica (Rothschild) and a small coterie of people intelligent enough to recognize his musical as well as his human worth. Beethoven, in an altogether different culture, experienced a fate not dissimilar. Along with J. S. Bach, Beethoven was surely one of the two most important composers in human history. The widespread recognition that came later does not make up for the neglect and stunning poverty of Beethoven's final years. Vincent van Gogh also died in poverty, unheralded and undone by his demons, but today his paintings are worth millions and hang in art museums around the globe. For Monk, too, no recompense is possible for the harm that was done him in his lifetime. I can only pray that justice and good taste prevail and that Monk's legacy remains strong for a very long time. For my own peace of mind, I must believe it will.

Max Roach once told me that he was in awe of me. In fact, I have been in awe of Max since 1945, when I was sixteen years old. Max was bigger than life for me. He played a role in the founding of modern jazz. His contribution to that historic movement stands alongside that of Bird and Diz. Like Jo Jones, his hero, the artistic fire and dignity that Max Roach brought to the world of jazz lifted percussive complexity and subtlety to the highest plateau. Max transformed the art of drumming into a serpentine accentuation, raising drumming to the level of lyrical punctuation and sophisticated melodic adornment. Listening to his earliest work with Diz and Bird in the 1940s, I am struck by the multiple ways he opened up temporal and emotional space within the music—space that invites or goads instrumentalists to romp freely with reinforced imaginative verve.

Max was the thinking musician's drummer, with a flair for adding a solid and discrete temporal feeling to a piece of music, unfolding like a flowing river. Max continually found new ways to frame prevailing expectations, crafting understated excitement with surprising percussive shading. As a man, Max was as constant as the tides. He was an autodidact, a thinker, and a reader. He ended his career teaching at the University of Massachusetts in Amherst, an appropriate calling for a man who gave such wise counsel to so many in the jazz community (to Miles Davis, among others).

Max had a predilection for enabling creativity and culture in the largest sense, which included dance and the spoken word. Many of his public presentations featured nonmusical arts. Max saw art as a multifaceted endeavor coming directly from the core of human hope and curiosity. He recognized that art articulates a fundamental searching that defines human life. Perhaps that artistic stewardship, demonstrated across decades of steady effort, is why Max received a MacArthur Fellowship.

Max never disappointed me. He carried history within him throughout his well-lived life. In the thrilling years of artistic revolution that flourished after the Second World War, Max helped to create something radically new. I am still in awe of his immense artistic talent and his enormous good humor, his perfect mix of pride and humility. He once described to me what I consider a unique "Max Roach moment." Apparently Max got on a bus in Manhattan one day soon after a fare increase had taken effect. He fumbled in his pockets for the right change. The bus driver looked at him briefly and said, "Sixty cents for senior citizens." Max arrived back home and looked in the mirror. He was stumped how any stranger knew that.

In 1956, while I was on the road with Earl Bostic, our band occasionally ran into Dinah Washington and her group. Dinah had just married saxophonist Eddie Chamblee, who left Lionel Hampton's band to be with her. Charles Davis was playing baritone saxophone and he led Dinah's group. That was when I met all of them for the first time. Instead of working with a trio, as did most other singers, Dinah fronted a septet, probably because of her new husband. Before she appeared on stage, Eddie opened the set with the band to get the audience a groove. It worked.

Eddie knew I was a writer and he got her permission for me to write a few things for the group. I wrote instrumentals and also some background pieces for her singing. She liked what I did and asked me for more. Eventually, I wrote full-blown orchestra arrangements for her recording sessions. Since I was traveling no less than she was, I often mailed arrangements to her. After awhile, whenever she came to a club where I was playing, she would announce loudly, "The Queen is on the scene!" She would head up to join us on stage even before I asked her. She just loved to sing. Her attitude was, simply, that she was one of the guys. On those evenings Dinah merely sat in, but she handled herself as if she were working her own gig, expending maximum energy and intensity. Doubtless, that is why musicians loved her. She was a pro.

After Art Farmer and I put together The Jazztet, we landed a gig at the Brooklyn Paramount. Brook Benton, Dion and the Belmonts, and Dinah Washington were also on the bill. I learned that Dinah and Eddie had broken up or divorced. I wasn't sure which, but during that week she sought me out for conversation more than ever before. I was divorced and she seemed to know that. Those conversations quickly got deep. I was not in the least interested in becoming husband number six or seven to Dinah, but I wanted to be kind to her. She misunderstood kindness for something else. Soon I was invited to her apartment for a home-cooked meal and tender loving care. Knowing that she had two boys of elementary school age who lived with her, as well as a full-time maid, I thought we would not be alone.

I went to her apartment on 145th Street. When I arrived, she opened the door, which I thought unusual since normally the maid would have answered the door. All the lights were dimmed, and an unnatural calm and quiet prevailed. There was no sign of the children, and no sounds except for some soft music on the record player. I asked about her sons. She had sent them to relatives for the night. Where was the maid? I inquired casually. She had given the maid the night off. I was trapped.

We had a fantastic dinner. Dinah could really cook. We ate and talked, romantic music enhancing my discomfort. It was excruciating. I was trying to figure how to get out the door without offending or embarrassing a very nice, horny woman whom I respected as a wonderful artist. It was not going to be easy. Finally, dinner was over, and the zero hour had arrived. I was the sucker in the crosshairs. Returning from the kitchen, she snuggled up beside me on the couch, as close as possible. Suggestiveness had given way to direct assault.

I saw nothing for it. I suddenly looked at my watch and exclaimed dramatically, "Holy cow! I'm fifteen minutes late for an appointment. I'm in real trouble now!" I grabbed my hat and coat before Dinah knew what was happening. On the pavement out in front of her building, I exhaled an enormous whoosh of pent-up breath. I had dodged an amorous bullet. From that day on, Dinah Washington always referred to me as "Reverend Golson." Only the two of us knew what she meant. Years later, in Detroit with The Jazztet, I heard the news of her death. So many who knew her were saddened by her departure from the musical universe. She was one of the guys, a genuine character, a great singer and performer. In many ways, she was a jazz queen, just as she wanted to be. We all loved our pal, The Queen. We lost one of our own.

CHAPTER 25

Curtis Fuller and The Jazztet

MY GREATEST PLEASURE playing with any trombonist has always been with Curtis Fuller. Curtis and I have played together, off and on, for more than fifty years, and I have played with him more than with any other trombonist. I know all Curtis's "in's and out's." He is the most sound-conscious trombonist I know. If his sound is not good on a recording, trust me: it's the fault of the recording engineer. Curtis's keen ear, so essential in playing jazz where the largest part is improvisation, is phenomenal. He hears everything.

Once during a New York recording session with Art Blakey's Jazz Messenger All Stars (additional members being Freddie Hubbard, Curtis, and me), we were working on a very difficult tune by pianist Walter Davis, Jr. The song was called "Uranus." The melody was not difficult, but the chord progression was. Curtis said he didn't want to solo on it. Freddie said, "Yeah! Those changes are kickin' your butt," and laughed hard. Freddie kept needling Curtis until Curtis turned and asked Walter to run through a chorus with him. As Curtis improvised with Walter, he created some of the most complex ideas I had ever heard on that tune. He was flawless and dazzling. He laid out everybody in the studio right there, including Freddie.

When he finished, he turned to the provocative horn player, whose mouth was agape. "See, Freddie, I know it. I just didn't want to solo on it."

Freddie said no more. An artist of the highest caliber had just exonerated himself, with rationality and artistic flair.

I first met Curtis while I was playing in Dizzy's band. We were performing at Storyville, in Boston, owned by George Wein, who soon launched The Newport Jazz Festival. One night an unknown trombonist came in with Diz and joined us. Our band was already complete. Nonetheless, the young guy took out his instrument, and we kicked off the set. An extra chair was set for him next to Al Grey, who held down the first trombone chair. There were no introductions. The band simply took off and roared as always. Eventually a trombone solo came up. The new fellow was right behind me. He stood up and began playing. I had never heard anybody play a slide trombone as though the slide did not exist. His playing was hip and soulful. He had the biggest sound I'd ever heard from that instrument.

I was delighted to think that he would join the band. He sounded like Miles Davis playing trombone. Afterward, Diz introduced Curtis Fuller, from Detroit. He wasn't there to join the band. Apparently, Diz merely wanted to hear what he could do. Curtis was lyrical, impressive, and fast as lightning.

Curtis and I became good friends. I was best man at his wedding. He married one of two immensely talented women who were each other's best friends. Amazingly, not long after, I married the other. Both were classical dancers who studied their difficult athletic art together for years in Washington, D.C. He married Judy Patterson, formerly with Katherine Dunham's dance troupe. I married Bobbie Hurd, formerly with the New York Negro Ballet Company and, for a while, the Washington Ballet Company in Washington, D.C., which was all white except for Bobbie. A year or so after Bobbie and I were married, Curtis called to see if I wanted to play with him at the Five Spot for two weeks. This was the original Five Spot in the Bowery, before the club moved up to St. Mark's Place in the Village. That gave me another chance to play with my buddy. The owners, Joe and Iggy, liked us so much that two weeks became a year and a half. Other groups came and went, but we became the Five Spot house band.

We were so confident of our gig at the Five Spot that we accepted a week at Birdland even though we were employed at the Five Spot. After all, there were two groups at both clubs. Surely with strategic planning, we could pull this off. The week of our double booking arrived and we began nerve-racking engagements at both clubs. We kicked off our first set on time every night at the Five Spot. Our employers knew nothing about

Birdland. We would finish our first set and, horns in hand without cases, jump in a cab to 52nd Street in midtown Manhattan. We always arrived at Birdland just in time for the second set—our set. That set completed, we raced back to the Bowery. How wonderful to be young studs with infinite chutzpah and inexhaustible energy. We nailed it, three trips each night. Close calls, but we had our new routine down. Everything was great the first few nights. But our plan soon fell apart. One night we were late finishing our first set at the Five Spot and barely made it to Birdland. Finishing our set at Birdland left us behind schedule back at the Five Spot. We sprinted back, but when we walked in, the second set band had been gone for a long while. People were patiently waiting, but what could we say? We wondered what Joe and Iggy would say.

We didn't wonder long; Joe headed directly toward us. We tried to look like two dedicated guys, devotedly returning, revved to go. It didn't work. Joe wasn't happy. "I don't know what you guys are doing," he said. With that, he fired us. We had outsmarted ourselves. I remember thinking about one of *Aesop's Fables*, where a dog crossed a bridge with a bone in his mouth. Seeing his reflection in the water, he decided two bones were better than one. He opened his mouth to grab the second bone and the first bone—the real one—sank out of sight. Our bone was now out of reach.

When Art Farmer and I decided that Curtis would be a member of our co-led group, Curtis named it The Jazztet. The name was just right. Curtis DuBois Fuller didn't let his childhood years in a Detroit orphanage prevent him from realizing his dream. He became one of the best trombonists ever. Years later, he learned that he had lung cancer. I thought I would lose my dear friend of thirty-five years. Surgery took one lung, but remarkably Curtis returned to the scene with artistic vengeance. The Jazztet, reassembled for a short tour of Europe, was back in gear. Art and I cautioned Curtis to take it easy, telling him we would cover for him. What a joke. Our revived trombonist played like someone possessed. He was as fast as ever. His sound was absolutely magnificent: big, warm, and round. He survived the operation physically and artistically intact. After our first song, Art exclaimed, "It's a miracle!" That miracle continues until this very day. Curtis's longevity has defied the odds.

Like Lester Young, Curtis possesses uncanny verbal abilities. He crafts spontaneous graphic caricatures. Speaking of "varicose veins," he'll say "very close veins." He might refer to a well-dressed fellow as "a man of the cloth." About a portly person who makes a strange or questionable state-ment, Curtis might immediately respond, "Fat chance."

At the outset, Art and I had almost mirror-like images of our desired sex-tet. Addison, his twin brother, would be our bassist. Dave Bailey became our drummer. Now we needed a pianist. I had recently met a sensational nine-teen-year-old piano player. To find out how sharp he was, I played a tune in a strange key. He ate it up. So we asked McCoy Tyner to join the sextet.

When I called McCoy, he responded as though he had been waiting for the invitation. Philadelphia is ninety miles from Manhattan. I asked if he was up to traveling that round trip distance most days. He surprised me. He and his wife, Aisha, had been wanting to move to New York. Art and I found an apartment for them. McCoy had a friend who owned a big Chrysler, who agreed to help them move. On the expected arrival day, I got a desperate call from McCoy. The Chrysler had broken down on the New Jersey Turnpike. Could I rescue them from the side of the road? I didn't have a car, so I told him to call back in half an hour. I called my pal John Coltrane and we headed for the turnpike. There was McCoy, standing by the dead vehicle. We loaded the young couple and all their boxes into John's car. I don't remember what happened to the driver and his disabled Chrysler.

We headed into Brooklyn, where their new apartment was waiting. McCoy and Aisha immediately made it a home. I rode back to Manhattan with John and we talked as we always did, arriving back at my place on 90th Street. When McCoy left our group a year or so later, he joined, guess who? John Coltrane. I saw John one night. "A fine friend you are—stealing our piano player." I was kidding. There were no bad feelings because, cre-atively, McCoy belonged with John Coltrane more than with us. History proved that right. In 1997 McCoy told me that John had expressed serious reservations about hiring him, because of the deep friendship John and I had shared since our neophyte days. Everyone understood the situation and McCoy really wanted to play with John's group in the worst way. Some things are meant to be.

As Art and I plotted the arrival of our new group on the scene, I thought we needed at least one song strong enough to make people think of our group every time they heard it. I wrestled with three different melodies and dumped two. The tune that resulted was "Killer Joe." The rim shot on every fourth beat derived from Dave Bailey. Without that accent, "Killer" would not have his seductive, sinister appeal.

One of The Jazztet's first gigs was at the Roundtable, on the East Side. One afternoon a week before opening, we were rehearsing there. The owner came in, wanting to know the name of the group. We had done everything except find a name for ourselves. He needed to know the name of the group before we left for the day. Curtis Fuller, with his uncanny gift for words, announced: "It's a sextet and we play jazz. We'll call it 'The Jazztet.'" Curtis and I had recorded an album for Savoy under his name a few years before. It was entitled "The Jazztet." So there it was—Curtis to the fore again.

The group was an immediate success. Columbia Records wanted to sign us. So did Mercury and a few others, too. We weren't looking for a big company. We wanted one that really cared about us and our music. With that in mind, we signed with Argo, a subsidiary of Chess Records in Chicago, run by Phil and Leonard Chess. They fulfilled their promises to us while we worked with them. Our first album was called simply *Meet The Jazztet*. Our new drummer was Lex Humphries. Soon "Killer Joe" was playing on jukeboxes across the country. We were on our way.

Just about all groups have personnel changes. Cedar Walton took over when McCoy left. He, too, eventually moved on. We tapped into Philly again, a promising young pianist named Kenny Barron. We gave him the piano book and rehearsed with him. Everything would be all right. After Cedar's last appearance, at Birdland, Kenny joined us. During that week, Harold Mabern sat in with us for one tune. His comping was so dynamic that Art and I both thought we needed him. Harold was playing with Lionel Hampton at the time, but he agreed to join us. That meant giving Kenny bad news. He was only sixteen, and we didn't want to discourage him. We confessed to Kenny that Harold had the flair we wanted. Kenny Barron has always been a hugely nice man. He replied that he understood (even if he didn't, really). We gave him two weeks' salary to let him know we were not heartless jerks. Of course, talent inevitably triumphs. Kenny became the most recorded jazz pianist on the scene. His stature continues to grow. He was inducted as a Jazz Master at Lincoln Center along with Bobby Hutcherson and Yusef Lateef. Now we laugh about that anomalous moment in 1959. Life's vagaries are circuitous.

Art and I kept our group together for roughly two years before we disbanded. The Jazztet was dead, we thought; yet twenty-four years later, in 1983, a European promoter named Alexander Zivkovic called me. Could we put together a group with J.J. Johnson on trombone? I called J.J., who was living in Los Angeles, but he was just breaking into the television and movie scene and didn't want to leave it. He was right. In Hollywood, if you drop out, you lose. It's not an industry known for loyalty. The promoter asked if I had a replacement. "We could put The Jazztet together again for your tour," I blurted out.

Bingo: Art and I contacted the other four. The truth here is that the Japanese are incredible people. Someone in Japan found out about this and invited us to come to play there before our European tour. We did so, and we also recorded an album while we were in Japan. Our new regimen called for recording on a variety of labels in order to avoid potentially oppressive contracts. The second iteration of The Jazztet was a different beast. My musical concepts had changed. I now wrote music with more space for improvisation. Nonetheless, its thrust did not abandon structure or group organization. I emphasized harmonic elements for their aesthetic and emotional impact. I also underlined the drama of lyric and narrative anticipation important to musical strength and compositional integrity. I explored intervals as if searching for gold. Greater use of the bass required considerable skill in execution. I felt the bass had not been used to its full potential. My view then and now is that bass carries enormous power. More should be done to liberate as well as integrate the bottom octaves into music, which is both infinite and genuinely eternal.

In 1957, two years before we created the original Jazztet, it received proleptic influence from Dizzy's big band concert at the Newport Jazz Festival in 1957. I learned something impossible to forget or overlook that came into play with The Jazztet. The business end of that band was handled with predictable routine. Diz had us travel by bus, if we had sufficient time to arrive comfortably. Organization was a high priority in our travel. We received constant reminders to keep our uniforms clean. After every concert, someone collected all of the sheet music, each and every individual part for all instruments—a crucial habit since those sheets of music represented who we were as an artistic organization. Symbolically, our sheet music was Dizzy Gillespie's band in miniature. However, when we arrived at Newport the afternoon before that July evening performance, Diz discovered that our music had been left behind at the last place we played. We had no way to get it before we played this event. What to do?

Diz informed us of the mix-up. I think every one of us was worried: could we play as a single throbbing unit without our accustomed written cues? The crisis had to be solved. We had never coped with a situation like this before. No prosthesis was available, no remedy or trick to call on. That night in Newport, Rhode Island, we would find out a great deal about our artistic worth.

As usual, we were introduced with considerable fanfare on stage, while we ourselves wondered what was about to happen. People plunked down their money and would not accept excuses about why a truly great orchestra stunk up the joint. The last thing the guy who has bought your records and has come to hear you roar like a Rolls Royce wants to learn is that some blockhead forgot your music and the whole band is wobbly. Imagine what the big-time critics for the jazz magazines and major newspapers would say. If we screwed up, they would be right to trash us. Grimly, we faced a do-or-die occasion, an unimpeachable opportunity to find out whether our band's assembled brain power and memory retention were as sharp as some believed. I, for one, was not certain. We filed onto the stage to an uproarious greeting in Peabody Park, its elegant cove before us dotted with sloops and yachts. The welcoming crowd might become a deranged mob if we didn't pass muster. It felt like showing up to take your doctoral examination stark naked.

I can only imagine how Dizzy felt, but when he raised his hand like a confident bullfighter ready to confront the bull, perhaps only my imagination perceived his hand slightly waver. The whole band hit the first chords with such force that I was startled. Suddenly I realized everyone in the band was doing what I was doing: playing with maximum conviction, every heart beating fast. We actually knew the music to perfection! As the set unfolded, it became clear to us that the sheet music was a crutch. We played so beautifully that Diz called my song, "I Remember Clifford." I thought he had made a mistake. I had written that arrangement only a few weeks earlier. I was shocked—but we hit not one wayward note, not a single clunker. That evening proved to me how capacious the artistic mind truly is. Once more I saw that great jazz musicians have an unrivaled capacity for musical depth and flexibility.

When The Jazztet was formed, we had a lot of sheet music to deal with. After awhile, when we played gigs the music stands began to bother us. We looked like slaves to the papers. Music stands proclaimed our bondage. Remembering the night at Newport, I called for a completely different rehearsal protocol. Rehearsals became sessions to file songs away in our memories. We worked through the entire book eventually, a substantial task, and committed everything to our personal internal song libraries. Our mnemonic dedication impressed our audiences. We played many complicated pieces without sheet music. I suspect our fans enjoyed our playing even more.

From then on, I called for memorizing sessions. We arrived at the studio on West 48th Street. Everyone received his individual part. We spent a half hour looking at the music, locking into place the notes and phrases, getting the structures and performance logic set in our minds and, only then, finally *imagining* that we were playing those parts. I allowed fifteen minutes for such visualizing. Then, it was all blowing. "Here we go!" Sometimes we refined things here and there, but for the most part, we played the music just the way I wrote it. Sometimes we surprised ourselves, finding that we could do so much in such a short time. I suppose the mind roams or soars only as far as we let it. Sometimes, if we push it further than what seems possible, it goes there with little effort. None of us in that original sextet had special powers of comprehension or memorization. And yet, we did it. Initially, it didn't seem possible, but no one said it was impossible. That anxious night at Newport in 1957, we discovered our triumphant coherence, just as Dizzy's fantastic orchestra bonded into a free, unfettered force of musical nature.

PART VI *Music and Writing*

What makes Benny Golson so singular—and globally influential—is his embodiment of what I have called "the life force" of jazz. . . . He has become famous, as have his boundless stories about his own self-discoveries, in and out of the jazz life, which have, in turn, opened up inner doors of self-discovery for his listeners throughout the world.

   —NAT HENTOFF

CHAPTER 26

Writing

A S A TEENAGER I became interested in writing songs in order to create music my pals and I could play in our ensembles. My first attempt, "The Maharajah and the Blues," was awful. Jam sessions of a sort took place in my basement: Percy Heath, Ray and Tom Bryant, on piano and bass, plus John Coltrane (then on alto sax). Sylvester Tillman played the drums and Calvin Marshall also played alto sax (he later became a choir master at an Episcopalian church in North Philadelphia). This was the ensemble that debuted my inaugural composition and arrangement.

"The Maharajah" was an irredeemable failure. Everything was wrong. The melody was crude. Mistaken transpositions were scattered across each part. Percy pointed out that I avoided designating a root in any chord for his part. The disaster I concocted made me I think I would never be a writer. However, I refused to stop trying.

Looking now at that fourteen-year-old fledgling saxophonist, I see that it was impossible for me not to craft pieces that were worse than dogs. I actually knew quite a bit about the piano, but it didn't help me write songs. I had no knowledge of lyrical and melodic concepts, no sense of song forms or structures, even less awareness of harmonic intervals, and absolutely no idea regarding tonal or instrumental functions. I did not understand how to make good use of notes, or how to set up anticipation or establish color, harmony, or rhythmic coherence. I had no idea how to make engaging use of common tones, or how to plot graphic musical events. I didn't understand the value of holding a chord to define weight and emotional value, or of changing a chord at an unexpected moment. Most of all, I had no idea how to make a song target the listener's *heart*. Beautiful melodies stir the soul. Because I was ignorant of all this, my initial attempts to write songs were utterly naïve. I was ambitious, but my execution was amateurish—uncorrupted love in the absence of experience or sophistication.

Tadd Dameron finally pointed me in the right direction in song writing. I was lucky to meet Tadd when I was twenty-one. We were in Bull Moose Jackson's rhythm-and-blues band in 1951, the year I first heard Frank Foster—a saxophonist who, sixty years later, remained on the cutting edge. I'm too old to be embarrassed now by the fact that, as an adolescent pseudo-hipster, I wrote whatever crossed my mind: "I Found My True Love in Mexico"; "I'm Finger Poppin' and Hip Shakin'"; "I'm Cool, Not Hot"; "Off on a Cloud"; "When You Find the One You Love." The titles were the best things about those bombs. With "Let's Find the Sun," I see now that I was ahead of the Beatles with my hope of invoking solar cheer. All of these disastrous efforts were necessary to my development. If I had known the changes to "Out of Nowhere," perhaps my song invoking cloud-like drifting would have succeeded. I actually beat Horace Silver to the notion of finger-poppin' grooves.

Slowly, I discovered what *not* to do. That lesson is of incalculable value. My apprentice compositions were a wasteland, but they helped me learn where I wanted to go as a writer. I see now that one has to be a nut case to pursue such daunting ambitions. My piano bench is a graveyard of my song-writing duds. Today, I do better, but I will say that that innocent kid's one prevailing virtue from the very beginning was an abiding love for melody, despite his ignorance of how to create it.

Melody is strong stuff, perhaps the essential factor in a song's longevity. Intervals frame melodies, create drama, and carry lyric power. When melodic and harmonic intervals guide song creation, the results more often than not are interesting, sometimes beautiful. I began writing in the mid-1940s, but I did not understand a song's inner workings until the mid-1950s. To this day, in the second decade of the twenty-first century, if I am listening to a song and every element and every note do not lie just right, I feel physical discomfort. When that composition finally hits my ear right, life is enjoyable again.

One of the first things I wrote after coming to understand the magic of song writing, in 1955, was "Stablemates," a rather odd creation. Other successful songs followed in due course. That elusive, unpredictable, much anticipated reward is, inevitably, an illusion. Success derives from an international network of listeners. No writer can decide that the song he has written is a winner. If people find delight or fulfillment in any of my pieces, my efforts are vindicated, and I feel blessed. Some supporters of my writing have been fellow musicians who recorded them. The acknowledgment of one's peers is the highest honor.

Sometimes music goes beyond temporal boundaries and formal restraints, eluding the laws of time and physics. In such moments, music escapes the fluid incarnation of "now." Metaphorically, it exists in an eternal realm where shape and limit are irrelevant. A sense of The Infinite is expressed—of unfathomable, unending life.

CHAPTER 27

Lessons

HAVE ALWAYS sought to avoid meaningless scale-line melodies in my writing. Little is required for scale-line thinking. The exception here, however, is the compositional genius of Thelonious Monk. Scale-line, who needs it? Check out "Straight, No Chaser." Very few songwriters can think that way. Considerable ability is required for most truly creative acts, except in the case of someone like Monk, who just followed what the scale dictated, in a process akin to painting by numbers. Finding meaningful intervals, one after the other, however, takes considerably more thought. I've written a couple of scale-line tunes. One is called "No Dancing." I recorded it in 1985 with Freddie Hubbard and Woody Shaw. They played exceptionally well, but I didn't like the piece. It's pedestrian and doesn't go anywhere.

What I usually try to accomplish are songs that stand out. I seek something out of the ordinary. The last thing I want is a piece that sounds fabricated and arbitrary. I want to create songs that feel natural, regardless of chord choice, tempo, syncopation, and note values. Most songs sit on my piano *in medias res*, awaiting further attention. They sometimes languish for weeks or months, or on occasion, years, before I return to them. Some I forget altogether. When I cruise through my dogs, I check abandoned songs to see whether I have brought to them the absolute best of which I am capable. Often, I change or reshape these songs completely. Even after I'm pleased with a song, I wait before sending it for publication. Music can be cruel and unforgiving. A song is either absolutely and completely right—or it's not right at all.

I write compositions with varying types of feeling and pacing, but my favorite genre is the ballad. Seventy-five percent of the songs I write now are ballads, melodies that tug at my heart. No doubt that is why I love Puccini, Chopin, and Brahms. They are maximum melodic maestros. In 1996, I began writing my own lyrics. I did this not from pride. I believe that a story lives within each melody. Any tale is best told by its composer. I have worked for years to understand the inner logic of lyric writing. It's not easy. I stand in awe of great lyricists. Jon Hendricks is a master of this formidable undertaking. I have let very few of my lyrics escape into the world. I'll continue to hold the rest, until I am sure of them.

When I write ballads, I think both instrumentally *and* vocally. Rather than call upon sonic or melodic generalities alongside a generic voice, I consistently draw upon two musical personalities deeply etched in my imagination: Art Farmer and Shirley Horn. I hear Art and Shirley within me as I write a ballad. I wonder how each would interpret the song I'm writing. For me, these two artists express the deepest soul of the balladic art. We have lost both Art and Shirley, but the way they articulated lyric beauty still haunts me. I love what they routinely expressed with such delicacy. I want my compositions to be as subtle and sensitive as was their art. Shirley and Art are unrivaled interpreters of melodic feeling.

In writing ballads, there are times I become so immersed in the music that my emotions overcome me. Since I often see an entire story unfolding as I work, my eyes well up with tears as if I'm heartbroken. The imagination has enormous roots in feeling as much as in intellect. One day, I was working downstairs in my Los Angeles studio, composing a song. I had decided to call it "Sad to Say." Though I was shedding no tears, Bobbie, upstairs, hearing this lament over and over again, grew concerned and came downstairs to ask me, "Baby, are you happy?" Of course, I was, but my mind was lost in the song's unfolding sadness. At that moment, I existed on two levels: I was working lucidly to write a somber song, intensified emotionally by my own private "audience of one." Bobbie was partly correct. As a listener, I was the saddest person on earth. Tony Bennett eventually heard that song and wanted to write lyrics for it. It was too personal. I refused because an *entire* narrative scenario was running across its songscape in my head. In Tokyo, soon after we lost Sarah Vaughan, I played it without accompanying lyrics. But this song is now one of the few with lyrics of my own composition that I have released to the world. The song was blessed by Shirley Horn's perfect voice.

I take inspiration from all kinds of sources. Sometimes, I compose melodies when I'm sleeping, often in great detail. I used to wake up briefly and note the melody, reassuring myself the tune was worth further consideration. I would go back to sleep thinking I would remember it in the morning, but in the morning, inevitably the melody was gone. I would then piously promise myself that the next time would be different: if I dreamed a melody, no matter how sleepy I was, I would get up and write it down. I figured I must have lost a few good songs because I was too sleepy to write them down.

Then one night, it happened again. I dreamed a fantastic melody. I awoke excited, convinced this was an important song, awaiting my lucid attention. I rubbed my eyes and went down to my studio. I quickly wrote out the melody, taking care to record it exactly as I had dreamed it. I didn't worry about chords or overall structural logic in the middle of the night. I could do all of that when I returned to my studio in the morning. I crawled back into bed happily. The song was a gift from the beyond. The song gods were on my side.

I popped up at dawn, ready to go to work on the tune. "What do I have here?" I wondered, my fingers prowling the piano keys. Wow, that sounds great—better than great. What a profound melody I had found! Yet somehow, it seemed vaguely familiar. Did I already write something similar? What does this remind me of? Then it hit me—I knew this melody. Holy moly! I dreamed "Stardust" as if it were my own.

I sat at my piano feeling like the village idiot. The one time I get up in the middle of the night to snatch a melody from a dream, I discover that I'm a plagiarist. Imagine what my dear mother would tell me! What would my dear pal John Coltrane say? Well, he would laugh, and he would make me laugh, too. Then I wondered about those many times I dreamed a melody, but didn't get up. How many songs had my unconscious imagination pilfered? Maybe I'm a thief when I sleep. Chastened, somehow I no longer dream bewitching melodies anymore. I write only when I'm awake. That seems safer, more rewarding.

Before I write, I must have a viable idea. I then let it percolate in my mind. When I think I've taken the idea as far as possible, I go to my piano. On rare occasions, I pick up my saxophone. Sometimes I continue, setting up a completely new idea. At times, after working on an idea for a while, I will abandon it although I do not destroy the idea. I file it with other glimmers of songful hope, now a sizable bundle.

Years ago, preservation of my manuscripts seemed unimportant to me. I had no idea what the significance or status of my compositions might later become. Like so many hopeful composers, I created without thought for the future. Writing new songs dominated my life. I had no time to ponder theoretically whether any of my jottings might be of interest decades later. Today, I keep everything.

I threw away the original manuscripts for "I Remember Clifford," "Whisper Not," "Stablemates," and two additional melodies written for "Killer Joe." For the latter song, I composed three melodies before choosing the one that became the song. To have those sheets now would certainly be interesting. All the original manuscripts that defined my legacy were pulped in forgotten garbage dumps. My habit was to rewrite clean copies. I threw away originals, with eraser marks, smudges, and tiny scribblings. With no idea of the importance they might later accrue, I filled up pages with songs and merely hoped for the best.

CHAPTER 28

"Stablemates" / MY FIRST RECORDED SONG

WENT ON THE ROAD with Earl Bostic, traveling all over the country like a person without a home. One night we played a dance in Wilmington, Delaware, fifteen miles from Chester, Pennsylvania, the home of my soon-to-be ex-wife. By then, I had made up my mind that I would move on with my life without her. Shortly after we began playing, I looked into the crowd and saw her face. She was a beautiful, beguiling woman, but in my deepest heart I knew it had not worked, and could not work, between us. Such realizations are profoundly sad. I did not want to be unkind to her. She had come with girlfriends; they were all smiling, obviously hoping for a fairy-tale reconciliation between us.

I did not want needless melodrama. When intermission arrived, I stayed on the bandstand, pretending to be absorbed writing something at the piano. As I expected, she sent word that she hoped to see me. I sent a succinct reply: I was working on a very important assignment, due the next morning. Thus, to live up to my own lie, I busied myself composing . . . something.

Serendipity rules the universe. When the intermission concluded, I had written fourteen bars that didn't make sense. Those fourteen eccentric bars got me off the hook. In the morning, I thought the song was demented, but somehow, I loved it; it represented my escape, and my optimism for the future.

The next night, another town, another intermission. I took another stab at my strange creation. Slowly, the tune started to make sense. Four-teen bars were close to sixteen, so there was no need to repeat the head (though, believe me, I tried to make that work). I wrote an eight-bar bridge. But I didn't like it, it was too ordinary. The next night, in yet another town, I reviewed the entire song. I had composed fourteen bars, followed by an eight-bar bridge, followed by a repeat of the fourteen bars. "Nuts," I thought, "it's cock-eyed." I tried as hard as I could to improve the tune, to impose a traditional structure on it. I couldn't.

Yet, somehow, I felt that the bizarre song was coming together. I was becoming bonded to it; it sounded right to me. Or else I was stuck with it, I wasn't sure which. Against all logic, the tune seemed to be working itself out, unless my ears had gone wacky.

Bostic's band played Boston quite a bit, and I had come to know Herb Pomeroy, a trumpet player who worked with a very congenial bunch of guys at a club called The Stables. Herb was aware that I had recently writ-ten a lot of songs, and even though I was playing with Bostic, he asked me to write a piece for his group—Herb on trumpet, as the leader; Varty Haroutunian on tenor sax; Ray Santisi on piano; John Neves on bass; and on drums Jimmy Zitano, who later joined Al Hirt—his Stable mates, as it were. "Anything you like," he said. "We'll play it." Pleased, I sent him this obtuse song, born from my mad scribbling, trying to evade my soon-to-be ex-wife. The song had caused me a great deal of wrangling, and it didn't have a name. But Herb loved it. It was odd and angular, not because, as Miles Davis later kidded me, I smoked funny stuff when I wrote it, but because I wrote it in a strange mood in a strange place, in an emotional tight spot. The motivation for its creation was desperate, but somehow, that evening's inverted enchantment was a blessing for my career. I wrote a song with a kind of ugly beauty. Creativity is perverse and marvelous and enigmatic. The song, of course, was "Stablemates."

Herb wrote me later to say that he and the guys loved the song. It was not as askew as I had thought. As I originally wrote the song, the chord for the first measure was a B-flat augmented chord. When Miles Davis recorded it, he changed that measure to accommodate two chords, an E minor seventh for the first two beats, and an A seventh for the third and fourth. His change dismayed me. I was extremely touchy in those days about people changing anything I wrote. Later in my career, I came to see things differently. Realistically, of course, I appreciated that Miles Davis recorded my song. Along with his bandmate John Coltrane, Miles was at the center of jazz awareness for legions of people. Miles introduced me into the big time, as a writer, and I loved him for that. Still, whenever I played that song, or arranged it for someone, I used my original chords. This was a losing battle, because anything that Miles did then was the Holy Grail. Everyone played it the way Miles recorded it. He also renamed Monk's "Round Midnight" to "Round about Midnight"; along with the changes Miles made to Monk's wonderful song, this did not please Monk. The simple fact was that Miles's influence was immense. He was The Main Guy. Eventually I changed my original lead sheet because everyone, except me, played it the way Miles did.

One day in 1956, working at the piano, I got a call from Les Koenig, president of Contemporary Records, in Los Angeles. He told me that he wanted to record me. I had to stop myself from screaming, I was so delighted at the prospect of finally recording under my own name. I agreed. We would do the recording in New York. Nat Hentoff, a man I deeply respect, was our artists-and-repertoire man. Knowing this was all new to me, he gave me every consideration possible. However, working as an artists-and-repertoire man on a recording session was new for him. I tried to be considerate, too.

I decided to record a nonet. I enlisted help from Art Farmer (trumpet), Gigi Gryce (alto sax), Jimmy Cleveland (trombone), Julius Watkins (French horn), Shahib Shihab (baritone sax), Wynton Kelly (piano), Paul Chambers (bass), and Charlie Persip (drums). Ernie Wilkins wrote one arrangement and Gigi wrote another. The rest of the tunes, I arranged. We also recorded a brand new song called "Whisper Not." Recording in stereo had just come into existence. We had two recording engineers in the studio: one for mono and one for stereo. They were located in separate places. The primary engineer, recording in mono, was experienced in recording classical artists. As a result, he used only two overhead microphones. All of us had our doubts about this. I had always been accustomed to playing directly into a microphone when recording. I kept wondering why Les engaged the services of a classically trained engineer, but since it was my first date, I wasn't going to make trouble. Besides, I was getting *five hundred dollars*. If you find the recording, you will hear how distinctly different the sound is between the two versions.

Not having recorded an album of my own, I was nervous. Les Koenig made sure the studio made food and drink available to us. Paul Chambers evidently drank a bit too much; when we were recording the last tune— exactly when I thought everything was in the bag—now Paul began playing strange notes. At first, I thought he had come up with an entirely new approach; then I realized he was lost. I stopped the take. "We'll try it again. Don't worry," I told him. Why make a person uptight by coming down hard on him? Things get worse that way.

We began again. This time Paul's bass stopped completely. I looked at Paul, who was bent over, looking at the music as if it were some strange animal. Slowly he laid his bass on the carpet and stretched out flat on his back beside it, as if he were bedding down for the night. I began to plead with him. "Paul, please get up. We're almost done. This is the last tune. Please, Paul!" He looked up at me, seeming not even to recognize me. I continued pleading, and finally he staggered to his feet. I didn't hold much hope for the last take. My initial recording date was hanging in the balance. The last song was the most important one. Paul picked up his bass and we began once more. Strangely, he played magnificently. We made it. Nat announced, "Great take!" I was transported with joy and relief. I hugged Paul, and he asked me what had just happened. I had been in more trouble than I realized.

That album was published as *Benny Golson's New York Scene*. The nearly disastrous take was "Whisper Not." This was the first of many albums to come. My second album was for Riverside Records. Orrin Keepnews was its producer and the co-owner of the company. The album was called *The Modern Touch*. Orrin wanted me to use several musicians whom he had in mind. When I found out who they were, I was in awe. I was still an unknown, so I was reluctant to call Max Roach, Kenny Dorham, and J.J. Johnson. They were all stars, and I didn't know them. Yet, when I called, they all agreed. I expected them to fob me off. Wynton Kelly and Paul Chambers had survived my first album with me, so that helped my confidence. Years later, I asked Max why he recorded with a total nobody. He said he had heard about me. For me, recording this album was the beginning I had been waiting for. From then on, it was up to me to make it happen. The greatest joy of my professional life has come from knowing other musicians, my peers. I have never let any of these people down. In truth, I have always tried to improve steadily.

I will never forget Nat Hentoff or Orrin Keepnews. Both men took a chance with me. I am sure Nat mentioned me to Les. From then on, both Nat and Orrin could always get anything they wanted from me. My office in Los Angeles has always been on notice: when Orrin calls, ask no questions, give him whatever he asks for. Both Orrin and Nat helped me when I needed it most, at the very beginning. What is more important than that? I will owe them until the end of time.

CHAPTER 29

"Along Came Betty"

ARL BOSTIC'S BAND played Dayton, Ohio, many times. I remember one night in the summer of 1955 in particular. The weather was nice, and I walked about four or five blocks from the Edmonton Hotel to the club. I passed a small building whose sign announced, "Holy and Sanctified Church." The place was usually empty, but tonight the intensity of the singing spilling into the street suggested the small storefront church was filled to capacity with worshipers. A small instrumental group accompanied the singers. I heard a full drum set, an electric bass, a trombone, and a tambourine, as well as hand clapping, some on the beat and some adding strategic, off-the-beat accents. The mixture of the two created a cross-rhythm that made me feel like dancing. It was really something to hear. Added to this was the soulful singing of the lead singer, probably the preacher himself, supported by the entire congregation, who all seemed schooled to reach the deepest possible feeling. The groove was so overwhelming that I had no choice but to stop for a moment or two. Somehow that moment extended. I stayed too long and arrived late for the gig. This didn't sit well with Bostic, but since I was usually on time, I received only a low-grade tongue lashing about responsibility.

Displeased with myself and annoyed that the congregation had been able to snare me with their infectious groove, I took my place on the band-stand and began playing. My eye caught the eye of a young lady who was enjoying our music. I would finish a phrase, lower my horn, and smile at her, a smile which was returned. During intermission I introduced myself to her and her friends. Her name was Betty Pritchett. The next day I called her, and we got to know each other during the period of the band's engagement. We corresponded by mail after the band left Dayton. Several months later, she decided to move to Philadelphia, where I still lived. She found a good job and settled in Philly. I had recently moved in with my mother and stepfather after divorcing my first wife. Betty found a roommate named Phyllis, who was white. I was now with Dizzy's band, which included Quincy Jones. So Quincy and I made a foursome with Betty and Phyllis. Several months later I finally had a chance to fulfill my longstanding desire to relocate to New York City. When I did, Betty stayed behind in Philly. She visited almost every weekend when the band was working in or near New York and when I was not traveling.

Betty Pritchett had an outgoing personality. Everybody liked her; after a while, many of my friends and colleagues knew her. Our relationship was so good that, when Herb Pomeroy in Boston asked me to write original pieces for his quintet, I wrote a song that I called "Betty, My Love." The title caused confusion at first because Betty was also the name of Herb's wife. I eventually wrote another one named after Betty Pritchett while I was playing with Art Blakey's Jazz messengers. This one, titled "Along Came Betty," became a standard in the jazz repertoire. Considerably later, the identity of the Betty in that song also caused confusion. Jazz insiders said I wrote it for my dear friend Betty Carter, whom I regarded as the greatest jazz singer in the world. It is fortunate that I never named a song "Sophia." Rumors can be difficult (sometimes impossible) to stop. Ridiculously, to this very day some people think "Killer Joe" refers to drummer Philly Joe Jones. It doesn't.

Betty and I were close for about three years. Eventually things changed between us, and even though I once thought I would marry her, the gap between us widened. I finally said good-bye. So I will clarify that "Along Came Betty" was written for a girl I cared about a long while ago, during my late twenties. I understand Betty is back in Dayton and doing fine. Of course, confusion has a life of its own. Ever since I met my wife, Bobbie, more than fifty years ago, people who meet me alongside Bobbie invariably say, "This must be Betty." Not true, but the alliteration between Betty and Bobbie has been somewhat embarrassing.

As a purely technical aside, I will point out that the last three notes coming out of the bridge in "Along Came Betty"—C-E-flat-D—were not originally part of the melody. I played those notes as a harmonic filler when Lee Morgan and I played the song in 1958, soon after I wrote it. We recorded it that way for Blue Note with Art Blakey's quintet. Those three notes fell firmly into place as an integral part of the song, so much so that Lee even played them in unison with me in concert. Of course, everyone thought that was what I wrote. I eventually changed the melody on the lead sheet to include those three notes.

Ultimately, song writing is an adventure. I admire all of the great composers and find many young writers whom I greatly respect. For example, bassist John Clayton writes not only with his pen but also with his heart. He understands how to touch a person emotionally. His writing is musical poetry, crafting memorable inner landscapes. I've come to recognize his writing whenever I hear it. A former piano player with my Los Angeles quartet, Billy Childs, also has impressive skills stretching far beyond the jazz repertoire. His superb writing ability allows him to compose for symphony orchestras with tact and intelligence. Billy has written major works performed by major orchestras, including the New York Philharmonic. Few people in the jazz world know this about him yet. He is a splendid pianist and writer. People will eventually recognize the breadth and depth of his talent.

In 1996 in Cleveland, I met another special composer. Neal Creque taught at Oberlin College before he passed away far too early. I met Neal when I gave a clinic at the Tri-C Festival in Cleveland. I concluded my portion of the event and a group came on stage to perform Neal's music. My ears almost fell off my head. I heard music of a type and quality seldom composed by writers today. Neal composed with both his mind and his heart, and his voicings were fresh and crisp. This man was a thinker. He knew how to give his music reach and motion, the power to explore sound, as well as engaging ideas. Surprisingly, I heard elements in Neal's work for which I myself strive. And yet his approach to composition was unique and persuasive. I heard singing qualities reminiscent of Tadd Dameron's writing, yet they were purely Neal's own. I felt immediately that it was a shame such a talented, hugely creative man was not a household name. He shared his knowledge and talent unselfishly, remaining in Ohio to dedicate himself to teaching. Neal was also a tremendous pianist. Had he pursued his career as a performer and writer rather than as a teacher, I am sure he would have entered the ranks of jazz notables. I hope Oberlin and its music students realized what they had in this distinctly creative person. I love what he did and the way he did it. Neal Creque, I salute you!

CHAPTER 30

"I Remember Clifford"

ONE VERY HOT SUMMER DAY in August 1956, I was appearing at the Apollo Theater, in Harlem on 125th Street, with Dizzy's band. Some of us were standing near the stage door at the rear of the theater on 126th Street. The theater was air conditioned, but we wanted daylight. On long days of practice, you feel boxed in unless you get outside now and then. Shows at the Apollo were scheduled close together, with a "B" feature film separating them. This gave musicians about ninety minutes off. On weekends the films consisted of two or three short subjects and maybe a cartoon. Mr. Schiffman, the owner, wanted to maximize his profit every week. As soon as we got off stage, we had approximately thirty minutes before the next show. Everyone performing had to be ready precisely on time. On weekends, instead of four shows a day we had seven. To make matters worse, the money was not great.

We waited for announcements backstage. First we would hear, "Half hour!" before our break, then a bell, followed by "All on!" Sitting behind our music stands, we waited for the stage lights to come to full brightness and for a voice proclaiming the band's virtues and announcing others who were appearing on the show. We would launch immediately into a "flag waver," a fast, loud opening number to stir enthusiasm. When the curtains opened, the whole band stand moved forward, toward the audience. Sometimes even we got caught up in the emotion of that well-plotted opening.

During our short breaks, some of the guys went up to Eighth Avenue, half a block away. They took a left turn, then about fifty paces more another left, to Bradock's Bar. Sometimes one or two guys overstayed their break. There were enough of us to cover any trouble and, in truth, trouble rarely happened in Dizzy's Rolls Royce big band. However, a classic case of intoxication at The Apollo occurred with a sax player, Morris Lane, in another band. As everyone gathered on stage at the end of the break, Morris was nowhere to be found. When the lights came up, the band began playing as the curtains opened. Morris was fast asleep in the first row. He slept through the whole set, inert and oblivious.

On this particular August day, a few of us glanced up 126th Street and saw our pianist, Walter Davis, Jr., making his way back, his gait distinctly unstable. Apparently he had indulged himself at the local watering hole. He was waving his arms randomly. We greeted his arrival with raucous laughter, knowing how Walter enjoyed his red wine.

But as he drew close, we saw that he was crying. Walter was a big guy and he was tough. His chilling words stopped us all cold: "Clifford's dead, an auto accident!" Every man froze. It couldn't be true. Rumors fly around without a shred of truth. Ron Carter once told me that, ridiculously, according to rumors he had already "died" twice. That day, we were stunned, muddled, feeling the worst emotions possible. And then the bloody bell rang. Dazed and nauseated, we trooped back out on stage and started our flag waver, the bandstand rolling forward as usual toward the expectant audience. But nothing could change the fact: Clifford Brown was dead. Our jubilant music belied the emotional catastrophe each of us was experiencing. I'll never forget those feelings or that performance. Tears streamed shamelessly down all of our cheeks. Our hearts were broken. We all loved Brownie as a man and we loved the wonderful way he played.

After the show, we learned the story: Bud Powell's brother, Richie, and his new bride Nancy, who had been driving the car, were also killed. They were traveling on the Pennsylvania Turnpike, on their way to join the other members of The Max Roach-Clifford Brown Quintet in Chicago. It was raining hard. Their car was passing a tractor-trailer. Apparently heavy spray from the truck's tires obscured Nancy's vision. The car slammed into a bridge abutment. Everyone inside died instantly. Clifford was asleep in the back seat, Richie on the passenger's side in front.

I was sick at heart for months. Clifford Brown was a close friend. I hadn't seen him much after he and Max began touring. Now, I would never see him again. A haunting pain devoured my mind and body. For a long time I felt a sinking feeling in my stomach whenever I remembered that he was dead. It was unreal and yet much too real. I thought about a photograph he had given me, which I neglected to have him autograph.

Clifford remained at the front of my thoughts and feelings for a long time. My usual habit during the day was to go to clubs where I was working in the evening, so that I could use the piano and keep my writing moving forward. I needed to write a song dedicated to Clifford's memory, if I could, something different than anything I had ever written. This song would emerge not from my pen, but from my heart. I loved Clifford so. It took me longer to write this song than any other. The notes had to *be* Clifford Brown.

I was almost afraid to begin, from fear of failure. Clifford deserved to be remembered for his accomplishments. Was I up to that? I felt compelled to try. My first foray was spent exploring possible intervals, which are often the heart of a melody. Intervals and the directions they take on have the power to frame and lift emotion. I always devote considerable time to finding the right ones. When I started on the melody, Clifford was my barometer. Would Brownie play this as a whole note or a half note? Would he pause *here*, or keep going? Would he play this up high or lower, or somewhere in between? This song had to recall Clifford's spirit, or I was wasting my time. As I conceived musical ideas, Clifford sometimes became so real within me that tears rolled down my cheeks. I was glad no one saw me, because had there been a witness, I couldn't have stopped my ears. Sometimes my ideas were effusive and needed to be distilled with care. Often I agonized. Was this sound and lyric motion Clifford's or not?

Dizzy's band had a two-week engagement at Peacock Lane. Just about every day we were there, I worked on the song. I was so engrossed in the process of creation that when it was finished I did not truly know what I had accomplished. I hoped the piece was something of consequence. I arrived hours before the performance on the last evening. Diz arrived early, too. This was a good chance to see what he thought of the song. I asked him if he would take a moment, and he sat down at an empty table by the piano. After a few bars, he took his trumpet from its case. He didn't know the tune, but he decided to play alongside it.

That was not the first or the last time Dizzy fooled me. He had a small plastic flask of kerosene that he used to lubricate the valves. He poured kerosene over them and then held the horn up to the light. Blowing through it, he sent a considerable spray of stinky kerosene over me, the piano, his table, and the floor. Maybe he was not paying attention at all. Undeterred, I finished playing the piece. "That's beautiful," he said. "What is it?" I felt encouraged. I said I might call it "I Remember Clifford." He asked if he could write an arrangement for the big band to record it. Jazz musicians are supposed to be cool, but inside I was bungee jumping into a delirious happy place. I was surfing Hawaii's dangerous pipeline—I was arm wrestling Jack Johnson. I said, "Sure," however, as cool as I could be. I wanted to say, "Anything you want, Mr. Gillespie, my hero, *il miglior fabbro!*" The legendary man had stepped right out of the photograph on my teenage bedroom wall, alongside Duke and Coleman Hawkins. Dizzy Gillespie had asked to record my new song! I was a nobody at the time; if I stood in Times Square all day every day for a week, not a single person would have recognized me. Suddenly I was a hilariously affirmed, transcendent nobody.

Dizzy's band had recently hired a talented eighteen-year-old trumpet player from Philly who was quickly making a name for himself. He had a recording date with Blue Note Records that was two weeks before Dizzy's scheduled recording date. He, too, wanted my new tune for his album. Thus, Lee Morgan was the first to record "I Remember Clifford." Diz's recording was soon followed by Donald Byrd's, recorded for Columbia. Before long, I received a huge surprise. I thought my tune was a trumpeter's song, but Sonny Rollins also recorded it, much to my delight. George Shearing's recording was followed by The Modern Jazz Quartet's recording, and soon after, by those of Art Farmer, Milt Jackson, and Oscar Peterson. Artists all over the world began recording "I Remember Clifford." Eventually I lost track of the order. While Nat Cole never recorded it, his brother, Freddie, told me that Nat used to play it in live performances. After awhile, I only knew who recorded my heartfelt piece when I read my royalty statement closely.

How grateful I am for this good luck. Other people crafted my success and recognition by their acceptance of my compositions. Perhaps the most wonderful acknowledgement came from Clifford's widow, LaRue. She genuinely loved the piece. By itself, that was more than enough for me. She knew Clifford better than anyone. Bobbie and I love her. My biggest regret is that "I Remember Clifford" derived from tragic circumstances. I wish I had never had to write it.

CHAPTER 31

The Ballad and "Weight"

NOTHING IN MUSIC charms us as ballads do. After he has written a ballad, however, the composer's artistic obligation ends (unless he then also orchestrates it). The performer's obligation never ends. Each time a musician plays a ballad, he must express feelings that come into existence only in performance. He is obliged to be in touch with feeling, as well as with the song's meaning and transparency. A performer's interpretation should not be the same each night. A jazz musician is obliged to discover different ideas and a variety of emotions along with many shades of expressive nuance. We could have asked Art Farmer about this. Art would address this question succinctly, emphasizing "the value of a single note." Consider what that concept suggests. Playing the same phrases nightly is like reciting lines one has memorized for a play. Even in the theatre, however, Hamlet's soliloquy will feel (and be) distinct each time an actor renders it on stage.

An extremely important element in playing a ballad is the "weight" of creative expression the musician brings forth. The need to play with varying degrees of weight should be intuitive once a musician understands the inherent nature of ballads. The weight, or feeling, given each note must differ as melodic movement requires. The outcome is an articulate emotional tapestry. If the weight of each note remained constant, the result would sound mechanical. A computer could play such music. In performance, one note inspires another into existence, creating a series of notes and phrases that we call musical "ideas." In performance, emotions (sometimes inspired by the notes themselves) suffuse a musician's mind and body. Although we do not think consciously about weight while playing, when we express feeling with *meaningful* sensitivity—always a matter of personal taste—at that moment we are exploring differences in notational weight.

How could it be otherwise? Notes are supreme when we play. Each note lends itself to lyrical ideas composed of certain intervals, durations, range, touch, and dynamics. Our emotions await notes that call them forth, though it might seem as if emotion determines the notes we play. Without question, feeling adds to our expressive range. But think about this. The birth of one note gives birth to another in an ongoing cascade (slow and deliberate, or more quickly paced) that inevitably carries a song forward. Each note leads in a certain direction and, thus, guides and determines what we express. A musician is judged to play well or poorly not because of emotions evoked or suggested, but because of *notes played*. Without talent and ability from intensive practice, emotions add nothing to a performance.

Let me drive my point home. If a player gets on a bandstand bursting with emotions yet possessing little talent or ability, sadly you are in the company of a man filled merely with unformed, inarticulate emotion. He might as well do magic tricks or acrobatics. Artistic taste and rational judgment play significant roles in musical performance. Even more important, the notes and phrases themselves carry weight and discernment, innate emotional rewards that shape artistic expression. Emotion in the universe of music derives from intelligence and notational control. This is inherent in the nature of artistic achievement. Art is ultimately the product of choice and of creation—of *making* things. It is not unfettered sonic (or verbal or pigment-saturated) ejaculation. Art, including music, depends on discernment and judgment. Of course, if we fail in such attempts, we feel frustrated. Unfortunately, some musicians express raw emotion without artistry. One certain indication of a lack of talent is the player who (often with a swagger) blows right by song structures, ignoring nuances of tonal articulation, abandoning techniques and instrumental skill in order to arrogate a "higher plateau" of avant-garde or, more accurately, artistically bankrupt pseudo-authority. There you have a person who thinks he can fool all of the people (including skilled musicians) all of the time.

One of the things most musicians cannot fully understand early in their careers, doubtless from paucity of life experience, is the depth of the ballad as a genre. I find today that there are (euphemistically) quite a few who do not understand that the ballad exists in a completely different world from other kinds of musical compositions. When my generation was learning to play, like every generation we wanted to be hip. For us, this meant that none of us ever wanted to play a ballad (not that we even knew how). We simply thought anything slow could never be hip. Whenever we tossed out suggestions for tunes in our jam sessions, now and then someone courageous would suggest a ballad. Somebody else would invariably snort, "A ballad?!"—as if a code of manhood had just been violated. We had no time for such foolishness. We were trying to prove how much musical muscle we had, playing "Cherokee" at supersonic speed. In those days, for us the name Louis Armstrong meant regression into the past. We wanted nothing to do with the likes of Pops. We were too hip. Years later, after maturing, we realized just what a powerhouse Pops was. Lack of maturity is a threshold everyone survives, with luck and enough years. Experience taught me that the real test of a jazz musician was not how fast he could play, but how meaningfully *slowly* he could play. Many players try to "hide" behind a barrage of slick runs and slurred notes (assuming they possess even that much ability). Speed demonstrates dexterity, an inconsequential skill on a ballad. Effusive blather becomes a dense forest canopy that obscures sunlight, bombast behind which immature players hide.

A ballad, played *like a ballad* where every note has enough duration to be heard and felt, invites some of the most beautiful musical moments possible, when played by a musician exploring a love affair with each note. Ballads are absolute in their devotion to feelings and to personal moods. Exercises and scales, nonmusical gymnastics, find no sanctuary there. A ballad reaches not the head but the deepest recesses of the human heart and soul. Imagine someone wanting to express love or worry, heartbreak and misery, with a flood of rapid words—that would be a travesty.

Dizzy Gillespie used to say, "Slow it down enough to chew a sandwich between beats; you'll find where everybody is." Diz marveled at Ray Charles who played and sang so slowly. It takes great ability to create music with deep value at a slow tempo. Also exposed at slow tempos is the *sound* of an instrument. Even the piano, the bass, and the drum kit have richer sonic quality at slow tempos. The beautiful thing about such tempos is the time and emphasis they afford to optimize sound. A player has "temporal space" to attain a tonality (or percussive sound) with meaningful instrumental life, then relinquished to natural sonic decay. People talk about a pianist's touch, but rarely a drummer's touch, though each drummer owns a distinctive sound. Drummers can be as sensitive as any other instrumentalist. Think about Max Roach and Mel Lewis or Jo Jones and Shelly Manne. They did not merely bang away. Ballads permit a musician to get the best sound from any instrument as long as he or she is "sound conscious" and knows how to express an instrument's inner sonic being.

Playing slowly puts added demands on any player. Perhaps the first rule of approach to a languid pace is to think about what sound you want to hear. The sound of an instrument, including the singing voice, is not governed by inadvertence and accident. Sound is not a given; sound is shaped, refined, enhanced, and sometimes perfected. Consider the improbable glory of Stan Getz's almost ethereal sound and Lucky Thompson's heavenly sonic excursions on both soprano and tenor saxes. Today, Harry Allen has a resonant saxophone worthy of angels. Sarah Vaughan's voice control was legendary, and anyone who sat near Hank Jones's piano experienced an almost symphonic complexity in the way he seduced and courted the instrument's full range.

In our youthful Philadelphia jam sessions, therefore, we shirked acquaintance with ballads. But the sessions were not wasted, because so many other things occurred that were necessary to our development. We learned to play together in tune. We acquired a broad repertoire of tunes and learned the correct chords. We honed our talent for the rigors of shared performance interaction. We learned the ropes and launched our careers. We improved by listening to each other and we learned to play harmony on a variety of melodies. However, maybe most importantly those sessions brought us into closer sympathy with each other, like iron sharpening iron. What I didn't know, someone else did know. What he didn't know, on occasion I did. This sharpening and sharing was accomplished intuitively. The medium of give and take was not words, but shared sound and feeling. We rubbed off on one another. Maybe that's why, with virtually wordless immediacy, we came to care about one another so passionately, to respect and even love each other. We were like sponges, despite our limited experience seldom missing important musical and human details as we soaked up technical knowledge and developed stylistic finesse. The best of our brood stuck with it. They demonstrated fortitude and courage. They were not wimps or quitters. Thus we evolved together and molded lifelong solidarity, even, I believe, beyond death's seeming finality.

My experience has been fortunate. Generations of jazz apprentices who came after us suffered a terrible deprivation when the educational value of local jam sessions dissolved. For us, because we were not wealthy, those sessions were as important as any academic training might have been. You may remember Ishmael, who tells the story in *Moby Dick*. He called his years at sea hunting whales "my Yale College and my Harvard." In land-locked Philadelphia, a crew of marvelously talented young guys—Jimmy and Percy Heath, along with Ray Bryant, John Coltrane, and me—set sail for some exotic location, like Ishmael's, never to be found. Yet, as we musical gangsters clung to our instrumental ropes, not only did we assist each other and discover profound friendships; we matured into successful futures. The musical universe now feels the inexhaustible buoyance of our collective mid-twentieth-century reach for lyric glory and spiritual affirmation.

Check out sixty-plus years of musical production. John earned immortality before he was thirty with his work in Miles Davis's first great quintet. He revolutionized the jazz heritage, before his much too early departure. Percy Heath was the rock of Gibraltar with The Modern Jazz Quartet, perhaps one of a very small number of groups whose work not only crossed traditional ensemble lines but also is likely to escape time's cruel forgetfulness. We recently lost my dear pal Ray Bryant. Seldom has anyone possessed such brilliance on so many levels. Ray also redefined the affiliation between blues and the jazz heritage. And Jimmy Heath, my heartfelt hero, continues to live and play as if years were nothing more than clouds scudding a cheerful sky.

PART VII *Icons*

Working on *The Terminal* (and with you [Benny] in that scene playing Killer Joe) turned me into not only a fan of jazz in all its permutations but also a man who can't live without it on my radio, in my iPod, and in my head.

—TOM HANKS

CHAPTER 32

Steven Spielberg and Tom Hanks

URING THE SUMMER of 2004, my wife and I were in Europe, where we spend the entire summer. I received a telephone call from my office in Los Angeles from my assistant, Sharon Malig, who told me that Steven Spielberg's office had called to find out if I was interested in appearing with Tom Hanks in an upcoming film. I told her I wasn't interested. She was surprised. Over the years I had been solicited by advertising agencies to audition for various parts. I was twice contacted by Woody Allen's office for the same reason. These invitations always turned out to be a waste of time. I assumed this call was similar. Sharon interrupted: "No, he really wants *you* for this." I didn't really believe it, but I returned the call, and we made an appointment in New York so I could take a screen test. Returning to New York, I went to a studio downtown and, on camera, spoke lines written for my film role. Those in charge liked it. But I knew what we had done wasn't quite right. I told them that "no musician I know would speak those lines on his own." We tried again, and this time the results were sent to DreamWorks in Los Angeles, where they liked my performance enough to request that my working quartet—Mike LeDonne, piano; Buster Williams, bass; and Carl Allen, drums—join me for the formal shooting of our scene.

We went to Montreal for the shoot. Steven had rented an abandoned airplane hangar and ordered construction of a nightclub set. He was considerate enough to invite my wife to join us. We checked into our first-rate hotel and headed to a nearby restaurant for dinner. Presently, the Maestro himself appeared, flanked by several assistants. I had never met him so I was reluctant to approach him. He seemed deeply involved in a significant discussion. One of his assistants came over to ask if, indeed, I was Benny Golson. I confessed the truth and started to get up. "Oh, no," she cautioned, "he'll come over here."

Sure enough, Steven came over and introduced himself, as if I might not recognize him. There was no seat for him. As I was about to snag a chair from an unoccupied table, he stooped down next to me. What a brilliantly personable man Steven Spielberg is! We talked about the film and about more personal things, too. Finally, I blurted out an awkward request. "Steven, would you please stand up? I promised myself, if I ever met you, there was something I would do, if I could." Without a clue what I had in mind, he immediately stood up, smiling. I hugged him and kissed him on the cheek. It made him laugh. I told him how much his films meant to me, how much I had admired him over the years. I also recalled the fact that the University of Southern California had rejected him for graduate school. "They must be quite sorry about that now," I asserted. "No," he responded. "I'm on the board of directors there and I decide who gets money every year." That made us both laugh.

Perhaps the odd thing about this relaxed repartee was Steven Spielberg's ability to make a person who has just met him feel at ease. He has a human quality that disarms one's anticipation of reserve or formality. I told him that I had first become aware of his directing from a TV movie called *Duel*, starring Dennis Weaver. The story involves an enormous oil tanker truck whose unseen driver threatens Weaver's car at high speed on a twisting, precipitous highway. The chase seems unendurable and without hope for Weaver. The film's power derives from creating sustained sympathy for a protagonist under extreme duress, intensified by the fact that we do not see the driver of the car murderously harassing Weaver and can only guess at his motive. I had never seen a film with such escalating tension and covert menace. That early film made Steven Spielberg stand out to me as different from film directors I had worked with. Spielberg possesses an extraordinary artistic vision and is profoundly in touch with his own feelings and with the feelings of others. Across his career, he has told powerful stories in a powerful way. If a jazz musician often seeks to tell a story (and Art Farmer and Clifford Jordan sometimes talked about connecting to a song's lyrics and their narrative meaning), then Maestro Spielberg is truly a jazz-inclined cinematic genius.

Why, I wondered, didn't other filmmakers discover such an engagingly intense point of view? Did I, Golson, have the temerity to think *musically* like Steven Spielberg? Was such a thought a form of self-inflation on my part? Perhaps proximity to a self-confident, yet sweet person like Steven caused me to identify with him. Or, maybe I was internally groveling, searching for an alter ego to attach myself to, or (worse) worship; since our artistic inclinations fall in different areas, there is no threat of unconscious rivalry. This much is certain. If I were to choose a model of cinematic story-telling to emulate in my song writing and in my playing, I could not choose a better model than Steven Spielberg's profoundly open-hearted example of lovingly created, affirmatively healing art.

In our discussions before the Montreal shoot, Steven told me that he was building a nightclub set for us. He asked what kind of piano I wanted. I told him I wanted a twelve-foot Steinway New York grand. When we arrived, the piano was on the set, tuned and ready to play. I'll put this succinctly. Steven is a first class man. Traditionally, whenever musicians are involved in a film, a large trailer is provided for them to share on the set. In Montreal, we *each* had a trailer, fantastically appointed. I mentioned to Bobbie that I would be delighted to drive this vehicle to Manhattan and park it outside our apartment building to live in for the rest of our lives. As they say in the 'hood, we were stylin'.

Just as we prepared to step in front of klieg lights and video cameras, Tom Hanks arrived to greet us. Between takes, he sat at the table conversing with Bobbie and pianist Mike LeDonne. That was when I finally learned the subject of our film, *The Terminal*. Prior to the shoot, I had had no idea of the film's premise and, therefore, did not know why I was recruited. In the movie, Tom plays a stranded airline passenger, who following a string of travel snafus becomes effectively incarcerated, to great comic effect, in a terminal at JFK Airport. His character, who hails from a fictional Eastern European nation, Krakozhia, has traveled to the United States to get Benny Golson's autograph. The back story is that the character's father is a jazz enthusiast who has spent years trying to get the signatures of every musician pictured in the famous 1958 photograph, *A Great Day in Harlem*, in *Esquire* magazine. He had collected all of the signatures except for mine. Hanks's character, a dutiful son, had promised his father he would get my signature. In the movie, I am thus the quarry being stalked. But horrendous bad luck dogs his efforts on the trip overseas. He lands at JFK to learn that Krakozhia, apparently a small country on the wrong side of East–West tensions, has suffered a coup while he was in transit. The U.S. immigration and naturalization agency will not accept his now-invalid passport. He becomes effectively a man without a country, unable to either enter the United States or go home. The unraveling of Tom's film persona elicited my painful awareness of the social and political fragility that anyone, so marginalized, inevitably feels. *The Terminal* is a complex, beautiful, and at times hilarious film about surprise, personal victimization, compensatory enterprise, bureaucratic punishment, and self-defense. Most rewardingly, it is also about the triumph of human solidarity in the face of injustice.

I was not prepared to play a film role. But I had the honor and the good fortune to work with the two most remarkable people in the film business. I feel unjustly blessed by the serendipity, by the vast upwelling of coincidence and spiritual *déjà vu* that made these events possible. I had no inkling I would ever meet or even chat with Steven Spielberg. He tapped me for reasons that had nothing to do with me, except that one day in the mid-1950s an inspired young photographer (Art Kane) assembled a gaggle of available jazz personages on the steps of a brownstone in Harlem. I remember that day with uncanny vividness. My dear pal Art Farmer joined me, and many of the people who were my heroes as I was growing up were also there that day.

In 2009, Jim Merod and I were involved in a public discussion at the Smithsonian Museum in Washington, D.C., about Jean Bach's film, *A Great Day in Harlem*, recounting the circumstances around that historical photograph. Our occasion capped a remarkable weekend that brought me to the Kennedy Center for an eightieth birthday celebration. Danny Glover served as emcee for the night's incredible festivities, and the president of Howard University and his beautiful wife were in attendance. My final album for Concord, *New Time, New 'Tet*, added punctuation to the regalia on display in the lobby. On the same weekend at the Center, my dear friend Kenny Barron received a Jazz Master's award from the Mid Atlantic Arts Foundation. With his usual effortless leadership under siege, Jim corralled me, Kenny, and Billy Taylor for memorable photos together. Earlier that night, Jim received a private seminar from Billy, who demonstrated, on video, his artistic exchanges with Art Tatum. The event in my honor took place in the main theater. Participants included Cedar Walton, Buster

Williams, the Clayton-Hamilton Orchestra, and many others. The night was unforgettable.

I have grown increasingly impressed with Tom Hanks's extraordinary ability to "be" any character he takes on. His talent is Shakespearean in its reach. Tom is the most adored actor of our generation, garnering respect from film to the Broadway stage. If one speaks to him of *Bosom Buddies*, a television series he starred in early in his career, he demurs as if it were a mistake. However, the show eventually launched him into the stratosphere. No actor I am aware of has so convincingly met radically disparate acting demands. Consider a random film trio: *Big* alongside *Saving Private Ryan* and *Road to Perdition*. These demonstrate the rarest kind of creative empathy with vastly different characters. Hanks is equally at home playing comic roles and portraying characters undergoing life-shattering devastation. His art is transcendent, his spiritual and cerebral interiority incalculable. I genuinely believe that Tom Hanks's art rivals the accomplishments of Armstrong, Tatum, Rollins, and Monk. In my world, no higher praise is possible.

Tom once sent me a DVD of his youngest son, on guitar, playing "Killer Joe" with his high school band. His oldest son, Colin, is a budding actor and the spitting image of his father. Rita, Tom's wife, is a great artist in her own right. Wow! Can she ever sing! I intend to bring Tom and Rita together in public to confirm my praise. Is so much talent under one roof legal? Once, between takes on the set, Tom leaned over to tell me that I had "no idea what an honor it is for me to do this scene with you." I was flabbergasted. Tom had that backwards.

Steven told me that he worked with Quincy Jones on *The Color Purple*. He was surprised to learn that Quincy and I had been roommates on long road trips back in our days with Dizzy Gillespie's band. I in turn was knocked out by his surprise. He stopped everything and dialed Quincy on his mobile phone. I told him to call Quincy by his nickname, "Tack." Q. was not home, but when I returned to Los Angeles, he reported that he had accused Steven of delinquency. "You've been talking to Benny Golson." When musicians expand the circle of their madness, anyone might need to duck.

Steven's wife, Kate Capshaw, arrived on set one day. He paused from our work to bring her over for introductions. No other director or producer I worked with in Hollywood ever did that. But this man is profoundly different in many ways. Kate is just like him: humble, friendly, and unassuming. The whole crew treats Steven like a loving uncle for whom they hold both affection and respect. When we completed our segment of *The Terminal*, Steven thanked me. It is still hard for me to comprehend that Steven Spielberg thanked me. The honor was mine. I sent him a lithograph of the manuscript for "I Remember Clifford." Steven's reply arrived soon. "This is my favorite composition of yours." He said he had heard me perform in Manhattan while he was in college—a discovery that confirmed for me that old age has rewards undreamt in youth.

Tom and Steven are both jazz fans. We stay in touch. Tom has accepted the idea of some day joining me at Soka University, where in early 2014 I enjoyed a two-day celebration of my eighty-fifth year above ground. When Steven learned that this book was forthcoming, he asked to read the manuscript. Jim, my co-conspirator, took it to DreamWorks' bucolic annex at the utmost outmost outback of the Paramount Studio compound, where he handed it to Marvin Levy.

A quick confession. Over the course of my life four events have been exceptional: receiving my first saxophone; meeting my wife; our daughter's birth; and visiting Steven Spielberg's inspirational, magical world. How I love this man. He represents everything that is wonderful and creative, routinely making the impossible seem normal.

CHAPTER 33

Duke and Strayhorn

OFTEN WROTE MUSIC for shows that drew upon that material afterward in shows elsewhere. In 1953 the comedy team of Stump and Stumpy (James Cross and Harold Cromer) hired me to write music for their new routine. It all worked beautifully with one exception. I was not paid. Because I knew we would all be in proximity for the entire summer, I didn't press them for my pay. When the season drew toward its end, I approached them. As soon as I appeared, they did a strange thing—something they thought would flatter me into silence. Mimicking their band with their voices, dancing enthusiastically while loudly humming my music, the two of them launched into the show's opening music. I was supposed to see how great they thought my music was. I was expected to be so pleased and flummoxed that I wouldn't mention the money they owed me. The first time, it worked. The subject of money got lost in their vaudeville act and the emotional dust they kicked up. A few days later I approached once again and was treated to a repeat performance. I was delighted that they liked my music, but their distraction routine was not a substitute for a happy bank account. The truth was that they didn't have the money.

In show business this often happens, and it seems to happen especially when you most need your fee or paycheck. A song writer's life is frequently precarious. I remember an itinerant song writer in New York who wrote tunes expressly for the purpose of selling them here and there for a few dollars. One of his songs paid twenty-five dollars, a sum he was very happy to receive. That song was "The Great Pretender." It sold millions of copies and earned an enormous amount of money for the person who bought it. The immense success that could have been his, but wasn't, catastrophically unbalanced the poor fellow's mind. After that, he was seen frequently near the Brill Building downtown, mumbling and gesturing to people who didn't exist, singing "The Great Pretender."

Eventually the show season ended for Stump and Stumpy, and I had not received my money. They opened again a few weeks later, however, with Duke Ellington and his orchestra at the now-defunct Paramount Theater on Broadway. If my writing accompanied their routine once more, I was told, Duke's orchestra would play my music. I decided to wait until that occurred and then make an unannounced appearance at the Paramount on draw day, when pockets became a little fatter. That November afternoon, I announced myself downstairs at the stage door (which everyone had to do) and took the elevator up to the floor where their dressing room was located. As soon as I stepped into their dressing room, on cue, they launched their act. This time I wouldn't hear it, and went straight to the issue of my money. Their well-rehearsed strains of my music faded meaninglessly in the stale air of their dingy room. I got my money, hung around for a few minutes, and left, not fully believing I had finally been paid.

I took the elevator down, but it stopped on the next floor to pick up another passenger. As the door slowly opened, into the elevator, without introductory overture, stepped the maestro himself, Duke Ellington. At that moment, Duke seemed bigger than himself. His commanding voice seemed to sing "Hello." He was a gentle man and silently elegant, his bearing relaxed yet regal. How can I adequately suggest his full magnificence? An Olympian hero stepped into the lift. This was the first time I saw Duke Ellington face to face. I expected no conversation since he did not really know me in person. I was shocked when he asked if I had written "the wonderful music for Stump and Stumpy?" How did Mr. Ellington know who I was? I was overwhelmed but replied sheepishly yes. He told me his band enjoyed playing it and that he looked forward to hearing it at each show. I could not believe my ears. For years, his photograph adorned the wall at the foot of my bed in Philadelphia. Here I was, a foot away from this musical genius. I wanted the elevator to descend two or three hundred more floors. When it jerked to a stop, Duke asked a final question: "Would you like to write something for my band?"

Zowie! How did my mortal heart endure this? These frighteningly encouraging words from the Master himself! I said I would love to do that. Unfortunately, we never had a chance to realize that notion. Nevertheless, Duke Ellington asked *me*, Benny Golson, at the time an almost complete unknown, if I would like to write music for his band. The Master had approached one of his eternally supplicating servants.

I never got to genuinely know Duke. My second son, Reggie, did. He and Duke's nephew, Stephen James, the son of Duke's sister Ruth, became very good friends as they shared the same interests: drums and Elvin Jones. Stephen often spent weekends at our place in New York. He and Reggie frequently traveled with the Ellington band on its bus to nearby engagements. The whole Ellington band, including Duke, knew Reggie. Duke once gave him a suit he was about to discard. I suspect Reggie begged him for it. Though the suit was many sizes too big for Reggie at fourteen, he insisted on having it cut down to fit. That cost me a small fortune, but it made Reggie feel like a king. I understood his desire and appreciated his good taste. In truth, I envied Reggie's relationship with Duke. I wished it had been me.

Twelve years after the blessing of my brief audience with Ellington, Bobbie and I moved from 92nd Street over to West End Avenue, ten blocks away but a new urban universe. Our rent jumped from $140 a month to $365. We had hit the big time. Or so we thought. I worried about whether I could come up with that kind of money every month. We laugh now, looking back to 1965. Everything has changed. My income escalated, but so did the price of everything. The Reagan years inflated the economic scale. Our new apartment was large enough that we no longer had to strategize about where to put new acquisitions: under the bed in metal storage boxes, behind furniture, or squeezed into closets designed for anything but wearing apparel. My subway stop was now 103rd and Broadway. I liked that.

Soon I began to run into Billy Strayhorn. Well, I suppose I should say I kept seeing him, usually shopping at one of the outdoor vegetable markets in our Upper West Side neighborhood. I was tempted, continually, to introduce myself, but something stopped me. I can't explain my childish hesitation. I should have gotten to know this elegant and mild-mannered man, because he had been a hero to me and because we were in the same line of work (if, at bottom, you can call jazz, the best job in the world, "work"). Nothing in Billy Strayhorn's demeanor was aloof. He seemed to me almost angelic. I have lamented my reticence for years. In retrospect,

I have no doubt that I would have learned things that only Billy Strayhorn could have imparted. I suppose I did not yet possess an adequate sense of professional brotherhood and artistic entitlement. I was not yet bullheaded enough in the sense of Socrates's admonition to his fifth-century Athenian interlocutors: to recognize that knowledge is elusive and that we must aggressively pursue the questions and discourse that mediate knowledge.

When Billy Strayhorn died, I realized just how foolish I had been. This brilliant man lived in my neighborhood at 106th Street, four blocks from my building. For years, one of the most profound composers and arrangers in history worked in and frequented our shared cityscape. I have often wondered what he might have said if we had talked. Would we have become friends? I have been told he was sweet and even sentimental. Those who knew him well attest that he was articulate and cheerful. I should have overcome my youthful hang-ups and introduced myself to him. Benny Golson, you silly dope!

I became aware of Billy when I was fourteen. His name was permanently linked with Duke Ellington's. At the time I came to know of their partnership, the two men had worked together for five years. I gathered that Duke worked closely with "Swea Pea," making good use of his remarkable talent as a composer: "Lush Life," written when he was a teenager (including the lyrics!); "Chelsea Bridge"; "Isfahan"; "Lotus Blossom"; "A Single Petal of the Rose"; "Raincheck"; "A Flower Is a Lovesome Thing"; "Day Dream"; "The Intimacy of the Blues"; "Blood Count"; and "Upper Manhattan Medical Group" are ineffable examples. When Duke hired Billy in Pittsburgh, he asked him to create a theme for the Ellington Orchestra. The result was "Take the 'A' Train." Even in eastern Pennsylvania, in the Philadelphia ghetto where I was raised, we knew the name of Billy Strayhorn from western Pennsylvania, though his name was always mentioned in conjunction with Duke's. Billy and Duke shared the same creative consciousness. One time, the older man called the younger with a task: to complete a multipart suite which the head Maestro had begun writing for the Queen of England. Duke was in Europe, Billy in Manhattan. The collaboration never failed. Still today—more than three and a half decades after Duke Ellington's death and nearly four and a half decades after Billy Strayhorn's—John Edward Hasse, curator of the Ellington Archives at the Smithsonian Museum, acknowledges that hundreds of as yet unarchived song manuscripts await attention. The creative output of these two accomplished and prolific composers was seemingly unending, defining thirty-nine years of unmatched artistry.

On May 31, 1967, not long after Billy Strayhorn's death, Duke wrote this tribute: "He demanded freedom of expression and lived in what we consider the most important of moral freedoms: freedom from hate, unconditionally; freedom from all self-pity (even throughout all the pain and bad news); freedom from fear of possibly doing something that might help another more than it might help himself; and freedom from the kind of pride that could make a man feel he was better than his brother or neighbor." As I read these words, I see within me Duke's beloved colleague at the vegetable market on 104th Street and Broadway. So simple, so wonderful and fleeting: an outright genius sought caloric sustenance like any ordinary person. Billy Strayhorn was anything but ordinary. To onlookers, he surely appeared an average mortal. He was not tall, handsome, or outwardly remarkable. He may have seemed like Sancho Panza to Duke Ellington's gloriously innocent Don Quixote. Or Boswell to Dr. Johnson, a talented man second to an elite superior. Since few had an inkling of Billy Strayhorn's mind and soul, his persona here on earth was vague, akin to a ghost or holograph. The Maestro and his dear "Swea Pea" were inextricably one. Their enduring art, derived from an unrivaled artistic partnership, reached the height of musical greatness, like Bach, Mozart, or Beethoven. Less than half a century after his departure, I am certain Billy Strayhorn's spirit continues onward to infinity.

CHAPTER 34

Coleman Hawkins

COLEMAN HAWKINS recorded "Body and Soul" in 1939, an iconic moment in jazz. The song remains a classic. When I was fourteen, in 1943, it was still popular and heard on jukeboxes in black neighborhoods. The first aspect of Hawk's playing that caught my attention was his full, round, and deeply mellow sound. Though I knew little about the saxophone, I felt he was doing something special.

When I began playing the tenor saxophone, Coleman Hawkins was my first idol. I collected as many of his records as possible. Across the years, I grew increasingly impressed. Hawkins could play anything at any tempo. On occasion he even handled "boot 'em up" funky tenor sax. Coleman Hawkins knew all the changes and every chord progression in every possible song, and he always played something mind expanding. Hawk played complex and intellectual music with great feeling. He was a master.

I could never imagine a time when I might play with Coleman Hawkins. I stopped thinking about it. In 1959, Eddie Costa (a pianist and vibes player who died later in an accident on Manhattan's West Side Highway) invited me to play a festival in Rhode Island. (It was not the Newport Jazz Festival.) He said Coleman Hawkins would play a song or two with us. The pressure was on. I would finally be playing with one of my greatest idols. That night when he walked on the stage, Coleman Hawkins seemed bigger than life to me. I had admired him for so long, it was hard to believe

I was sharing a stage with this legendary man. I remember the only song we played, "Perdido." Years later I found out that this concert was recorded. I didn't question that fact (whether permission had been granted for the recording) as I usually do. I was far too happy that the evening was documented. Imagine this: Hawk waiting to make his entrance, to play with us. While he waited, he was listening to *me*. I recall that the pressure felt paradoxically warm and uncertain. Can you imagine the master of your instrument listening to you and watching you? When he joined us, he didn't try to steamroll me. Coleman Hawkins had as much compassion as he had talent.

For years I have been compared to Coleman Hawkins, Don Byas, and Lucky Thompson. That is heady company. There are jazz critics who behave as members of a cattle herd when they assess a performance or a musician. They repeat what critics before them have written, loyally following the lead bull back to the barn at sundown. Sometimes this must surely be unconscious. Reviews of my playing, over a considerable span of my career, provide a case in point. First, in the early years, most tenor players were more sound-conscious than the tradition which evolved later and which defines the present trend. A wide vibrato disappeared under the (scandalous at the time) influence of Lester Young. The Prez offered a new concept of what a tenor saxophone should sound like. He wanted to move forward, thank goodness.

Coleman Hawkins came into my life over sixty years ago, followed by Don Byas and Lucky Thompson, and I immersed myself in their art. I wanted to play and sound like them. But times change. People change. Playing styles change. Later I picked up on Dexter Gordon because he was so hip. I paid close attention to Lester Young, but I loved Dexter's approach so much that I worked hard to sound like him. Coleman Hawkins, Don Byas, and Lucky Thompson disappeared from my jazz life. Like most aspiring musicians, I underwent changes, many rejected. Such experimentation caused me to stop playing for several years. Slowly I realized that no musician can or should be defined by another player's accomplishments. That searching, and its attendant uncertainty, caused me to wrestle with myself. At no time, however, did I return to my formative stage or re-entrench myself in that earlier jazz era.

I need to satisfy myself, not someone else who has ideas about what I should do. I hope people enjoy my work, but I am obstinate on the importance of every musician crafting and perfecting his or her own sound and style. Not long ago, I read a review in which the writer claimed, "Benny Golson gets close to Coltrane's reedy sound." This was a favorable review, and I appreciated it, but I wonder if the putatively "professional" critical institution operates within bounds of reality or fantasy.

It is strange that critics seem to associate a big tenor sax sound virtually exclusively with Hawkins, Byas, and Webster. What about Gene Ammons, whose sound was incredibly big? Chu Berry, Jimmy Forrest, and Ike Quebec were all sonic monsters. In recent years, Joe Henderson, Joe Lovano, Joshua Redman, George Coleman, Jerry Bergonzi, David Sánchez, Grant Stewart, and others have also offered "big" sonic footprints. I fear that some critics access "sound" and the whole stylistic palette by adhering to an archival saxophone legacy that keeps their ears frozen in jazz antiquity. Such anachronistic critical assessment has no value. When I read a review of my playing, or of another musician whom I admire, and I find such out-of-touch commentary, I shake my head in disbelief. A critic should aim to report accurately, but if he can't hear what is going on in the music—or is too lazy to *listen* instead of merely "hearing"—he fails in the professional discernment required of him. Jazz, its players and listeners, are all cheated.

In defense of jazz writers and critics, they have a right to their tastes and opinions, of course. My hope would be for everyone involved in jazz to attempt to understand serious musical creativity when it appears, even if it falls outside their parameters of immediate enjoyment. For my part, I cannot dwell where I dwelt musically fifty or sixty years ago. That would be like driving a car while twisting to look over my shoulder through the rear window, a dangerous undertaking. A driver might arrive late or not at all.

The older I become, the more I feel humbled and affirmed by the immense obligation to perform at my best each time I put the horn in my mouth or sit down to compose. But the critic, too, has an awesome responsibility. Shouldn't he be thoroughly knowledgeable about the field he critiques, as well as about the performer, since his writing casts light and dark on individuals as well as on the art form itself? Unfortunately, we have few genuinely knowledgeable, tried-and-true professional jazz critics working on the publishing scene now. Jazz is not the big news it once was. But for any paper or "critic" to simply repeat, even in part, a previous writer's comments about an artist is the lowest form of critical effort. Many of my reviews, both good and bad, compare my playing to the work of Hawkins, Thompson, and/or Byas. After awhile, such comparisons take on a life of their own. They become the framework for assessment, a viewpoint that is unchallenged even if it is incorrect. A writer's life is easier if he can dust off some variant on a longstanding critical tradition in order to meet a deadline. Some writers have claimed I have a wide vibrato. I don't. Others say I sound like Hawkins. If the theme of "the big tenor sax sound" is in play, then the critic will invariably invoke Hawkins and Byas. Sometimes the exaggeration goes further to claim that I actually *sound* like them. That would be scandalous if it were not such an outright joke. Wiser, more knowledgeable critics describe me in a variety of informed ways. Naïve reviews are not necessarily negative. Many are favorable and I appreciate them, but they reflect a diminished level of professional and journalistic awareness.

In the mid-1960s, many critics said I was trying to play like John Coltrane. They were right. However, is John the only viable reference when a sax player produces an abundance of notes? How about Johnny Griffin, Sonny Stitt, or Earl Bostic? Kenny Garrett and Ron Blake as well as Chris Potter and Donny McCaslin all luxuriate in notational excess, as do seemingly the majority of young players today. I gave up that needless pursuit. Imitating John could only lend further testimony to *John's* enormous talent, eclipsing my own artistic nuances. Over the past two decades, I have heard too many young tenor players who think they can emulate John by copying his mannerisms. They want to be the reincarnation of John Coltrane. When critics touch upon my career, I wonder why anyone would expect me to abandon advanced technical sophistication only to regress twenty years or more back toward Coleman Hawkins or Don Byas or Lucky Thompson, who are now wonderful echoes from our majestic, if antiquated, jazz past?

My pursuits five or six decades ago came from youthful energy. Both my achievements and my excesses came from moving forward, not backwards. If a critic thinks I am still back where I started musically, perhaps his ears are homogenizing stylistic and expressive differences under the reductive rubric "Golson." From my humble beginnings as a musician, I have always fought to move ahead. The truth is that, if we allow our creative growth to cease or slow, it soon becomes a memory. That may be the fate of a scholar as well, if his commentary and annotations to history become meaningless footnotes to life. Moving forward is a condition of committed artistry, with or without recognition. An itch within, to overcome false confidence, nags at my mind and heart.

Regardless of how well they write, critics often do not understand that when musicians stretch themselves artistically, a joyful serendipity sometimes occurs. We stumble upon surprises, things we did not know we were seeking. They pop up right in front of us—in fact, inside us—and we wonder where they came from. Critics rarely comprehend the origin of such creativity. For the most part, neither do *we*. These experiences create anticipation and excitement in a musician's life. I have been told that such experiences fall under the heading of "the sublime"—a mysterious sense of self-revelation and self-overcoming. That sounds right to me, although far more common in my long career as a composer and player has been the recurrent sense of never being satisfied, feeling the gnawing insatiability of imagination's urging and beckoning. Artists, musicians, move in a forward direction, we hope. That is the lure, the goad, and sometimes the illusion. We hope the future is fulfilled with substantial creations. Coleman Hawkins invented the tenor sax, within the jazz heritage. My long life, within the reach of his life's work, has not sought imitation but the splendor of his example.

CHAPTER 35

Art Blakey and Thelonious Monk

IN 1947, while I was in college at Howard University, I began to listen intensively to Art Blakey's recordings. His stick control, his flexibility and precision with time, and the mind-boggling coordination among his hands and feet fascinated me. Art was unique as a drummer. He could get four different rhythms going at the same time: two distinct rhythms with his hands and two with his feet, his four limbs independent yet wholly synchronized. Each separate rhythm was perfect on its own. If you listen to Art's introduction to Monk's original recording of "Straight, No Chaser," you'll find that he did all of this. Exactly.

Art quickly became one of my favorite jazz musicians and so he remains today, fifty-eight years after he called me in 1958 to join him as a sub one night at the Café Bohemia. It was an opening night, a Tuesday as I remember. I was fresh from Philadelphia and had been in New York only a few weeks. I had worked shows at the Apollo Theater with Reuben Phillips's band. A few weeks before Art's call, I played a concert at the Renaissance Ballroom in Harlem (sadly, as of this writing recently demolished). It was memorable for me because I owned photos from concerts there that featured many of my boyhood heroes. That gig helped me feel as if I had arrived on the big-time jazz scene. The evening in Harlem featured four saxophonists: Joe Henderson, Jimmy Heath, Booker Ervin, and me. Cedar Walton played piano. I found out that night that Joe Henderson could really play. He was great then, and he only got better. Joe was a thinker who did not believe in serving warmed-over offerings to his listeners. His mind was explorative. It was impossible for him to regurgitate memorized scales or repeat patterns like a parrot. Joe was always self-challenging and, thus, stimulated others. I met him in 1956, when Kenny Dorham introduced us. I always called Joe Henderson "The Lima Flash" because he grew up in Lima, Ohio. He never seemed to mind that nickname.

I had been given a heavyweight jazz welcome at the Renaissance Ballroom, a sort of Manhattan baptism by musical immersion, so I was thrilled when Art called. He needed a sub right away. Although he didn't know me personally, he had accepted someone's recommendation. His voice on the phone sounded concerned. I assured him I would be there that evening. He told me what I would be paid, having no clue I would have done it for free. I was overwhelmed with happiness by the invitation.

I was clueless what to expect that night. We didn't have a rehearsal, so I had to wing it. I would also draw on what I knew about Art's playing from my records. I had never played with such a propulsive, swinging percussionist and I enjoyed myself from the get-go. Art had a way of playing that seduced you and engaged your whole body. He made *everybody* feel like playing. Immediately I thought that was as close to paradise as I was likely to experience on stage. Our arrangements were fairly simple; in fact, that disturbed me somewhat, as I describe later. But I enjoyed the feeling completely. Art threw so much energy and so many surprises my way that I soon forgot everything else. At the end of the night Art asked if I could return the next night. Without thinking, I blurted, "You got it." The prospect of continuing was irresistible. Art Blakey—Wow!

Once again the following night I was beside myself with joy. The thought that hundreds of jazz players would die for this gig kept crossing my mind. I wondered how many musicians knew what it was like to play with this hurricane force. Art was a phenomenon, a rare and utterly natural talent. He didn't know how *not* to swing. I was undergoing the mercy of Dr. Blakey's musical scalpel, my attention sharpening, growing leaner and fitter.

At the end of the second night he asked me to finish the week. Better, he wanted me to join the group permanently. I told him I would be delighted to complete the current gig, but I aimed to establish myself in the city. My plan was to land writing assignments, to compose music for television and advertising, so I needed to cultivate that work. Art understood, though he was disappointed. In truth, I was enjoying myself more each night and really didn't want it to end. Nevertheless, I had career moves to pursue.

By our third evening, however, I still hadn't gained full insight into Art's overwhelming press rolls. The third night I came to understand them completely. During one of my solos, to my dismay Art's invasive press rolls thundered right over the musical statement I was making. I found myself standing on stage pantomiming. Nobody could hear my horn, or would have known if my horn were silent—even I couldn't tell the difference. Art was giving me a heads up. My habit was to play smoothly, and not too loudly—a type of restraint that had no legal or professional place in the presence of his stentorian press rolls. Somehow I still didn't get it. His ponderous rolling accents usually occupied two bars. This one, however, lasted four bars, and Art dropped it on me at the end of a chorus, underscored with a loud cymbal crash precisely on the downbeat of the following chorus, then further accented by another crash. Then another. It was calamitous—raw percussive mayhem. Then Art shouted across the stage at me, still swinging, not missing a single beat: "Get up outta that hole!"

I was shocked. But I continued playing, realizing that I was not playing aggressively enough for Art's style. "He is right," I thought. "I *am* in a hole and I've got to climb out." I began to try to play ferociously and increased my volume. Neither Art not I ever mentioned this event afterwards, but we both knew what had happened. Certainly I understood what he had done. It was a version of Bird's moment with Jo Jones, when that most elegant of drum maestros threw a cymbal across the stage at Bird. Art's explosive outburst greatly benefited my playing.

Art Blakey's drum style was famous for these thundering press rolls, which he developed under the influence of Big Sid Catlett. When Art came to New York from Pittsburgh, Big Sid heard Art's potential and made himself Art's coach. One thing that almost drove Art nuts was Sid's advice to play only eighth notes, two taps to every beat. Art practiced this for an hour straight, over and over. It was so boring, he said, he felt he was going crazy. Art wanted to *bash*, but he continued his assignment at varying tempos. When a tempo became fast, the exercise became harder. Art persisted. Out of such monotonous practice, Art's famous press rolls evolved. Obsessive practice, linked with talent, often creates success in performance. John Coltrane had such strenuous, rigorous dedication.

My third night at Café Bohemia was extraordinarily revealing. That night I would learn more than one lesson. Thelonious Monk arrived and listened to a set. When I came off the bandstand he was waiting for me, rocking on his heels, clasping both hands behind his back as he did when something profound was on his mind. I was nervous but eager to hear what he thought of my playing. I knew Monk slightly, but he had never heard me play in person. Instantly, Monk fired off an observation. "You play too perfect!" I knew this wasn't a compliment, but I didn't understand what he meant. Monk stood swaying, a giant of a man, completely silent. He looked at me and waited to hear if I had understood what he told me. Art, listening nearby, knew what Monk meant but said nothing. They let me stand there like an idiot. Art snickered. I was thoroughly perplexed and uncomfortable. What was this man talking about? After a long interval, Monk continued. "You've got to make *mistakes* to discover new stuff!" The light dawned. I had a moment of epiphany: I needed to make drastic changes.

When a jazz musician reaches a certain degree of accomplishment, he cannot hang near the wall. He must expose himself—reveal what he is made of. I saw what Monk meant. If I played only what I knew, what I was comfortable with, then I would continue playing only *what I knew.* Comfort, deriving from self-protection, is a selfish mistress. It makes a musician phobic about mistakes. Over time a persistent fear of glitches crowds out the spirit of openness to new musical possibilities. I have witnessed this many times over the years. Fear, timidity, avoidance of risk, or protracted uncertainty all define failing talent. Creativity comes to a standstill when a musician will not risk playing a strange phrase or attempting a difficult interval, or trying a fresh approach to a familiar song. Monk was right. Mistakes are the price we pay to proceed with faith and strength into the future

On the fourth night, I came to work ready to play like a crazy man. I would blow anything that came into my head, whether it made sense or not. Nothing could thwart my advance. I was loaded for bear; I was willing to go skinny dipping in Central Park or walk naked through the Village. My mantra was "Get up outta that hole." I would court mistakes and risk purple excess. For these lessons, I have been grateful ever since to Art Blakey and Thelonious Monk. Those sobering nights at Café Bohemia were where I began my doctoral degree as a jazz musician.

But this particular night still had a surprise in store. I had my mojo cranked, when Charles Mingus arrived with his wife. He got into a scuffle with a patron at an adjoining table. From the bandstand we watched the melee while we played "Out of the Past," a peaceful song I had composed (far removed from aggressive energies). This song now unfolded calmly, incongruously. In a rage, Mingus brought a beer bottle down on the victim's head, which the man deflected with his arm, the bottle flying into the bewildered crowd. It was a Friday night and the place was full. On stage, I envisioned the next day's headline: "Mingus Starts Fight Serenaded by Golson's Anthem." As in a Charlie Chaplin silent film, the brawl up front was unrelated to the soothing lyrical underscore. Mingus and his adversary rolled on the floor next to the bandstand. We played on. The besieged fellow got a tight bear hug on Mingus from behind. Mingus began growling. The room emptied out. Nobody paid a check; the truncated set was on the house. Art's drum pulse suddenly ceased. Art headed toward the front, carrying his drum seat, which was a large, heavily modified motorcycle seat, of a type used at that time by a number of drummers. I asked Art what he intended. Nonchalantly, Art replied that he was "going to break up the fight." I thought he was out of his mind. Jimmy, the club owner who lived directly across the street, arrived, dressed in his pajamas, slippers, an overcoat and hat. The place was completely empty, the night's revenue down the drain. Separately, both brawlers cleared out, Mingus having made his mark once again.

CHAPTER 36

Blakey and The Jazz Messengers

MONK CAME BACK the following night. It was cold outside, so he wore galoshes, a Russian fur hat with the flaps down over his ears, thick gloves, a heavy scarf, and, best of all, sunglasses with tropical bamboo temples. We invited him to play a song or two with us. To join us on stage, he had to part a curtain to the left of the bandstand and climb a few steps. He disappeared through the curtain, and I'm sure we all thought he would need a moment or two to unbundle his winter garb. But he popped in view immediately, still encumbered with his heavy clothing, and sat down at the piano without so much as removing his gloves. We kicked off a tune and Monk dug in, the bulky gloves not slowing him down in the slightest or seeming to cause him any discomfort. It was one of the wildest things I had ever seen on stage. However, I was in New York now, and after all this was Thelonious Monk.

On Sunday, my last day at Café Bohemia, Art approached me, his manner distinctly casual. "Benny," he said sweetly, "I've got a week in Pittsburgh soon and I know you don't want to leave New York. This is only six days," he reasoned, "and it won't hurt your plans: you can get right back." I saw that he was right. One week would be all right. Art Blakey was The Man when he sat behind those drums. Why not do it? Just one week.

Trust me here. Art Blakey was just as clever away from the bandstand as he was on it. He had a plan and I was part of it. I didn't know that. So we hit Pittsburgh, and two days before closing at the legendary Crawford Grill, he approached me again. "Benny, didn't you attend Howard University some time before coming to New York?" "True," I shot back, "how did you know that?" "Oh, I heard it somewhere," he said vaguely. "I was thinking you must know Washington, D.C., pretty well and maybe have quite a few friends you could visit. I suppose it's like a second home for you." I agreed. "Well, I've got a gig at the Spotlight Room for a week and this would be 'ol' home week' for you down there, seeing so many acquaintances again."

Art's right, I thought. It would be good to see old buddies again. I said yes once more. That decision was, without question, the best and most fortunate I ever made in my entire life. If I had not joined Art on that gig, I would never have met Bobbie. The events of that week were divinely inspired. I am forever grateful that Art conned me into joining him. We were launched, even if that fact dawned on me only slowly. Art had already lined up many other gigs after that. He wanted me. In Washington, I fell in love with the most amazing young woman on earth. My not wanting to leave New York was never mentioned again. I had, indeed, become a member of The Jazz Messengers. Art was a shrewd old fox.

During our week at Café Bohemia, however, I noticed that Art's repertoire didn't include any strong, self-identifying arrangements. I also noticed other things that bothered me. After a few days, I decided to talk to him about my concerns. Looking back, I cannot believe I said the things I decided to say to him.

I confronted Art during an intermission with a series of extremely presumptuous observations. I began something like this: "Art, you should be a millionaire." How's that for a bold opening? It got his attention. Somewhat taken aback, Art responded openly. "A millionaire, what do you mean?" Never could there be a less defended chin for my next jab. "With all your talent, you should make much more money." (Somehow I had learned how much his group received for the week at Café Bohemia; the money was terrible.) Next, I told him his lack of punctuality was atrocious. "You leave the bandstand for a fifteen-minute intermission and disappear sometimes for an hour. At the beginning of the night, you and other members of the group are frequently late . . . in fact almost always." Art was totally attentive, so I plowed ahead. "You're undependable and unreliable, Art. You're a risk for anyone who hires you."

Art's eyes widened in disbelief. "This green upstart punk is saying these things to me," he must have been thinking. "Who is this kid?" But he let me go on. "I heard Smalls Paradise *never* wants you to work there again, because you were late all the time. Is that true?' A pause and then his admission: "Yeah-h-h, I guess so." I pressed on with my lecture. "Procrastination cannot be a way of life," I informed him. "In the long run it makes things more difficult and hinders aspirations. It is selfish, since other musicians are almost always involved." I blathered on, assuming Art would be aghast at my remarks. But he was looking at me with interest, apparently unoffended.

I continued. "When guys nod off on the bandstand," I told him, "it looks unprofessional. I'm not used to that, Art. It bothers me." He listened intently. "Have you ever been to Europe?" I asked. "No," he said, embarrassed. I coiled for the knock-out punch. "Honestly, your name should be known the world over as one of the greatest drummers." I was expecting Art at any moment to tell me to mind my own business. Instead, he looked at me with those big, sad cow eyes of his, and asked quietly, "Do you think you can you help me?" My reply was still more presumptuous. "Sure, Art, if you do *exactly* what I tell you to do."

Did I really say such a preposterous, self-inflated thing to this giant of an artist? But Art took my critique in absolutely seriously, and meekly asked me, "What should I do?" I had saved the worst for last. I ordered him to get a new band. "O.K.," Art agreed, "tell them they're fired." Now I knew all of these guys, and I could never bring myself to fire them! How could I? I was not even a member of the band! I had no authority whatsoever. We went back and forth. "You tell them." "No, *you* tell them." Finally, Art struck on a solution. I would join the group and become the musical director. I reminded him that I didn't want to travel. I said I couldn't join the group but that I would help as a nonmember. I continued lecturing him: I believed in him, because of his fantastic talent, and I truly wanted to help, though I wasn't sure it was possible. I told him that, intuitively, I felt I could help, but he needed to find people for his band whose talent was commensurate with his. That was the key, I insisted. "O.K., then," Art blurted, "I'll tell them Benny said they're fired." I was horrified. I emphasized that he was the leader. I was *not* in the group. This was not a nuance. At last, Art got it. However, before he would let anyone go, he asked logically, "Do you know anybody we can get to replace them?"

I did. On the trumpet, a nineteen-year-old musician who had played in Dizzy's band with me: my roommate, Lee Morgan, from Philly. On piano, a fellow who played with Chet Baker and elsewhere around New York: Bobby Timmons, also from Philly. On bass, a guy who had played in Bull Moose Jackson's band along with Tadd Dameron, Philly Joe Jones, and Johnny Coles, and had also played electric bass with B.B. King: Jymie Merritt, again from Philly. "What's this Philadelphia shit?" Art wanted to know. "Listen, Art, they all can really play. Serious stuff, understand? They all just happen to be from Philadelphia. Heck, when you think about it, we're from Pennsylvania . . . even you." Art laughed. "You're a great salesman, Golson." High praise from the master of the con.

I followed Art's urging and invited these cats to join the group. All said yes. These events, including my recruitment of the band, occurred over a span of three weeks, including our initial meeting at Café Bohemia and our gig at the Crawford Grill. I organized the new group and rehearsed them. Art wanted us to finish the gig in Pittsburgh before he engaged a new tenor sax player. We went to the Spotlight Club afterward, and one week turned into two. He originally planned to hire a new saxophonist after the D.C. gigs, but over the course of those three momentous weeks, I became completely absorbed in building The Jazz Messengers' future. Art's infectious percussive jubilance, and the rope-a-dope games he played with me, won me over. In the midst of this melodrama, too, occurred the most important event of my life: I became a different person starting the moment I met Bobbie Hurd. My developing romance with Bobbie profoundly influenced all my career moves, henceforth.

I told Art we needed songs that people would closely identify with him and with The Messengers. "If all you do is execute jaw-shattering solos, complete with inimitable press rolls after the guys do their stuff, you're another drummer at the top, like Buddy Rich, Cozy Cole, or Louie Bellson. But where's your difference? What distinguishes you artistically?" I was on Art's case again. "If you bring up the rear each time a tune is closing and just about worn out, then you're a mop-up man. You become the musical janitor. Do you really want to lead a great band from the rear, or worse, from the alley, where the janitor sweeps the musical dumpings? You've got to have something that features *you*—from the very beginning."

He agreed. We kicked ideas around. Finally, I said to him, teasingly, "You've played everything there is to play except a march." We almost hurt ourselves laughing. But I suddenly stopped laughing. "Wait a minute, a march—we can do that." Art was skeptical, but I had an idea. He was convinced it would never work. A march, by a jazz group? We must be nuts to even try. "Art," I reassured him, "I don't have anything military in mind. Something like the Grambling State band plays—a march with soul, with a certain hipness, you dig? A march unlike all other marches." Art was convinced there was no such thing. "You can help me make it so," I told him. "I'll go home and see what I can come up with tonight." I was living with my aunt in Graham Court, at 116th Street and Seventh Avenue, in Harlem. That corner was a small crossroads of the black world in Manhattan. It rocked on weekends. I often opened my large window all the way, to soak in the scene on the street below. Especially on the weekends, I heard epithets of every description, car crashes, accusations, screams, vilifications, friendships beginning and ending, alcohol-infused merry making, out-of-tune singing, prostitutes' disputes with their pimps. I loved all these sounds. This was my New York! Duke Ellington's "Harlem Airshaft" drew from these human tapestries. Albert Murray's wonderful books also capture these emotional, existential scenes. Wynton Marsalis, a New Orleans boy, sat at Dr. Murray's knee soon after he arrived in Manhattan from Louisiana. He absorbed the Harlem ambience, along with lessons from classic Basie and Ellington albums. As a young Turk not yet thirty, I drew inspiration from these scenes as I set to writing my march of dubious consequence. I worked on a second-hand, out-of-tune upright piano I had purchased just a few weeks earlier. Fifty dollars, delivery included. Someone had attempted to repaint it, then abandoned the effort, so that the piano was half black and half green—like Harlem. A writer doesn't need Rolls Royce quality to create something in touch with the universe. Everything I wrote with The Messengers I created on that piano, a beautiful-ugly monster that helped my career enormously. It was a friend I eventually gave to Curtis Fuller when I got a new one. I wonder if Monk's tune "Ugly Beauty" was inspired by an abused upright piano on Sugar Hill.

The following morning, I had the march. I called a rehearsal. Art wanted to know what he should play. I answered him with a question. "Do you remember the drum and bugle corps that marched through our neighborhoods?" He did. "Sometimes the bugles stopped. Only drums and cymbals: rhythm, rhythm, rhythm—medicine for the spirit. Kids followed them in delight for blocks well outside their neighborhoods. Everyone got caught up in the fun." He asked, "How will you guys know when to come in?" Art was on occasion a worrywart, but it was simple. His role was to play a roll off. "We'll come in on time," I assured him. I had become accustomed to saying, "Trust me."

I called the tune "Blues March." Lee and I got into the spirit of the melody, and then we were ready. Art dug in and made the march his own. The rest is history. No one else has ever played it like Art did. I wish I had a live recording of "Blues March" with Art Blakey at the helm. Over the years, as The Messengers evolved, playing "Blues March" became de rigueur. I also put the finishing touches on "Are You Real?" during that period, and "Along Came Betty" became a staple as well.

Bobby Timmons also had a little tune he used to play between songs. This snippet was soulful and funky, only eight bars long, not a full song. When he played it, he would almost always say, "That sure is funky." Bobby played it nightly, *sotto voce*, for months, but because it wasn't a complete tune, nobody paid much attention to it.

This changed when we played a club in Columbus, Ohio. I called a rehearsal on arrival. Everyone wanted to know why; we had our act together. But I felt we needed to move the group forward somehow. A tune of seductive intensity was missing. When we started rehearsing, I called first for this funky fragment of Bobby's. He thought it had no value. "Aw, that's nothing," he insisted. But I saw in this small scrap the makings of something wonderful. After all, he already had eight bars, which, if repeated up front, could serve as an opening sixteen bars. The same riff could be the last eight bars. Adding an eight-bar bridge would make it a standard thirty-two-bar tune. That's why we rehearsed that afternoon. We put silent pressure on Bobby to write a bridge. He worked reluctantly, while the rest of us sat at empty tables in the club, conversing idly. After about thirty or forty minutes, he called me over to the piano. "What do you think of this?" He played a few bars, but they lacked the feeling of the original eight bars. "I don't think I can do this," Bobby confessed. He wanted me to do it. I insisted it had to be *his* tune. I loved the eight bars he played all the time, I said; I knew he could do this.

Bobby went back to work. Twenty minutes later, he called me over again. I played the new piece. That was it! The snippet had expanded into a song, carrying the same feeling as the original eight bars. We set to work learning the new tune. That evening, gauging the audience's mood, I announced we had a brand new piece, something really special, and they were the first audience to hear it. We began. Although Marty's club did not have a dance floor, people began dancing, finger popping, and doing soulful jive. The joint really rocked. "Moanin'," fresh out of the cradle, was a hit, as I knew it would be.

By now I had set goals for The Messengers. I invented a kind of evaluative "scalogram" on which I organized the challenges facing the band in order of difficulty. Accomplishments at one level would indicate our capability to achieve aims at lower levels. I knew we had to set sign posts to measure our movement forward. The first challenge we set was for Small's to hire the group again. Art told me to forget it; that would never happen. I had gotten in the habit of picking Art up on the way to our gigs, in order to ensure that we started the first set on time. I was a hard task master, demanding that everyone return punctually from intermissions, including Art. He didn't oppose me; we were progressing well. I also took charge of the money, which was increasing steadily. To ensure that we looked professional, I made one substantial draw for the whole week and required everyone, Art included, to draw cash from me during our engagements. We now had financial autonomy and did not confuse or irritate club own-ers—or ourselves.

When I suggested we dress uniformly, Art demurred. I noted that peo-ple *see* a band before they hear it. Visual signals are valuable. The Messen-gers needed to convey a sense of self-worth, even before we played a note. The high quality of our performance would confirm an already established viewpoint. Art resisted a bit, but I didn't back down. To compound my temerity, I asked the Shaw Booking Agency, who secured gigs for us and with whom I was already working closely, to book a concert for us at Town Hall in Times Square. Town Hall was an upscale venue; The Messengers would perform in tuxedos. Art thought I had lost my mind. I held firm. The reviews of our performance were fantastic. But I wasn't done.

I called Jack Whitmore, the key man at the Shaw agency. I asked him why Art and The Jazz Messengers had never toured Europe. His answer was simple: no one ever pursued that goal. I told Jack that I wanted that accomplished immediately. I would take care of whatever needed to be done before we left. Jack went directly to work.

Before touring Europe, however, we needed a new album. I called Alfred Lion at Blue Note Records and asked why Art's band had not been recorded in such a long while. Alfred said something like, "Art is already involved in so many things." Such a superior artist, I retorted, should per-form and record regularly. Regularity and global exposure helped not only musicians but also audiences, record sales, and, therefore, profits—includ-ing Blue Note's. A whimsical belief that overexposure was a detriment was not a legitimate excuse for slowing an artist's advancement, I told Alfred. I urged him to come to one of our appearances and hear what the group was currently playing. He agreed. Sure enough, after he heard our live act, he recorded us. I had planned the entire album, which he accepted. Fundamentally, I pushed The Messengers to the top with my positive attitude and energy. I avoided being offensive, yet I insisted calmly but firmly that everyone do as I asked.

With Blue Note, I argued for adding several details to the album. First, I wanted a particular photograph on the cover, a head shot a photographer had taken of Art as we toured the States. Alfred complied. I wanted the album to be entitled *Moanin'*. Done. Everything I wanted was carried out, across the board. I was a young upstart, and I sometimes couldn't believe the success of my efforts on our behalf. But I always acted as though whatever I asked for was normal. I expected everyone to comply, and they did. Whatever I said to Jack and Alfred evidently sounded logical, feasible, and professionally useful. Perhaps my instincts were sometimes prescient. Of course, my efforts succeeded mainly because they supported the remarkable talent of Art Blakey. I merely acted in the capacity of someone underscoring, or occasionally directing and enhancing, the value of that talent.

"Moanin'" was a hit. We heard it on jukeboxes wherever we went. In droves, people were becoming aware of Art Blakey and The Jazz Messengers. Increased fees were now a solid index of our mounting popularity. Art no longer questioned *anything* I said.

We flew to Paris via a brand new form of air travel—a jet. The trip to Paris by 707 took five hours, instead of twelve. We landed at Orly Airport, exhilarated. We had finally made it. Jymie Merritt missed our flight, but joined us the next day. Paris was a dream, a first for all of us. Art invited his friend Bruce Wright, a sharp, erudite, and accomplished attorney, who later became the Honorable Judge Wright on the New York State Supreme Court, to join us. He and I were roommates on that European tour.

We played the Club Saint-Germain in Paris, one of the most notable and elegant venues on our itinerary. The audiences were enthusiastic, and each night, we tried to outdo ourselves. People had no choice but to love us because of Art. The band was window dressing around his luminescence. Hazel Scott, a classical and jazz pianist and the former wife of Congressman Adam Clayton Powell, Jr., lived in Paris then. She came to the Saint-Germain every night. Lucky Thompson, one of my teenage idols, lived in the Hotel Crystal, across the street from the club, where our group was staying. He too came often to hear us. On that trip I also met Don Byas, another of my youthful idols. To my delight, we became friends. One night I looked up from the stage to see Don Byas and Lucky Thompson standing at the bar listening to me play. That night I really came to understand the feeling of *pressure*. A French group worked opposite our band, led by violinist Stéphane Grappelli, a dear, talented man with an abundance of feeling for music. Kenny Clarke ("Klook") was also living there. He and Don Byas were American jazz expatriates in the City of Light.

Artistically, Kenny Clarke was created from the same mold as Art Blakey. He always had a deep, contagiously swinging groove. Years earlier, when most jazz drummers were arriving at their groove by way of a 1–2–3–4 beat on the snare, rolling a beat here and there, sometimes from the high-hat cymbal, Klook went to the ride cymbal (mainly relegated to crashing accents) to carve his groove. His peers thought he had taken leave of his senses. Today, Klook's method is common. He was the initial drummer with The Modern Jazz Quartet. He left them for life in Paris. I had always wondered what playing with Klook would feel like. I soon found out. The club owner at Saint-Germain came up with a clever idea that we all loved: he hired Klook to join The Messengers one night. He and Art played at the same time with our group. I couldn't believe it. Two drummers of the highest propulsive order, swinging, hip. I'll never forget the experience. Words cannot describe the energy and the feeling on stage that evening. We then took this idea into the Olympic Theater, the venue where Josephine Baker became famous. During this tour, Art built a formidable name for himself in the European market. The Jazz Messengers thrived, too, and that name gained a cachet of genius in the jazz world, too. Art Blakey's inimitable talent created from every group of "messengers" he fronted an awe-inspiring force.

Eventually the time arrived when I had to leave the group. In March 1960, I had been with Art for almost a year and a half. My leaving was sad for both of us. We had come a long way together rapidly. We both learned a great deal about music and business and life. I urged Art to stay the course. Wayne Shorter, a powerfully creative saxophonist and composer, replaced me. When I think of Wayne, I remember a time when he was vying for a place in the sun. I had been in New York only a short while when Wayne called me to ask for a few lessons. I was taken aback. I had heard him play. "What can I show you, Wayne, that you don't already know?" I laughed. Wayne was sweet and modest, and I admired his thirst for knowledge. I continue to look at Wayne Shorter as a jazz hero. Wayne draws from a bottomless well of brilliant musical ideas. His work has made life more exciting for all jazz lovers. I think Herbie Hancock would endorse that fact.

Art and I never lost contact. Whenever he felt he needed another viewpoint on a problem, he called me. I remained an emeritus Jazz Messenger. I knew Art Blakey intimately; he revealed all aspects of his life to me without shame or reservation. We had an unself-conscious give and take. I don't think Art would mind anything I have shared here, because it is truthful. It accurately reflects who he was, as well as his sometimes startling teaching methods. Art Blakey was revered, not only by his fans but also by his fellow musicians. Art also had a rare talent for identifying artistic potential. He could hear musical strength and ability from a distance. Where others might find a young player intriguing, but remain uncertain about his talent, Art always identified ability unambivalently and knew how to cultivate nascent talent. He was a master at coaxing energy and intelligence from suspended possibility or obscurity into achievement. When his plebes matured into refined stars, they were symbolically anointed by Art. They gained knowledge, confidence, and poise under the aegis of his tutelage.

Art Blakey's Messengers were figuratively incorporated as a school or college with one teacher, Maestro Blakey. He could be didactic, though his tutelage was subtle and accumulative. Working with Art, one came under his influence naturally. A natural and spontaneous man, Art led by his enormous and unprepossessing self-confidence.

Earmarks of Art's instruction were "swing" and "fire." Art taught us how to articulate emotional ferocity, and how crucial the living heartbeat of musical pulse is to the storytelling power and seduction of lyric expression. Sometimes a player's development was amazing. Was Art's college successful? Consider its graduates: Horace Silver, Kenny Dorham, Jackie McLean, Lee Morgan, Cedar Walton, Hank Mobley, Freddie Hubbard, Wayne Shorter, Wynton Marsalis, Michael Brecker, Geoffrey Keezer, Brian Lynch, John Hicks, Bill Hardman, Buster Williams, Curtis Fuller, Spanky DeBrest, Walter Davis, Jr., Mulgrew Miller, Donald Harrison, Joanne Brackeen, Terence Blanchard, Jymie Merritt, James Williams, Billy Pierce, Javon Jackson, Bobby Timmons, Benny Green (the American), Keith Jarrett, Peter Washington, Valery Ponomarev, Steve Turre, Reggie Workman, Chuck Mangione, Randy Brecker, Craig Handy, Frank Lacy ... and Benny Golson. There are more, but this roll call suggests the man's pedagogical abilities.

I have written at length about Art Blakey because I had to. I want no important gaps in my autobiography. Art's life history shaped many productive and successful careers. Had there not been a College of Art Blakey, the jazz heritage would be far poorer. He helped many musicians find their way. Art never received a medal or official commendation for his contribution to music or to world culture. However, those of us who played or studied with him knew his daunting authority and carry some of the glory of association with him in our hearts. In memory of this special man, every day, many of us silently thank Art Blakey.

CHAPTER 37

Kenny Dorham and Lee Morgan

MET KENNY DORHAM in 1954, before I moved to the City. I had heard many of his recordings in Philly and while I was studying at Howard University. When Earl Bostic's band played, I would sometimes spend a day or two in New York. Kenny perfected a particularly hip way of weaving in and out of chords that I loved, but I could never figure out how he did it. One day I called him, and asked him if he could enlighten me as to how he achieved this distinctive sound in his approach to chords. At first he didn't see what I meant. His technique was second nature to him, and it took him a while to absorb the logic of my question. Finally he understood what I was asking. "O-o-h-h, wow!" he exclaimed. "I've never explained it to anyone before—no one ever asked."

Over the phone, I could hear him trying to figure out how to make sense of it for me. His explanation was one of the wildest, most aberrational I had ever heard. "Well," he began, "when I come to a chord and I want to do something different, I come in from the side and jump on it. Sometimes I come in from the front, but quickly back up." When he finished, he seemed proud of his bizarre explanation. Although we had been on the telephone for quite a while, I was too embarrassed to tell him I didn't understand a thing he told me. I thanked him for taking the time to share such personal information and said goodbye. I hung up not knowing a jot more than before I called. I stood in the same spot for a few seconds, shaking my head in disbelief. I never did tell him that I understood absolutely nothing he said that afternoon. Kenny's hipness was too deep and subtle for me to understand.

Thinking about all this, I realized that Kenny played with the same indirectness and obliquity I had just heard when he talked. His playing always offered something allusive, unexpected, and endlessly interesting. He developed a habit of teasing anticipation that became an earmark of his virtue as a trumpeter. Without recognizing it, I had always been delighted by that "sideways" quality in his music. Now, in conversation, I saw that he *spoke* sideways as well, in a manner vague, teasing, figurative. A habit of irony or poetic approximation was rooted in the man's psyche. He searched for back doors and side entrances for his utterances, ducking inside musical and verbal expressions from odd angles. He may have been protecting himself from direct emotional exposure, unexpected, dance-like movements misdirecting or obscuring his aims. The simplest thing to account for in Kenny's playing was its tonal allure, a firm but gentle, prowling quality. He gathered chords as if they held secrets that too much sunlight or too much attention might destroy. If he were an accountant, you would want to keep your eyes on his books; Kenny would move the decimal point precisely where it would not be looked for, when you least suspected it.

Did he put up a smokescreen for me, to keep his stylistic secrets to himself? Or did he speak sincerely, guilelessly but perversely, as he played his horn? I suspect the latter. He was capable of only this mode of expression, whether personally or musically. I viewed him as innocent and undefended. Others have noted that Kenny was an ambiguous yet unself-conscious fellow, by turns shy and oddly self-aggrandizing. Although he was consistently good natured, when you spoke with him, he could make you wonder where he was coming from or where he was headed. He was a fabulous musician and a confusing man.

Ten years after I first met Kenny, jazz promoter Monte Kaye assembled an all-star overseas tour dubbed "Jam Session." Our first stop was Japan. Along with Kenny and me, the group included Freddie Hubbard, Cedar Walton, Jackie McLean, Reggie Workman, and Roy Haynes. In Tokyo, we checked in to our hotel. We knew that in Japan, jazz fans are more persistent and more eager to get musicians' autographs than one finds in most places. People would wait in the hotel lobby for hours, hoping to snag an autograph from one of us when we came down in the morning to eat breakfast. Sometimes they were even more determined to find us. We all had rooms on one hall, and one morning before breakfast, we were still relaxing upstairs. All the doors were open and we were wandering in and out of each other's rooms. Five or six female jazz enthusiasts found our floor and sauntered down the hallway. To everyone's surprise, Kenny walked into the hall buck naked, greeted the women and continued talking, oblivious to their discombobulation. The guys were flabbergasted; the women fled. Kenny looked at us as if to say, "What's the problem?"

Once in New York, Kenny had a suit custom made that caused quite a stir. I cannot imagine another man who would wear it; the tailor might have sewn it together on Mars. We didn't want to embarrass Kenny, so we said nothing. But on the stage that night it was clear that, although his performance was as hip as ever, the audience didn't hear a note he played; the suit was a blinding distraction.

No one I knew ever broke the "Kenny" code. He was engaging and hip, a term that fits Kenny better than anyone else I could name. His personal energy elevated everyone. He was great to be around, seemingly constantly ready for action. He was almost a coach or team leader to us, albeit with an eccentric style of "leadership." When he picked up his trumpet, you were in for a treat. I never figured out his technical or improvisational tricks, and I seldom had an inkling what he would say or do, musically or otherwise. To this very day I miss Kenny Dorham.

In 1956, a new boy in town exploded on the New York jazz scene. Lee Morgan had just come to The City from my hometown. He was only eighteen, still unspooling a rare silk thread of astonishing talent. Lee made an indelible impression on everyone who heard him, commandeering extraordinary lyrical talent and technical ability. Lee had perfected one of the strongest embouchures I had ever heard. His chops must have been made of steel. He joked about the size of his lips, often noting that he was the only player who could play the trumpet with a tuba mouthpiece. This always got a laugh. Lee Morgan was an unexpected delight. We all regarded him as a treasure when he played. And he knew it because everyone told him so.

Lee was brash and self-confident—cocky, actually, although he had great respect for Clifford Brown; from the beginning, I heard it in his playing. Arrogance is sometimes synonymous with great talent, perhaps particularly in a young person. Like most highly gifted people, Lee gained perspective with time. He was certainly not a malicious person. His smile and laughter were equally for everyone. He matured quickly in every way, including musically. Lee was extremely bright and a very fast learner. Later, he would

laugh at how he acted when he first came to New York. I always thought
he felt his pontifical behavior was expected of him. It had been a long time
since anyone as young and talented as Lee came on the jazz scene.

I was playing with Dizzy Gillespie's band when Dizzy hired Lee. The
move was wise for both parties, but especially for Lee. He would now rub
shoulders with the Master every day. Diz was keenly aware of Lee's outrageous talent. Diz was a magnanimous man, with nothing to prove, and
he featured Lee prominently. Diz allowed Lee solos that had been his
own, before the new kid joined the band. I was astonished when Diz gave
Lee the solo spot on "A Night in Tunisia." Dizzy wrote the song and it
was always associated with his swooping, unrestrained trumpet. But Dizzy
unselfishly wanted people to hear and appreciate this talented kid from
Philadelphia. Diz gave Lee his permanent stamp of approval.

In those years, band members shared hotel rooms. Quincy Jones and
I had been roommates, but when Lee joined the band, Quincy was leaving. I don't remember the details; Lee may have replaced Quincy. Lee
and I became roommates. He continually asked me questions about past
events and players, trying to learn their significance in jazz history. Already
abundantly talented, he pursued knowledge ceaselessly. He was naïve and
brilliant. He quickly memorized Dizzy's book.

Lee Morgan was a special person as well as a rising jazz "phenom."
In any band, many personalities exist side by side. The Ellington band,
for instance, was a model of divergent, brilliant eccentricity for more than
half a century. In Dizzy's band, Lee was a natural comedian. His antics
kept us laughing. He could play-act any character effortlessly. He became
the incarnation of Kingfish from the Amos and Andy radio and television
series. He morphed into Ray Charles. He could walk like someone with
very bad feet or like a teen hipster in the ghetto. His imitation of John
Wayne's swagger and drawling speech was hilarious.

Lee was a prankster. Riding the band bus, he sometimes administered
a "hot foot" to a sleeping band mate—not one match but many, lining
the entire inner edge of a shoe. We plotted his take-down when he was
sleeping. Lee habitually snoozed with his head back, mouth wide open.
The time finally came, late one night. We were all dead tired. Lee was
fast asleep. I fashioned a large piece of paper into a funnel, filled it with as
much salt as it could hold (a quarter of a cup or so) and placed it into his
invitingly open mouth. Lee dozed on; there was no reaction until the salt
dissolved. Then we saw his tongue begin moving rapidly. Soon, as the salt

liquefied and slipped down his throat, the taste must have become overwhelming. He woke up with a grotesque look on his face. He could not imagine what was happening. Our hilarity brought him abruptly to reality. "You're dirty guys," he blasphemed.

During intermission one night, we placed a small piece of cellophane over Lee's mouthpiece. Positioned in the shank of his trumpet, it prevented air from passing through. We came back on stage for the next set. Diz kicked off and, of course, Lee couldn't get a sound from his trumpet. It was completely blocked. He struggled fruitlessly with his instrument and began cussing. We kept straight faces. "Something's wrong with this damn horn." His dark face turned red. Half way into the tune, he figured out our gag. Being a practical joker himself, he didn't get angry, but laughed with us all.

When we became roommates, I discovered that he wore pajama bottoms instead of underpants. I asked him why. Underpants gave him leg rashes, he told me. His choice of underwear must have been uncomfortable in summer, but he didn't complain. The guys often teased Lee that he was "all legs." We called him High Pockets. He never took offense. Lee Morgan was maturing well. He laughed when we did.

CHAPTER 38

Sonny Rollins

TRY TO USE the word "genius" sparingly. I make two exceptions: my lifelong friend John Coltrane and Sonny Rollins. For nearly six decades, Sonny has brought glory and refinement to the art of the tenor saxophone. He has conducted a public love affair with his horn. It's a special partnership, a confederacy of forces that lifts Sonny high above earth, while at the same time allowing him to fully express his humanity. Sonny Rollins owns the saxophone the way Einstein owns the theory of relativity.

Sonny Rollins is a poet for the ages, both a storyteller and an ironist. His stories are elaborate and engaging, his irony swift and deep. And yet his art is not esoteric. On one hand, he pursues his craft with the patience of a man assembling a ship in a bottle. On the other hand, he is persistent and selflessly devoted to the amorous exploration of sound and musical meaning.

The term *rhetoric* is important in understanding Sonny Rollins's art: melodic rhetoric, musical phrases chosen intelligently, with precise aware-ness of each note and its emotional impact. Sonny speaks with his horn the way John Milton spoke in his epics, with knowledge of the tradition he car-ried forward and eloquent understanding of each phrase. Poetry read aloud is musical. Sonny Rollins creates long melodic narratives on stage. He is an iconoclast unrivaled in the history of jazz. I cannot rank him; he is a musi-cal universe all his own. How fortunate we are to be on earth while Sonny creates his sonic archipelagos, evoking the redemptive, gorgeous world we share. Has any musician ever played as *cheerfully* as Sonny Rollins does? Is there a happier beat than Sonny Rollins's calypso rhythms? When was the last time you listened to him play "Hold 'Em, Joe" with Mickey Roker's tom-tom beating underneath? Take a brief vacation. Put on that song, and your feet will soon be dancing.

In 1958, Sonny recorded "I'm an Old Cowhand" on his *Way Out West* album, for Contemporary, with Shelly Manne. I still listen to it. I'm convinced that his playing there represents the full capability of the voice of our instrument, the saxophone. Sonny doesn't toss off a stream of aimless missiles. He offers a steady flow of contemplative, soulful notes that are tactile and heartfelt. In the midst of an essentially comic song, the feeling conveyed is spiritual. Hearing him bring new life to an obscure and otherwise forgettable tune, one says, "Yes, Lord!"

I truly believe that Sonny could arise from deep sleep in the middle of night and play something heart-rending, delicate, and powerful. His métier is jazz and the saxophone is his loyal servant. Time is corrosive but, in Sonny Rollins's case, time has also been his ally. His dreams are now our dreams. Sonny's genius is like sunlight, which once dispersed cannot be recalled.

I have always contended that any serious jazz musician must exemplify two forms of originality: of sound, and of expressive style. Today, perhaps because many musicians pursue formal academic training where my generation honed our skills in jam sessions, young musicians too often sound alike in concept, style, and tonal production. I must admit, they frequently demonstrate a technical facility and an expressive velocity that are absolutely astounding. Surgically precise, and brilliant, but needing room for the heart's deep feeling, many young players sound alike. The same person (or musical persona) sometimes seems to inhabit dozens of young players. True individuality is lost.

Sonny Rollins represents the opposite of today's trend toward technical virtuosity and polished professionalism. Few musicians have ever been as distinctly *themselves*, as instantaneously identifiable as individuals, as Sonny Rollins. One or two notes, and you recognize Sonny. He often quotes from someone or something in jazz history, but the allusion only adds to the musical meaning he produces. He punctuates phrases with his own personality. He may offer a period when you expect a question mark—or slide toward elliptical phrasing where someone else would choose staccato. You can never plot Sonny's moves. Young players could learn from him: some lock into patterns, as if to prove that memorization and consistency of execution are more important than creativity and daring.

Sonny internalized and extended the great tradition of tenor players: Coleman Hawkins, Chu Berry, and Lester Young. Like their playing, his is as fresh now as when he started. In great art, time stands still. That sounds mystical or silly or just plain impossible. Yet that is what we find in the work of artists such as J. S. Bach or Shakespeare, or when we contemplate a glorious ruin such as the Roman Coliseum. Hamlet defines human possibilities more fully than most people alive will ever do. The Coliseum haunts us with the juxtaposition of its enduring physicality coupled with the spectacular carnage that took place there. The elder Bach describes the complex beauty of the cosmos, in more ways than one could grasp in a lifetime. In the annals of jazz, a secular liturgical music filled with love and despair, celebration and lament, Sonny Rollins stands with these giants. There will only ever be one Sonny Rollins.

CHAPTER 39

Great Performances | OSCAR PETTIFORD,
RON CARTER, BILLY HIGGINS,
BILLY TAYLOR,
AND WALTER DAVIS, JR.

WHEN I THINK of Oscar Pettiford, wonderful memories flood my mind. Like Lester Young, Oscar came from a musical family in Minneapolis. Milt Hinton convinced him to leave Minneapolis in 1942 for Manhattan. He quickly became one of the most recorded bass players of that era. Oscar was a happy-go-lucky guy with an inordinate talent for the bass. Many thought he was the successor to Jimmy Blanton. When I moved to New York, I was in awe of Oscar. When he asked me to write arrangements for his big band, I was thrilled. Oscar refused traditional configurations, and among other innovations, his set-up included a harp.

Over time, we recorded albums with significant jazz stars and many other notables. 1958, the year I went to Europe with Art Blakey and The Jazz Messengers, I discovered that Oscar was playing there. He was living in Europe briefly, not as an expatriate. He had recently had a terrible automobile accident somewhere in France and narrowly escaped death. He awoke in a hospital with an ugly scar extending from his bald head to his forehead, a memento of his vivid good luck. I ran into him on the Left Bank. He was smiling as always. Oscar was working, but I had the night off, so he asked me to come hear him. I agreed. Harold Nicholas (of the Nicholas Brothers' Hollywood tap dancing fame) came with us. Intermission had just started when we arrived. Oscar welcomed us and got us a table. There was no piano on stage, no drums in sight, just a small round stage that resembled an oversized bass drum tipped on its side. Oscar's bass rested there. The stage was not big enough for a trio, I thought, assuming that a small piano would be rolled out as well as a small set of drums. I was wrong. Soon maestro Oscar Pettiford was introduced, in French, and Oscar headed to the miniature bandstand. He picked up his bass to check tune—no drummer or pianist in sight. I was bewildered. This was about to become an enlightening night for me.

Unaccompanied, Oscar launched into "Stardust." The man was playing the gig by himself—solo bass, all night, every night. I was astounded. A few minutes into the set and I forgot about piano and drums. Oscar, alone, consumed our attention. He was playing melodies along with his own accompaniment, double and triple stops: two and three notes at the same time. He played high in his thumb position and well down on the neck, never once picking up his bow. It was all pizzicato, a bravura performance. I was barely able to contain myself. I knew Oscar, but I had never met *this* Oscar. When the set was over, I couldn't wait for him to join us. "Oscar, I knew you played the strings right off your bass; I didn't know anyone could play like that!" He chuckled, a bit slyly. That performance was a tour de force, redefining for me the meaning of bass playing. I am thankful I had the rare privilege of hearing Oscar Pettiford in that stark setting. I have told the story of that evening to many musicians. Alas, that was the last time I saw Oscar Pettiford.

Another rare and startling evening for me took place at Sweet Basil, in the Village, where I went to hear Cedar Walton's trio. Ron Carter and Billy Higgins played bass and drums, respectively. I walked in during "Round Midnight," soon after the second set started. Monk's song is one of my favorites, so I was glad I arrived in time to hear it. In the second chorus, Ron seemed to find notes that had nothing whatsoever to do with the song's original structure, but each note was infatuating. On and on he went, each fresh inspiration trumping the last. Now and then, a player comes upon notes that are aberrational but enchanting, but usually, he soon returns to the foundational structure of the song. This time, Ron didn't turn back; he had his own thing going, against what Cedar was playing. Miraculously, it worked. Ron worked against Cedar, yet with him. The tension felt beautiful and vivid. Ron tried something daring, masterful, and fresh, and created a new and entirely compatible structure. I sat transfixed. Ron Carter has artistic guts and vast imagination. He has the technical facility to effortlessly execute his most dangerous ideas. When he came off stage for intermission, I sought him out to ask how he came up with his risky creation. He smiled and replied, nonchalantly, "You can't keep doing the same ol' thing, all the time."

During that same set, Billy Higgins dug in on a drum solo. Billy possessed an epicurean musical palate, and he played tasty things as always. Suddenly, unexpectedly, he abandoned everything, except for his bass drum. Straight up, he played a bass drum solo. I was shocked. In itself, such a solo is unusual, but Billy's playing was astonishing. The audience made not a sound. Even nonmusicians recognized that this performance was special. I have still never heard anything else like it. Rather than a long bass drum break, he crafted a solo within the entire solo interlude, a sonic world unto itself. I am glad I stopped in at the Sweet Basil that evening, or I would have never experienced the improbable inventions that Ron and Billy tossed off with such élan.

Another high point in my life: Around 1997, I was playing in Italy with a saxophone group called Roots. Also appearing on that program were Cecil Taylor, Kenny Barron, and Billy Taylor. Cecil gave a fascinating solo performance which included a spoken word segment. Then Roots performed, and, finally, Billy Taylor and Kenny Barron played together, accompanied by a rhythm section. In a breathtaking performance, they explored the jazz heritage with sensitivity, boldness, and symbiotic camaraderie. I had heard Kenny "stretch out" like that before, but in all the years I knew Billy, I never heard him reach the heights he touched on that elegant evening. Billy embarked upon interplanetary travel. His playing was dazzling, nimble, unpredictable, a merciless excavation of the imagination. I was so glad to hear Billy in person. I'll never forget that evening, or Billy's extraordinary pianistic conversation with Kenny Barron. Billy had established his authority as a pianist back on 52nd Street in the 1940s, and he continuously brought unrivaled elegance to jazz: his respect, class, and gravitas influenced multiple generations of musicians as well as audiences.

There are other times on stage, or in a club, when nothing special happens. A set can go downhill much more easily than it may take off soaring. You try all night to get off the ground, and you don't ever leave the runway. These times are terribly frustrating, yet we all know they happen. Art Farmer always worked to prevent such nights. He felt that any "bad night" might be the only time someone heard him play, and forever after that person would remember him at his worst. Any jazz musician knows that hope for a good night in performance has as much chance of satisfaction as a knock on the door from room service. Sometimes we have off nights but still get rousing applause. On those nights, I feel like apologizing, instead of bowing in thanks. You come off the bandstand thinking, "I could have done *this*. I should have tried *that*." Clark Terry was right: Fooled 'em again.

Another preposterous occasion occurred when Walter Davis, Jr., was traveling with me, on tour in Japan. We were playing a gig in the northern city of Fukuoka. Our concert concluded early, and we headed to a restaurant that featured an organ player, a young black girl from the States. We ordered dinner and listened to her play and sing. A small grand piano also sat on the small stage. After she finished her set, she came over to say hello to us. When she recognized Walter's name, she asked him to play. I had never heard Walter play solo piano, and frankly I didn't think his style lent itself to that. Walter was a Bud Powell devotee.

But Walter agreed, and he acquainted himself with the piano, musing over the keys with evident delight but not really playing anything discernible. Then he slid into "My Funny Valentine." It turned out he had something to say on that piano. Walter played without a trace of Bud Powell. His touch was delicate, a complete departure from his conventional approach. I was startled to see Walter not only caress the keyboard but also elaborate the heart and soul of the ballad. My ears were opened to a Walter Davis, Jr., quite unlike the man I had known so long. He was sensitive, nostalgic, adventurous, beguiling. I listened and wondered if anyone else had ever heard him play like this—or if anyone else had ever touched the piano keys this way.

As he probed the ballad, Walter became another person—perhaps the person he usually tucked away. His tender rendition of "Valentine" completed, he began a medium up-tempo tune, drawing on techniques I was not expecting: Art Tatum runs, the melody moving from his right to his left hand; stride, adding secondary melodies; bop inversions; his own iconoclastic inventions; and more. If I had not heard this superlative performance, I would never have believed it. Walter Davis, Jr., playing like this? Why hadn't he recorded this part of his pianistic repertoire? I had a feeling, uncorroborated, that he did not want to be known for playing like this. I find it a pity, perhaps even a jazz tragedy, that his legacy does not include this brilliant material. This piece of Walter's genius is unfortunately unknown to the world. That evening was a revelation and delight that I will always cherish. Walter passed away far too young. I never heard him play like that again.

Charles Mingus, Benny Goodman, Gigi Gryce, and Horace Silver

A YEAR OR SO after I arrived in New York, in 1957, I finally met Charles Mingus. He called me, and, after the hellos, asked me without preamble: "I've heard that you play subtones. Can you do that for an entire song?" I told him I could. (Subtones are subtle smoothings, in playing a single note, that make its sound more enchanting.) Mingus hired me right there. He wanted me to play only subtones on an upcoming Columbia recording session. At those sessions I met Teo Macero, who later produced Miles Davis for Columbia and who was, at the time, producing Mingus's album.

It might have seemed as if Mingus was not prepared for the recording. He constantly made changes, but he was a composer with a vast understanding of music. He could easily choose among ten different versions of any song. Ideas ran through his imagination like electricity coursing through a wire. Settling on a final version must have taken considerable discipline and discrimination for Mingus; recording everything he had in his mind for every tune would not have been physically or economically possible.

I was intrigued watching him conduct the group while also playing bass. His bass appeared to become subliminal, but the appearance was deceptive, as every note he played was important in the scheme. His nonchalance when he conducted was also confounding. Sometimes he laid out while he was also talking. When we were recording, he was audible, demonstrative, and surprisingly uninhibited. The band was capable of playing without him. He held his bass like a toy, gesturing with the other hand, pointing: "You next, then you, but stop right there. You two play together and put your cup mute in. Stand up and play free over here." And so on. To trombonist Tom McIntosh, who is a serious Bible student, Mingus once ordered, "Okay, Jesus, you're next." His demeanor was like a busy factory foreman, and his music was strongly constructed. Mingus was fascinating to watch and listen to. Sometimes he seemed to have an enormous amount to say, his words coming fast and effusively. He spoke quickly to keep up with the rapid flow of his own thinking. Almost everything sounded urgent. I suppose it was; creativity is like that. Frequently he expressed things crudely, on purpose, so no one could mistake his meaning. Most of the time, everybody got his message, and the music came out exactly as he intended. Mingus was a musical architect, building right on site, blueprints unfurling from his fertile imagination.

His song titles were 100 percent his own devising. Nobody else could come up with those titles. He didn't care what people thought of his eccentricities. During these sessions, he wrote a piece originally called "If Charlie Parker Was a Gun Fighter, There'd Be a Lot of Dead Asses." That title was revised on the published album, but it took some moxie. Just as he asked me, all I did on those sessions was play subtones. Booker Ervin was his regular sax player and he took the solos.

I learned a lot about Mingus during those Columbia sessions, but later I was to learn much more. He invited me and my wife to his house for dinner one night. When we arrived, we discovered he had asked about ten of us, including Burt Goldblatt, the photographer, and his wife. Before the meal, he set out a giant bowl of popcorn. No one touched it except Mingus, who wiped out the entire bowl himself, before the meal began. The entrée was delicious—chops of some sort, if I recall. Most people, when dining out or entertaining guests, do not gnaw steak bones down to the last morsel. This was, however, Charles Mingus at home. He devoured not only his own but everyone else's as well, asking each of us in turn if we intended to finish our chops. Every guest, in turn, passed him their plate, off of which Mingus then cleaned every last bone of all remaining vestiges of meat. He worked his way through every plate at the table. None of us looked at him as crude or gluttonous. This was simply Charles Mingus.

Mingus was heavy then, but at other times he was thin. No doubt this reflected how he felt about his body at a given time. During one of his thin periods, I was working at Birdland with Diz. Mingus came in dressed to the hilt. He looked like an English barrister, complete with a black derby and a cane. He had rented a large limousine that waited curbside for him between clubs. By the end of our set, I had seen his attire but, when I came upstairs and saw the limousine, I looked at him with exaggerated approval and exclaimed, "Look out, Charlie Mingus!" He gave me one of his happy smiles and drove off into the glare of Broadway's glamorous lights.

I met Benny Goodman soon after moving to Manhattan. Our first meeting was cursory. Not long after, he called to ask me to write music for his band. He also asked me to join him as a saxophonist. Benny was preparing for his first tour of Russia. I always experienced Benny as a little strange. I never quite knew what he was thinking. He didn't talk much, but once he started he kept going, divulging ideas as if he had been waiting for the right moment.

Benny and his wife came to hear me one night at Café Bohemia in the Village. He wanted to record some of my material. I was flattered. I had been aware of Benny Goodman all my life, well before I embarked on a jazz career. His late 1930s Carnegie Hall concert was an enormous recorded hit. No one in America could escape hearing it dozens of times on the radio and elsewhere. I was disappointed, however, to find that he paid very poorly; he had no desire to part with much of his money. In the end, I did not take him up on his invitation to join the Russia tour, because his offer was underwhelming. Perhaps he thought the honor of playing with him would substitute for full payment. I did write an arrangement for him for "Somebody Loves Me." I received $125. His brother Harry, who years before played bass with the Goodman band, was a contrasting personality, very outgoing and talkative. He had become successful in music publishing, which is how I met him, unrelated to Benny.

At one of the rehearsals for the Russian tour—before we found out how poor the pay would be—I remember Benny walking around the studio, stopping here and there, apparently to casually adjust his reed. He was actually checking out everyone's chops, slyly leaning toward the person he was evaluating. Zoot Sims was the other tenor player and Doc Cheatham was with us that day. Benny called a blues in D-flat, a key that sometimes presents a problem for players who are not thoroughly familiar with all the keys. When he wanted to hear someone solo, he pointed to him. It soon became ludicrous. He was pointing all over the place.

When members of his staff called us aside individually to discuss fees, the rehearsal thinned out dramatically. A few of us had fun later, mocking Benny as a cheapskate. However, my uncle Robert, who worked as a bartender at Minton's Playhouse during the club's glory days, said Benny often dropped in there when he was working in New York, to sit in with the cats who were jamming. Others in his band sat in, too. Jamming was more important in Benny's life, I guess, than making payroll.

I remember the summer of 1951 quite well: one sultry day after another in the Big Apple. I was making plans to move permanently to New York, a city of hope where I felt confident I would realize my dreams. The streets were crowded with cars, the blaring of random horns underscored by epithets from hot, irritated drivers. One heard myriad unintelligible conversations, human voices buzzing like invisible, hungry locusts. The city's tall buildings were sentinels, silently protecting nothing in particular. It seemed to me as if everything that could possibly happen was happening in New York, squeezed into the amplitude of a day. Was that true, or was my perception distorted from years of anticipating my move to The City? It didn't matter. I was in New York.

I met Gigi Gryce on such a day in the summer of 1951. Gigi was a nervous person who evinced a conspicuous quirk. He constantly cleared his throat for no apparent reason. When he did so, he expressed an indefinable, high-pitched sound. Several months earlier he had suffered a nervous breakdown. Now he appeared emotionally fragile. Yet, for all the strange things I saw in Gigi, I came to see his genius, too. He was quiet, not self-aggrandizing, making his talents easy to overlook. Despite his shyness, he was extremely vocal about other people's talents. He championed his peers, just as Clifford Brown and John Coltrane did. Gig had numerous accomplishments, but to learn about them one had to probe and cajole, and rummage through his past. He found it painful to disclose the symphonies he had written that were never performed.

Gigi supported and encouraged all of us, both musically and personally. By 1953 he and I had become inseparable friends and business partners. We had two publishing companies. When Bobbie and I got married in 1958, Gigi was my best man. He was also there when Brielle, our daughter, was born. Over time, we recorded together often. Art Farmer played with us on many of those sessions.

One of our sessions comes vividly to mind. Jimmy Cleveland, trombonist, hired us to play on an album he was recording for EmArcy, a subsidiary of Mercury Records. Gigi and Art were there, Hank Jones was playing the piano, Osie Johnson was on drums, and Milt Hinton played bass. A difficult section required Jimmy and Milt to play in unison. Milt nailed the bass line like it was child's play, but Jimmy had problems. He made several attempts but kept making mistakes, becoming more embarrassed with each take. Finally, even though no one had said a word, he took the horn from his mouth in exasperation, exclaiming: "Don't a living ass say a word!" We couldn't contain ourselves any longer. Everyone, including Jimmy, laughed hysterically. That broke the tension. He then blew through the take effortlessly.

Around the same time, in 1951, I first met Horace Ward Martin Tavares Silver (his full formal name). From the first, I sensed Horace Silver had a great deal of energy. He was slight in build but had immense drive. After a set, he always came off stage drenched with perspiration. He gave audiences everything he had, and they loved him for it.

Horace had a unique way of playing the piano. He began his career as a tenor saxophonist in Hartford, Connecticut. Perhaps his saxophone training influenced his piano playing. His left hand romped like a drummer leading a charge. In all the groups Horace led, his style told you it was *his* band. He controlled the group's sound from the piano. He imparted an identity and character that could only be his. This ability is important. Stylistic differentiation prevents blandness. The essence of jazz is individual personality, along with group energy and ensemble flair. A number of major jazz players (and labels) tapped into Horace's talent, including Miles Davis. He played on Lee Morgan's first date with Blue Note, when Lee became the first to record "I Remember Clifford." Horace was a joy to watch during that session. He made me feel like dancing—and I can't dance a lick. That tells you how infectious Horace Silver's playing is.

Perhaps most compelling is his uncanny ability to create memorable tunes. Horace is a master tunesmith. I suspect he could have retired nicely living on his ample royalties, but Horace was too creative to rest on his laurels. He moved to Los Angeles during the time I lived there. One day he called to tell me why he had left New York. He had been living in Manhattan's uptown Lenox Terrace, in a very nice area inhabited mostly by blacks. As he was about to embark on a long tour, he told the doorman of his building that he would be away for quite awhile and asked him to keep an eye on the place. No doubt Horace either tipped him handsomely or promised him a great tip on return.

The tour successfully completed, he came home directly to his apartment. Home feels like paradise after a grueling tour. He opened the door and found his apartment stripped bare: furniture, curtains, rugs, clothes, silverware, books, records, personal items, every last belonging, gone. Horace couldn't believe his eyes. Of course, when he inquired, no one knew a thing.

I wondered about the helpful doorman. Did Horace tip him ahead of the trip? Would the wipe-out have occurred if he hadn't asked that doorman for a favor? The event shattered Horace's affection for New York. He moved west and bought a beautiful home in Malibu. I think he was happy there. The last time we were together was in Hollywood in 2005, when Horace and I, along with Jon Hendricks, received President's Merit Awards for lifetime achievement at the Grammy Salute to Jazz. Horace's legs were giving him trouble. Sitting with us in the first row, Horace was helped to his feet by my friend Jim Merod. He was weak but visibly pleased. Horace's music can never be thwarted. The Horace Silver I have known was unstoppable.

CHAPTER 41

Peggy Lee and Diana Ross

I FOLLOWED PEGGY LEE from the beginning of her career. I first heard her sing with Benny Goodman's band, a tune called "Why Don't You Do Right?" She left Goodman and married a guitar player named Dave Barbour. They made a few recordings together, including the big hit "I Know a Little Bit about a Lot of Things." I never dreamed I would some day write music for Peggy Lee. In 1983, a producer at Capitol Records in Los Angeles called me to ask if I would consider arranging an album of music for Peggy. In the course of that project, I came to know her well. She was a perfectionist, kind, loving, and humble. People adored her.

Peggy Lee was one of the most professional people with whom I ever worked. I once asked her if I could have a photograph taken with her at home in Beverly Hills, for a brochure. She not only agreed; when my photographer and I arrived, she was ready, with her hair coiffed and her make-up on, dressed in stage attire—as if this were a performance at an elegant club or concert venue. I knew then that she was a professional of the highest caliber.

During the recording at Capitol, she refused to be overdubbed. Peggy insisted on making the album the old-fashioned way, alongside a live orchestra, in real time, no gimmicks. Her performing schedule did not permit us to complete the album in Los Angeles, so we completed it later in New York. By the time she arrived back in Los Angeles, the album was mixed, completed, and ready for release. However, when she heard it, she wasn't happy. "The orchestra is not loud enough," she said. "I can't hear Benny's music clearly." By then, I had written for many singers, but none had ever complained about the volume of the musical accompaniment. Often the musical score was treated almost as a throw-away. I frequently wondered why money was wasted paying musicians, and paying me to write music nobody would hear vividly. Peggy cut through all of this. The album was remixed the way *she* wanted to hear it. After that album, I wrote music for her New York and Las Vegas appearances. We developed a wonderful professional relationship and a warm and lasting friendship.

Peggy was an extremely talented lyricist. In 1993 we began collaborating on songs. During our early years, she threw lavish parties on New Year's Eve. It was at those parties that I got to know Johnny Mandel. Everyone who was "anyone" in Hollywood attended Peggy Lee's New Year's parties. Everything she did was fun and relaxed, as well as distinguished. Peggy had elegance and class, as an artist and as a person; the same cannot be said for everyone in Hollywood. When I wrote music for her Las Vegas and New York appearances, I would sometimes attend the openings to help make sure everything was in order for Peggy. She was in a class all her own.

In 1972, Motown Records made a film about Billie Holiday's life, called *Lady Sings the Blues*. The lead actress would need to both act convincingly and sing like Billie. Motown called upon one of its own: Diana Ross, who after many years with The Supremes had become a star in her own right, signaled by the change in the group's name to "Diana Ross and the Supremes." Diana's talent was extraordinary, though she needed grooming for the role of Billie. The part was a boon to both her and the label, a perfect confluence of marketing and artistic interests.

After the picture was completed, Michel Legrand was called in to write the score. Diana's musical director, Tex Briscoe, a trumpet player, was in charge of completing the arrangements for the songs she sang. He asked me to help with the writing. During the recording session at Paramount, Diana gave birth to her daughter (who later became a singer herself). Diana and I chatted and I found her to be congenial and down to earth. Though she was a superstar, she carried herself without an inflated sense of self-importance. She was delightful. I fell in love with all that she represented. In 1993 when she was preparing material for an album, I received a call from her producer, Ben Sidran, who was a recording star himself. He hired me to arrange one of the songs. Arriving at the studio, I discovered old friends waiting there: Roy Hargrove, whose playing she loved, on the trumpet; Barry Harris, on piano; and Ralph Moore, on tenor sax, whom Diana hired along with nine or ten others so she could dub her voice over my arrangement. While the band recorded, she listened in the engineer's booth. After each take, I joined her, to hear the results. After the third take, Diana paid me an unforgettable compliment. "Your music gives me chills, Benny," she said. She had sung music written and arranged by some of the greatest arrangers who ever lived. I was truly gratified. Who doesn't enjoy praise? Sometimes it makes us work even harder.

From an early age, I saw many things that made no sense to me. I came to see that women rarely got credit for what they did. Too many men seem to think women are not worthy of full respect, compensation, or recognition. My word "seem" here is itself unseemly. Clearly, many of my gender resolutely do not give their wives, mothers, sisters, or female friends and co-workers the respect or the financial, legal, emotional, and professional compensation they deserve. History attests to the repeated injuries and usurpations men have inflicted on women. In many places in the world, sexism is still official state policy. It is painful and demeaning, an absurd joke, that men and women essentially live in different worlds. This state of affairs accounts in part for the many comic and polemical portrayals of perennial "misunderstandings" between the sexes.

Sexism has prevailed in the world of music as well. Traditionally, women played piano, violin, cello, flute, perhaps the accordion. For a long time it was unthinkable for a woman to sit down behind a set of drums or to pick up a bass, trumpet, or saxophone. But women are not slow-witted creatures who cannot succeed on their own. Some comedians tell us that, in the end, women are superior. Finally, however, across the past three decades I have been gratified to see more women joining the jazz rank and file, adding depth and new ideas to the jazz heritage and helping to take the music forward.

I hope our musical culture arrives at the point where, in speaking of a woman's talent, we can say, "She's great," without reservation when it is deserved, and without a deprecatory wink between men. If a musician is great, she's great. Period. I have traveled all over the world and heard women excel on every imaginable instrument. Their numbers are growing. It's wonderful, the late arrival of justice, even if unfinished.

Look at the amazing women now on the jazz scene: Maria Schneider, composer, arranger, big band director, and Grammy Award winner;

Esperanza Spalding, bass player, Grammy winner; Diana Krall, pianist and vocalist; Anat Cohen, clarinetist and tenor saxophonist; Terri Lyne Carrington, drummer; Geri Allen and Renee Rosnes, pianists; Mary Fettig, alto saxophonist; Mimi Fox, guitarist; Carla Bley, band leader and pianist; Anne Patterson, saxophonist and big band leader; Lori Bell, Ali Ryerson, and Elise Wood Hicks, flutists; Regina Carter and Yvette Devereaux, violinists. The tradition of great female vocalists continues: Dianne Reeves, Mary Stallings, Jackie Ryan, Claudia Villela, Sara Gazarek, Maucha Adnet, and Amy London. A very special pianist, Jimmy Rowles, spiritual and artistic companion to Ben Webster, Coleman Hawkins, Lester Young, and Charlie Parker—who recorded Billie Holiday's final albums with Sweets Edison for Verve—raised a daughter, Stacy, who became a highly respected trumpeter. Tragically, like Clifford Brown, Stacy recently met a premature end in a late-night automobile accident.

This list is partial at best. It points to women's artistic powers in a world needing their genius, dedication, creativity, and brilliance.

CHAPTER 42

Milt "Bags" Jackson, Larry Young, Joe Farrell, and Tony Williams

RED NORVO AND LIONEL HAMPTON brought the vibraphone into prominence before the Second World War. They both began their careers playing the xylophone. With its hard wooden keys, the xylophone was little more than a novelty musical instrument. Unlike a piano, its notes could not be sustained, so it was used mainly to add splashes of sound and excitement to an ensemble. To achieve a semblance of sustaining notes on the xylophone, a player must roll the notes the way a drummer rolls a snare. That technique was also necessary on the marimba. As time went by, a new instrument was invented, reminiscent of the xylophone but with metal keys and a sustain pedal: the vibraphone. The pedal allowed notes to be sustained without percussive rolling. A small motor permitted a player to add vibrato. Norvo and Hampton switched to the new instrument. For a few years they became known as the two most accomplished players on what later came to be called "the vibes."

Milt Jackson told me that he was launching his career as a singer in Detroit, when he heard the vibes for the first time and was seduced by their sound. He soon perfected playing the instrument. Before long he gained recognition. Milt's style was completely different from Red's and Hamp's. Milt was hipper, and since he had absolute pitch, he heard every nuance, interval, and off-key dissonance. Dizzy Gillespie always told his guys to slow the tempo and "find out where your band mates are." "Bags"—as Milt soon became known—laughingly insisted that the blues in D-flat, at any tempo, accomplish the same thing. Benny Goodman thought so, too. I marvel, laughing, at the Socratic manner in which these two, through different routes, reached the same musical wisdom.

But Bags was not satisfied with the way the vibraphone was designed. He wanted a more vocal quality. Bags felt the action of the vibes was too fast and too mechanical. He aimed for a slower, soulful sound. Somehow, he figured a way to relax the motor and control his vibrato speed. Thus, he created a sound of his own.

I first heard Bags with Dizzy's big band at the Apollo in the late 1940s. His vibes, at that time, were still metallic and thin, but his passion for the instrument made up for the inadequate sound. He soon replaced that instrument with others of higher quality. Years later, I told him that his vibes on that evening with Diz's band sounded like they were falling apart. Bags said, "They were."

Other vibes players emerged, but Bags had a unique style. You might say that Bags's vibe was the sound of the vibes (you dig?). When he played, he made you believe he was meant to do nothing else in life. Why else would John Lewis ask him to join The Modern Jazz Quartet when it formed in the 1950s? Bags's vibes became central to their sound, along with John Lewis's clever, sometimes awe-inspiring arrangements. The Quartet played music the way Picasso filled canvases with startling images and engaging colors.

I first recorded with Bags in 1957. Art Farmer played with me on that session. Remarkably, during the summer of 1997, Mike Hennessey, a journalist and promoter, arranged a concert allowing us to revisit that event. Mike chose Kiel, Germany, for the concert. Along with Art and me, he recruited Bags, Max Roach, Niels-Henning Ørsted-Pedersen, Kenny Kirkland, and Toots Thielemans. Bags's playing that night was so beautiful I didn't want him to stop. Art and Bags played "Thinking of You," a gorgeous rendering on which I played background harmony. Their playing surged through my body. I fell in love that evening with the song, and with the astounding intimacy of their playing. Soon after that event, I began playing that bewitching song with my own quartet. Talking with Bags, no one would know how great a master he was. Like John Coltrane and Clifford Brown, Milt Jackson was a musician for the ages.

Certain circumstances carry a lingering impact. In my life, three events stand out with exceptional vividness. One was playing with Larry Young.

Larry was an immensely gifted jazz organist who grew up in Newark, New Jersey. He had recorded a couple of albums that impressed me. In 1957 I got a call from an organist, whose name I no longer remember. He wanted me to play with his organ trio every Wednesday at Club 85 in Newark. That job lasted quite a while, although I did not make every gig. Joe Farrell substituted for me whenever I couldn't come. One night, the leader asked if I minded if another organist sat in. I felt it was considerate of him to ask me, but since he was the leader, it was his decision. At the beginning of the next set, the leader announced the new organist, Larry Young. I didn't recognize him. But as the set unfolded, I got to know him very well. Larry was extremely hip. Playing with him was a joy. I was stoked. Larry Young was a monster organist.

We talked on the phone several times after that night, but we never played together again. I would have loved to record with him; sadly, he died before it could happen. I have never heard anyone play the organ like him, before or since. There are many very good jazz organists, but none like Larry Young. We lost a fantastically and uniquely musical person far too early. He had a great career ahead that would surely have increased our collective joy.

The second event was meeting saxophonist Joe Farrell in 1957. Joe and I became good friends. When he couldn't make a gig, I subbed for him, and he in turn covered me. Bobbie and I got to know his family. After we moved to Los Angeles, we saw Joe whenever he came to town. Years later, in 1986, I heard that Joe was hospitalized in Los Angeles in poor health. I went to see him. Leaving his room as I arrived were Airto Moreira, the Brazilian percussionist, and his wife, the jazz fusion singer Flora Purim. I didn't know them then. We exchanged greetings. Joe's appearance shocked me. He looked so helpless. His voice, a shadow of what it had been, broke my heart. The man was very sick. As we talked, he mentioned two of my tunes: "Stablemates" and "Along Came Betty." He told me that he had always had trouble with "Betty" but—he added proudly—he could "play the snot out of" "Stablemates." That touched me very much because, as he told me, tears rolled down his cheeks as if he knew he would never play these tunes again. My eyes were wet as well, because I knew he was right. A few weeks later, Joe was gone, leaving me with wonderful memories.

The third event was playing with Tony Williams. Throughout 1957 I played as a tenor for hire with rhythm sections in a variety of cities. In Boston, I played Connolly's with a trio that with my inclusion became a quartet. The drummer, named Floyd, was the leader. We played well that week, and the crowds were good, too. Friday night the place was full and the audience enthusiastic. Friday night is almost always the best night—the end of the workweek, often payday. After the first set, Floyd told me that a fellow he knew had brought along his twelve-year-old son, who played drums. He hoped the kid could sit in. "Are you kidding?" I asked. Friday night was important, the culmination of our week. Letting people "sit in" just about always disrupts the mood and the groove, but especially when the guest is a total amateur—in this case, a *twelve-year-old kid*. Floyd pressed me. "This kid plays pretty good. I've heard him." I thought, "Aw, man, why me?" I agreed he could play one tune, if Floyd promised to come back immediately after that. I told him we didn't want to lose the group's vibe.

Intermission over, I dreaded going back on stage. Floyd grabbed the mic and, with great fanfare, introduced the new drummer, Tony Williams. The name meant nothing to me. I was perplexed. Why the big deal here? I asked Tony what he wanted to play. He said, "Anything." What tempo? I asked. Again, "Anything." Well, I thought, we'll soon see. I kicked off a medium-tempo tune and got the shock of my life. This young cat Tony had all sorts of things going on behind me. The high-hat cymbal was chomping away, 1–2–3–4, an attack I had never heard before. His ride cymbal beat was fantastic; meanwhile, he created excitement on the snare drum with his right hand. The whole thing was *together*, with pockets of crazy accents popping up all over. The kid was twelve! The darnedest thing I ever heard from such a young drummer. After we finished the tune, Floyd headed back to the bandstand, as we had agreed. Now I was embarrassed. I didn't want him back so soon; I was knocked out by this young fellow. I waved Floyd off and asked Tony to play another one. And then another, and another. Not long after, of course, the seventeen-year-old Tony Williams joined Miles Davis. The rest is history. One night in Amsterdam thirty years later, in 1987, when Miles's quintet and my quartet played the same venue, I asked Tony if he remembered that night in Boston. He did.

CHAPTER 43

Wynton Kelly and Chick Corea

I BECAME AWARE of Wynton Kelly when he played piano with Dinah Washington during the early 1950s. He always set her up magnificently. His timing was flawless. I saw him as a great accompanist, a sideman, but I had never heard him "stretch out" in a trio or small ensemble. When I finally heard him playing straight up jazz on a recording, I was delighted and surprised. He played with the same sensitivity I heard with Dinah. Eventually, Wynton and I played gigs together. Working with him was like having him plugged directly into my mind. Comping behind me, he inspired me to want to play to my utmost.

When Wynton joined Miles Davis, the quintet also included John Coltrane, Paul Chambers, and Jimmy Cobb. They sounded so strong and so right that, when I prepared an album for Mercury Records, I asked Miles's permission to use his trio and he agreed. The album was titled *Turning Point*. I arrived at this title because I felt my life changing in important ways. My viewpoint was maturing, and I was beginning (or at least *trying*) to hear added nuances in my music. That great trio helped me to express my ideas and brought enormous simpatico to my album. When we finished, Miles asked jokingly if he would receive a commission.

Wynton seemed to hear everything. His ear was uncanny and precise. Musicians sometimes say another player has "big ears." Ironically, Wynton Kelly had only one good ear; he was deaf in the other. If I approached him on his deaf side, he quickly turned so his good ear faced me. That move was almost humorous. We laughed frequently when he swirled abruptly toward a voice, but so did he. He was a realist. However, I do not remember his deficiency ever hindering him from creating amazing music.

Wynton joined Dizzy Gillespie's band in 1957, while I was playing with them. The music he crafted in that context was different from what he played with Dinah or in small groups with me. He adapted his style perfectly to fit the complex setting of Dizzy's big band. Wynton always knew what to do in every circumstance. I loved his playing enormously. I hear vestiges of Wynton Kelly's magic in other pianists today, those who are established as well as musicians emerging on the scene.

One day, years after I arrived in Manhattan, I got a call from a drummer who, although he was not very talented, ploughed forward and managed to snag quite a few gigs. He was a lovely guy. Could I work with him on the upcoming weekend? The money was decent—barely. The gig was in Canarsie. As I recalled vaguely, Canarsie was out "in the sticks," at the end of some subway line. I had never met anyone from Canarsie. I accepted, wishing the job were already over. I needed the bread.

Despite my unhappiness about this silly gig in East Bumchuck Nowhere, I knew that a professional can play under any circumstance. Charlie Parker and, later, John Coltrane often played with inferior musicians. Bird insisted, "Everyone has something to say." He was right. Sometimes that "something" shows itself clearly, other times not. I asked my drummer pal cum nemesis who else would join us on the gig in the Lost Outback. He named a new guy, Chick Corea, who lately had been freelancing around the city. That news delighted me. I had heard of Chick Corea. I no longer remember who else played that night (strategic forgetting, perhaps), but it turned out Canarsie was indeed the end of the subway line. It felt like the outer edge of civilization.

I arrived, leery. Chick arrived a bit later. We had never played together, so we cobbled together a few tunes we both knew. Slogging forward, however, we realized something was amiss. We were not told the neighborhood was German—and patriotic. Our playing was tolerated, but we became aware of comments of a nationalistic flavor directed our way. Finally, the denouement: the owner of the club asked us to play the German national anthem. Chick and I looked at each other, startled. Our neophyte leader pleaded urgently with us to comply. I asked Chick if he knew it, because I surely did not. Amazingly, I foggily recalled a few bits, and Chick, some-how, recalled a few other bits. I cannot imagine now why either of us knew even part of the German national anthem, but indeed, each of us knew half. Hard-chiseled faces stared at us; we could see the crowd would take no prisoners. The crowd waved beer steins unsteadily but emphatically, shouting gutturals which we could not understand but intuited. The air was heavy, almost menacing. These patriotic burghers aimed to end their evening singing their nostalgic hearts out.

It was do or die. I would not wish such torment on my least favorite colleague. We were playing for the firing squad. Of course, they saw I was black. How could they reasonably expect a black guy, without notice, to play the German national anthem? Reason was not their strong point; they had been drinking fine Pilsners and draft ales for hours. I had never been to Germany (although years later, Germany became my other home). I knew the words "bratwurst" and "sauerkraut." If we displeased them, would they beat us up in the trenches of Canarsie? Was there no exit at the end of the subway line? We were implored to switch from jazz to heroic nationalism. Today I chuckle manically, remembering that evening; sometimes a guy trying to earn a few bucks has his rear in the wrong place. I reached for inspiration from a jazz-derived Hippocratic Oath, as Bird and Diz had showed us. Do not disrespect your band mates. Do not let down your aver-age, raging weekend mob.

The crowd screamed itself hoarse. Bleary-eyed, semi-drunk faces began to appear bloodthirsty. What had Chick and I stumbled into?

I had no idea how to begin. Bless Chick Corea; somehow, he began playing that tune which once so dreadfully enchanted a different militia. Chick played a few bars, then faltered, arriving at the limits of his recollec-tion. Fortuitously, we came to the part I knew, and I picked up the melody as if I had played it many times. Somehow, together, we worked out the entire German national anthem. We milked it as if our lives were at stake; maybe they were.

When we finished, the delirious crowd cheered. Who'd've thunk? We were heroes now; we had conquered foreign territory, like Peter Sellers's rag tag conquerors in *The Mouse That Roared*, invading Manhattan. Drunk or sober, the crowd loved us. We achieved success. We were finally "in" with this crowd, just as the time came to depart. A bevy of nostalgic German roughs escorted us safely to the subway, where we caught the last train from

Canarsie, finally free of worry that European S.S. agents might detain us to discuss problems regarding a beloved song slaughtered in their pub.

That unforgettable evening in New Jersey, Chick and I arrived at the fork in the road that Yogi Berra often talked about. Yogi was right: when you come to an unexpected quandary, take on the challenge. We did. Saved by teamwork, Chick Corea's and Benny Golson's jazz pincer unit escaped under siege, to uproarious effect.

CHAPTER 44

Miles Davis and Geoffrey Keezer

MILES DAVIS was an intriguing, almost always significant figure, on my horizon. He influenced all of us young jazz players starting in the late 1940s until he left the scene. But the Miles I knew deviates from standard accounts of his legendary complexity.

When John Coltrane and I aspired to become sax players in Philly, we were together almost every single day. Constantly searching for new sounds and ideas, one day I bought, for a quarter, a used seventy-eight-rpm Charlie Parker disc that I had never heard. When I spun it on the turntable at home, I received a huge surprise. I had heard many great trumpet players: Charlie Shavers, Roy Eldridge, Dizzy Gillespie, Buck Clayton, and Pops. The guy on this album was unique. I memorized his solo on "Now's the Time."

It was, of course, the one and only Miles. I shared the disc with John, who also marveled. Who was this guy? Where did he come from? Miles began receiving more attention, and we heard his style evolve. Dizzy told me years later that Miles dogged his apartment on Seventh Avenue in Harlem. Miles came by so often that he irritated Lorraine, Dizzy's wife. Miles was nothing if not an opportunist and he knew that Diz was the one player who could teach him what he needed to learn.

Years later, Gigi Gryce and I played a week's gig in Chicago. Miles was living there, probably because it was close to where he grew up, near St. Louis. I had come to know Miles slightly. He came to hear us and asked if he could sit in. I told him I would ask, but that the club owner was strange. As I expected, the owner said, "I'm paying you guys to play, not somebody else." But, I explained, this was not just "anyone," this was Miles Davis. That meant zero to him. "I don't give a damn who he is," the owner shot back; "I'm paying you guys, not some stranger off the street." I let Miles know the bad news. Later, after a rhythm-and-blues gig Blue Mitchell and I played in Detroit, I had to disappoint Miles once again. He came in to hear Blue, I think, and when the evening was over Miles asked if he could snag a ride to the other end of town, where he was staying. The group leader was our driver. When I asked him to give Miles a lift, he refused. "Tell that guy to walk. I'm not a taxi." For Miles, such rejections became unforgettable sources of disappointment.

Miles was not at heart a nasty guy. He was sensitive. He had grown up in an upper middle class family and enjoyed financial advantages John Coltrane and I never had. Unprepared for unaccustomed slights, he developed private emotional callouses. He crafted a variety of retaliatory maneuvers to preserve his self-regard.

In those early days, Miles's voice was high-pitched, soft and innocent like a young boy's. Over time his vocal sound grew rough and raspy. His personality, too, became gruff, often insulting, a transformation that doubtless paralleled the difficulties he suffered. Being Miles Davis was not easy, I am certain. His talent and ambition were evident. He looked carefully at his options, but he made moves that others might not have risked. Before Miles formed a working group for extended tours, he recorded a number of albums for Blue Note and Prestige. He was paid very little by Bob Weinstock at Prestige, but those albums established his alluring reputation. Before his leadership credentials were fully vetted, he shuffled from one ensemble to another. Pegged as a low-wage sideman, he recorded with great musicians, including Thelonious Monk, Lucky Thompson, Sonny Rollins, J. J. Johnson, and Bags. His professional limbo ended in 1949 when he released *Birth of the Cool* for Capitol Records, with Gerry Mulligan and Lee Konitz. That publication made a significant mark. *Birth of the Cool* featured great arranging and exotic songs such as "Boplicity" and "Israel." Its beguiling sound harkened back to Claude Thornhill, projecting a sense of skating fluidity. However, his nonet was not a working group that could travel and create a lasting legacy. The group was featured briefly at the Royal Roost in Manhattan and made a brief foray in France, and that was pretty much it.

When Miles finally assembled his own quintet, Hank Mobley played the tenor sax. Hank's career was gaining stature as his Blue Note albums gained critical acclaim. When Hank left, Miles needed a replacement. Philly Joe Jones, their drummer, recommended John Coltrane. Before their first recording, Miles asked John to identify another song they might record for the session. And that is how "Stablemates" found its way onto their initial album, helping my career immensely.

Miles often asked me what I was smoking when I wrote "Stablemates." He enjoyed teasing me about the odd structure of that song. Years later, I was asked by a Korean promotional group to organize a tribute to Miles. Their budget allocated $35,000 for each night's performance. I could hire a strong trumpeter to play the role of Miles himself. But why fall short? I called Miles, thinking he would want this gig himself. He behaved peculiarly during the call, never replying directly to my invitation. He joked the way he always did about "Stablemates"; several times, he pleaded brusquely, "I gotta go now." I was perplexed. We knew each other well, but the call ended with neither a firm "no" nor a vague "maybe," though I was offering him a large sum of money for a small amount of work. I realized that, for whatever reason he didn't want the gig, he had chosen not to insult me, as he so often did people he didn't like.

Not long after that confusing phone call, I had a chat with an agent who was booking Miles in Europe for several events. I learned that Miles's fee for an evening was not $35,000, but $95,000. I called Miles and confessed that although I knew he was doing very well, I had had no idea just *how* well. Miles saved me from embarrassment in that strange conversation.

I must admit, in all our years, Miles never once insulted me. Because his initials were M.D., I called him Doctor Davis, which made him laugh. In school, he had been called "Little Doc Davis" because his father was a dentist, though I did not know this until recently.

One night at Birdland, where I was working with Diz, Miles came up after a set and dropped a compliment on me that still means a great deal. "You left nothing for me to play," he said. Maybe that praise has stayed with me for so long because John Coltrane was also playing with us that night. He told me that, if I drank, he would buy me a drink for what I had just laid down. Such words from Miles Davis and John Coltrane, holy moly! It's all downhill after that.

Once my group and Miles's appeared during the same week in San Francisco. We both stayed at a hotel down the street from the famous

Blackhawk Club on Broadway, where he was playing. After finishing our gigs one night, we hung out together in his hotel room. His former pianist, Red Garland, had been a boxer who, surprisingly, fought a round or two with the legendary Sugar Ray Robinson. There is no doubt in my mind that Miles Davis would have loved to be a championship boxer. That night, he bent my ear for hours, talking excitedly about this boxing technique and that boxing tactic. Playfully, he used my body to exemplify his points. (I was younger then, and better suited for a live punching bag.) That night I took a few swats that stung. Friendship sometimes needs limits.

When I was in college at Howard University, I remember a freshman who looked just like Miles. He carried a trumpet case under his arm. It was unsettling. One day I went up to this fellow and asked him if anyone had ever told him he looked just like Miles Davis. "He's my brother," he shot back. I had just met Vernon Davis, Miles's younger sibling.

Miles's style at every point in his career was without imitation or derivation. He did not remotely approach the facility of Dizzy or Freddie Hubbard. His art was personal and distinctive. He went deep into the music, into unexplored shades and colors. Miles Davis's playing touched people's hearts and souls. No one else ever approximated his depth of feeling or the mysterious quality that he perfected over time. You heard the private, sensitive man in such playing. He was dubbed The Prince of Darkness, but I think his difficult behavior was prompted by an urge to ward off uncertainty, and to prevent and avenge insults. I suspect he wanted to prove what he had always known about himself: that he carried a special musical authority, a delicately lyric, artistic nature that deserved complete respect.

I also believe that on occasion Miles behaved perversely just to amuse himself. He was not, as I knew him, a bad man or an evil person. Miles was complicated, but his relationship to music was not complicated. Musically, he was always defiantly himself. Unlike most musicians, Miles congenitally refused to hide a flubbed note. If he hit a sound wrong, he was as likely to emphasize it as to seek resolution. He could sustain a skewed or distorted note until, by sheer duration or following some abstract logic, the error resolved itself—as if stubborn insistence upon anything that opposed a listener's expectation had the power to create new beauty or other worlds.

Another special musician I have worked with is the pianist Geoffrey Keezer. I first met Geoffrey when he was a nineteen-year-old kid from Eau Claire, Wisconsin. Many things about Geoff were noteworthy. In fact,

Keezer is the only contemporary pianist whose genius approaches that of Art Tatum. At nineteen he already possessed a tremendous repertoire that included not only tunes of the current era but also many reaching far into the past. How could a pianist so young command these relics with such authority? How had he even learned of them? When Geoff played with The Jazz Messengers, Art Blakey acknowledged his talent by giving this remarkable young man his own featured spot in the trio and, equally unusual, allowing him to call tunes. Art had a longstanding reputation for nurturing young players, but he went further with Geoff than with most. The decision was wise.

James Williams, an extraordinary pianist in his own right, brought Geoff's powerful talent to light. He touted Geoff to everyone who would listen. Fortunately, Art believed the rave reports. I saw Geoffrey before I heard him play. I would never have guessed he was a vastly talented jazz pianist; he looked like a student from an expensive prep school. He was shy, but he obviously greatly respected musicians from the era preceding his.

On the bandstand, Geoff Keezer explodes into life. I enjoyed every night I played with him. He rarely did anything the same way twice unless an arrangement dictated. I have played with hundreds of pianists and heard all of the great ones. Geoff Keezer was constantly awe-inspiring. Musically, he has a bottomless well of ideas and an astonishing range and daring of conceptual brilliance.

After Art Blakey died, Geoff's career accelerated at a fast pace. I hired him a couple of times to play with my quartet in New York, and also engaged him on one of our European tours. I offered minor suggestions about his playing, and always when I next heard him, he would have far surpassed my expectations. He was a musical phenomenon. I hired him for a week at the now defunct Connolly's jazz club in New York. That entire gig was a revelation. I heard things from Geoff that I had previously heard only from Art Tatum. I was astounded. In 1996 I engaged him on an album featuring songs associated with legendary tenor saxophonists. That album, *Tenor Legacy*, included Branford Marsalis, James Carter, and Harold Ashby. Geoff was absolutely brilliant. Later that year, he joined me on a European tour conceived by Mike Hennessey, a pianist and former journalist (and executive) with Billboard magazine. Mike's wife, promoter Gaby Kleinschmidt, was also instrumental in arranging that tour, called "40 Years of Benny Golson's Music: Whisper Not." The line-up included musicians who had been involved in my career, some dating back to the beginning and some newcomers: Jon Hendricks, Art Farmer, Brian Lynch, Curtis Fuller, Geoff Keezer, Dwayne Burno, and Joe Farnsworth.

On that tour I found myself overcome by young Keezer's phenomenal playing. He frequently converted things I had written out note-for-note into sounds, phrases, and melodic explorations that I had never imagined. When he embellished chords, or changed them completely, Dwayne Burno, a young bassist with an incredible ear, was always right there with him. Their pairing was consistently breathtaking, like sun surging through billowing white clouds. Although "genius" is a word to be used sparingly, it describes Geoff Keezer's pianistic majesty. I'll never forget hearing him play one song with his right hand and another with his left. Independent of the other, each song was perfect. I confidently contend that this still youthful pianist is sneaking into Art Tatum's territory. Geoff's imaginative prowess and technical ability have inspired my own playing and writing.

I have encouraged Geoff many times to stretch as far as his talent will permit. He hears things instantaneously and is impossibly alert. Strange new songs pose no problems for him. Whatever he hears, he can play. Some of his ideas may seem aberrational initially, but Art Tatum's playing blazed a similar trail. Creativity and artistry are not subject to approval by an Aesthetic Adjudication Council. New things do not always please the ear at first. Consider the early scorn directed at Thelonious Monk, Dizzy Gillespie, and John Coltrane. Perception changes, and acceptance matures. Innovation creates the conditions of its own reception. Also, new offerings become more polished and more explicable as they develop a framework for listeners' expectations. This is what happened to John Coltrane in his last decade. When John first joined Miles Davis, many listeners heaped disdain on him. "Miles is great, but who is that tenor player?" I heard many false prophets pontificate at John's expense. I am reminded, in another genre, of the story-telling genius of Steven Spielberg. His talents would still be a rumor had he followed a conventional cinematic course; instead he changed the history of film. Distinctive talents and new artistic visions likewise sustain the jazz heritage. Appreciation came finally to John Coltrane, Dizzy Gillespie, Art Tatum, Bud Powell, Bill Evans, and now Kenny Barron. I have loved playing with Geoff Keezer. Even he, I am sure, does not always know what he will bring to his next performance. I, for one, am delighted by the surprises he perpetually offers. I hope to have the privilege of playing with Geoffrey in the future as often as possible.

Golson's Funky Rule of Thumb is in play wherever I look. Artistic impediments lurk everywhere. Too many mentalities at work on a project—decision by committee—dumb it down. Surely you have noticed that multiple talents in a single person confuse the music-consuming public. A trumpet player cannot also be a serious composer, and, of course, a splendid pianist cannot also be a singer. The result of this homogenized production logic is that musicians are "branded" with a commercial identity. This evolved capitalist cultural wisdom ("Keep it simple, stupid") places a talented musician under the full manipulative control of handlers who concoct an "image" for their client. These "suits," as they are dubbed in the 'hood, want things done their way—or else.

Both Sarah Vaughan and Carmen MacRae were excellent piano players. As I've mentioned earlier, Sarah once came into a club where I was working in Los Angeles. When I asked her to sing a number, she chose "The Man I Love." My young pianist did not know the tune. So Sarah not only sang; she also accompanied herself beautifully—typical Sassy, and characteristic of her many talents. A few more examples: Jack DeJohnette plays both drums and piano. Terence Blanchard plays trumpet and piano (he told me he wished his trumpet playing reached the level of his piano chops). Freddie Hubbard played trumpet and piano. Kenny Garrett plays alto saxophone and piano. During a rehearsal in Germany, the piano player was late and I witnessed Kenny burning it up on the keyboards. Wynton Marsalis plays trumpet and also composes and arranges; I've heard him play drums well, too. Joe Chambers plays drums and piano and writes songs. Ron Carter plays bass and composes. A little known fact is that Kenny Barron plays bass with great proficiency in addition to his majestic piano playing. Nick Brignola played every double-reed instrument as well as all the single reeds. Who says a person should be recognized for one talent alone? It is redundant to assert that the world is crazy. Shakespeare's plays show how infinitely surprising are human inclinations and identities. We find a harsher type of craziness in the micro-managers of the art world, some of whom rival Iago or Lady Macbeth in their destructiveness. May our dreams and talents escape such madness.

CHAPTER 45

Mickey Rooney, Redd Foxx, Jersey Joe Walcott, and Muhammad Ali

WHAT A CHARACTER Mickey Rooney was, as bombastic in real life as on the screen. We had a rendezvous at his house in Beverly Hills one day. When I got there, no one was home. I decided to wait for a few minutes. Suddenly an automobile horn blared dramatically in the distance; I wondered if someone was being rushed to the hospital. But moments later the car swung into view, tires screeching. It was Mickey. He skidded abruptly to a stop and jumped out. He raced toward me, apologizing. That was Mickey Rooney. He came and went with flare. Mickey once invited me to dinner with him and his wife, Carol. He would cook something special, he announced. When I arrived, he invited me into the kitchen to watch him cook. I don't remember the name of the dish, but he was an artist in the kitchen. He placed a layer of Mexican tamales at the bottom of a pot, then a layer of vegetables followed by another layer of tamales, still more vegetables, and so on until the large dish was filled, ready for baking. I didn't know what to expect, but it tasted pretty good.

At the time I was writing for his Las Vegas act. We had a routine for writing songs. Mickey sat at the piano, doodling. He could mimic any instrument in the orchestra, a feat that entailed emitting various strange sounds while stomping his extremely loud heel unrelentingly on the wood floor. His method was crude, but he got his point across. Mickey was a talented man in many ways. Jerry Mayer, another fellow who was just getting started in show business at the time, putting together spoken routines, sometimes worked with us. Mayer went on to become a producer of many successful television comedy shows. He took me with him to Las Vegas to make sure everything was ready for Mickey's opening. We planned to collaborate on an independent project that never materialized. Now and then Jerry and I spoke on the phone, sometimes about Judy Garland. He and Judy worked together for years at MGM and were very close friends. Her loss caused him great pain. I know that many years later, Jerry still deeply lamented his dear friend's death.

And then there was Redd Foxx. If there ever were a person who could look the blues in the eye and make it buckle, it was Redd Foxx. We met in 1948 when we were both students at Howard University. Redd was as funny offstage as he was in performance. His brand of humor was different: street jive that hip people understood, because they saw and experienced the things he built his comedy on. He could give anything a funny twist. Redd just looked at the world comically. After I left college, I lost touch with Redd for several years. When I saw him next, we were featured on the same bill at the Apollo Theater in Harlem. I was performing there for the first time, playing in Bull Moose Jackson's band. Redd appeared as part of a comedy team that later became "Slappy White and Redd," and still later "Foxx and White."

We were completely surprised to see each other at the Apollo, a small reunion of sorts. We had both made progress toward realizing our hopes, but he confessed that his journey to the stage had not been easy. He had encountered many problems in New York, and sometimes slept on the street. Winter was the worst because he had no overcoat. He told me that he would slip his arms out of his sweater sleeves and fold them on his chest, like a dead man in a coffin, to conserve his body heat. When he ran from the police (usually for something petty), he told me, his method of self-defense was to streak full speed around a corner and glide like a hockey puck under the nearest car. He was so quick the police never found him and never figured out his routine. They must have thought he had supernatural powers.

Around the time I moved to Los Angeles in 1967, Redd did, too. By then, he had gained quite a bit of fame and was making plenty of money. He bought a club, which he named "Redd Foxx," and I went to see him one night. When I pulled up, he was standing out in front. He didn't know I was also in L.A. Surprised, he asked me with mock paranoia if I was following him. His club prominently displayed memorabilia he had purchased from the Apollo. What memories that evening brought back!

Soon after that, Redd's career shot forward, and he got his own NBC television show on NBC. *Sanford and Son* was an instant success. Redd brought to his performance the same delivery he had perfected on nightclub stages. A visionary executive at NBC saw the wisdom of tapping his talent. The move was shrewd for both sides.

Not long after, Redd bought a building and set himself up as an enterprise. When Redd became successful, he did not forget where he came from. He remained the same funny guy I always liked. He never talked down to me in any way. One sunny day, walking near Sunset and Vine in Hollywood, I heard someone yell from a car, "Benny Golson . . . hey!" It was ol' jailhouse Redd Foxx. Redd achieved many of his life's goals, though they took a long time. Unfortunately, he died in the midst of his greatest success. When I think of him, I hear his raspy voice and his goofy drugstore wisdom. I chuckle with quiet understanding.

My uncle Robert, back in Philadelphia, was getting on in years. One day on the phone he mentioned casually that Jersey Joe Walcott's son was a good friend of his. They were teammates in a checkers club. (In fact, Uncle Robert informed me that at that time, he was a champion, one of the foremost checkers competitors in Philly, news that floored me.) The great Jersey Joe Walcott, in my estimation, was an unsung boxing hero, although that appraisal was lost on many. Uncle Robert asked if I would like to meet Jersey Joe. Of course I would! The next day, we arranged a date for me to come down from New York. The great boxer's son would bring his dad, and we would meet at Uncle Robert's house.

The day arrived. Toting my video camera, I went to the checkers club, where my uncle was waiting. A car pulled up, carrying Jersey Joe Walcott, in the flesh! I started my camera rolling. Watching him haul himself out of his son's car, I saw that the years had been kind to him. He was still a tight bundle of muscles. I stood to greet him, as excited as a little kid meeting a department store Santa Claus. He smiled at me. I tried to hold my camera and hug the big guy at the same time. Despite his accumulated years, Joe Walcott still had the wily shuffle that boxers employ to stalk opponents. The moment was fantastic for me. I was touching history.

At Uncle Robert's house, I turned on my video camera and situated myself in front of my hero. I listened intently as he talked about his career. I fired him a question when I could. For forty-five minutes, I was living a dream, listening to and videotaping the one and only Jersey Joe. When the big man finally left, I watched one last time as he did that cagey boxer's shuffle back to the car. The visit was magnificent, but when I played back the tape, I found that I had gotten inadequate light balance. Jersey Joe was only a silhouette in the video. My heart sank. But at least I could hear him speaking to me on the voice track. I still treasure that tape. Jersey Joe Walcott was a great boxer, and, I learned that day, a sweet guy. The memory remains important to me.

Later, in the mid-1980s, I had another encounter with an iconic boxer. Early one morning in Los Angeles I stood on a corner, giving *Watchtower* magazines to passing strollers. A custom-built car drove slowly by. Its uniqueness clamored for scrutiny. Muhammad Ali was at the wheel. Hard to believe, but it was him. I lost all restraint and shouted, "Hi, Champ!" He smiled and waved, and drove on in the stream of traffic. My eyes followed him down Wilshire Boulevard. Two blocks down, he made a "U" turn and headed back. When he was directly across the street, he made another "U" and pulled to the curb where I stood. The window came down. The Champ beckoned me over. The door opened. "Get in," he told me. I did. He wanted to know why I was on the corner handing out "those magazines." Aware that he was Muslim, I explained the views of Jehovah's Witnesses. After five minutes or so, Ali thanked me. I got out of the car, and right before saying goodbye he politely asked me my name. "Maybe we'll get together sometime," he concluded. I thought he meant he would probably come that way again and we might talk again. I thought no more about it.

Not long after that, a friend of my son Reggie, named Porter, called me. He was a very close friend of Muhammad Ali. Surprisingly, we all lived within a few blocks of one another. Porter told me he spent a lot of time at Ali's house. Ali had reported our meeting on Wilshire, and mentioned me by name. Porter explained that he was a friend of my family, as well, and that we lived only four blocks apart. Ali told him to invite us over to his place.

Porter picked me up and we went together. The butler let us in, and, sure enough, everyone knew Porter. We were escorted to a sitting room, where Ali soon entered. What a massive man he was. I had seen him face to face when we sat in his car, but had not taken in his full size. "I told you we might get together again," he joked. We all went down to his basement. There I discovered the *real* Muhammad Ali. He was an amateur magician, and he insisted on performing tricks for me. Boxing never came up the entire time I was there, nor did religion. Muhammad Ali was relaxed, at home, and delighted in his hobby as a magician. He did trick after trick. At one point he walked past me and I heard a kind of flick near my right ear. When I looked, he wasn't there. I know what he did, but I don't know how he did it. Ali was childlike, almost giggling. Half an hour later, a photographer from Holland, who had come to shoot a series of photos with Ali, joined us. Greeting me earlier upstairs, Ali had forgotten about the photographer. He now introduced us and asked him to "get photos of Benny and me."

The fellow clicked away, catching me and Ali in all sorts of poses. I now very much wish I possessed one of those photos. Just one shot would do. The photographer said it was no problem. "Until you get them," Ali jumped in, "I'll give you one I already have." He handed me an eight-by-ten color photo, and signed it on the spot. That photo hangs in my recreation room in my Los Angeles home. But the promised photo of me and Ali never came, and I still regret that I don't have a memento of that wonderful afternoon. I am glad I met Ali, a playful kid who is also a giant of a man. I have his autographed photo to prove it. Although we planned to meet again, shortly afterward he divorced his wife and moved away. Meeting Muhammad Ali and seeing his magic show constitute a veritable coonskin on the wall of lasting memory.

PART VIII *Verses and a Coda*

Many musicians and fans worldwide admire Benny and
his music. Benny's great contributions to music, jazz
in particular, have generated increasing appreciation.
Benny Golson is a truly unique voice at the highest
level of achievement. My deep admiration and respect
for all he has done are echoed over the globe.

 —KENNY BURRELL

CHAPTER 46

Notes on Starting Over

N THE EARLY 1980s I began playing seriously once again, while I also continued to work in Hollywood movie studios. The road to regain my full jazz confidence was long and hard. Nearly eight years had passed since I played my horn in live performance on a regular basis. Returning was very strange. I had to relearn many skills I once took for granted, and much of the subliminal knowledge a professional jazz musician acquires. My good luck was immense. I had very, very good musicians supporting me as I tried to climb out of my hole. In retrospect, I almost cannot believe the collegial support I received. As I tried to reestablish myself over a period of several years, these musicians extraordinaire stood side by side with me to revive my aspiration to front a quartet: pianists Patrice Rushen, Bill Mays, Billy Childs, and Gildo Mahones; bassists Fred Tinsley (also a bassist with the Los Angeles Philharmonic), Louie Spears, and Bob Magnusson (a former French horn player with the San Diego Symphony Orchestra); and percussionists Roy McCurdy and Al "Tootie" Heath. Could any hopeful "advanced recruit" seeking reentry to the jazz world aggregate by sheer chance such an ensemble of brilliance and kindness? All of these remarkable people helped make real my reemergence as a jazz musician.

My quartet played in and around Los Angeles, a very large territory. We didn't try to make a big splash; I didn't know if I was ready for such a thing. Regaining my lost proficiency was difficult. I almost had to emulate, in middle age, the obsessive efforts of my dear boyhood pal John Coltrane. The uncertainty was agonizing. I gave the effort 100 percent and received 50 percent, or less, in return. *Benny Golson, saxophone player,* sometimes felt alien and out of reach. I sometimes wondered if my own horn had a vendetta against me. Had I jinxed myself in my heedless youth, with my blithe confidence? Had I ever really appreciated my art, or my horn, or my own great luck as a musician? I felt trapped. Creative doors that had once opened effortlessly within me now resisted, like doors in a fun house.

Intervening against frustration and the prospect of failure, as always, was my wife, Bobbie. She has given me everything a person could hope for from his eternal paramour. She was always able to help me put discouragements into perspective, or make disappointment lift. When my view was distorted, she focused me. I knew if I were to triumph, I would owe it to Bobbie's belief in me, and to the amazing goodwill and solidarity of the good-hearted musicians who propped me up. I escaped humiliation and artistic degradation because of those talented cats, their ferocity and their friendship. At times, I was my own adversary. Trust me: some of my performances in that period were terrible. Those fantastic musicians helped save my creative life with their encouragement. I don't know if they know that; I hope they do.

I sometimes imagine that the most horrible outcome of drug addiction for an artist must be its utter emptiness, its repetitive, stark dependency on temporary false highs. Innocence, desire, and aspiration are destroyed. At some point, the addict gives up. The void within leads to hopelessness, and to personal and imaginative decline. I have never used drugs, and yet a similar black and white choice once defined my future. Returning from the tyranny of creative loss was a musical resurrection for me.

If you have ever struggled to reinvent yourself against self-doubt or long odds, imagine the impact of someone whom you respect telling you that, regretfully, you don't sound the way you once did. You don't have it anymore. Even if such an opinion is well-intended, the feelings of inadequacy and failure that it generates swamp the insight. Anger, directed at oneself, is a temptation that solves nothing. Risking further loss and failure, regaining access to imagination's elusive power means investing huge amounts of time and painstaking effort to unlearn old routines and habits. Remaking fundamental neural patterns in the brain can be terrifying, requiring focus and will power, seeking traction in emotional quicksand. Artistic recalibration involves replotting the total immersion of consciousness and feeling. The brain creates "reality" for itself, reconstructing how one is as a person as well as an artist. This is not just brushing yourself off to head back into battle. Within a context of disorientation and radical uncertainty, an entire cosmos must be remade, within one's own head. Think about this carefully before you try it! Even at the relatively advanced state of scientific and neurological sophistication that we have achieved in the twenty-first century, scientists do not fully understand how all of this occurs in the brain. The "mind" in all its complexity evolves within the serpentine folds of the brain's redundant electrical networks, charged by billions of neurons.

Many people readily accept "change" in most human spheres—in fact, they are frequently disappointed when change does not occur—yet nonetheless demand that an artist never change his style of expression. A trumpeter no less than a painter is expected to settle into a recognizable mode of expressive exploration. Stylistic evolution is perceived as deviance. Picasso's manic figural manipulations over time make Miles Davis's multiple musical personas seem catatonic by comparison. Yet, the stodgy critic greets the agonized artist with dismay and unconscious hypocrisy. The critic has a day job. His financial stability depends on upholding middle-brow standards. An advocate of normalcy, he scolds, "You had a good thing going—now you junk it?" Meanwhile, he is decked out in the latest threads; the tumult of fashion is fine with him. He drives a late-model car; he does not perceive the irony. But do not violate the critic's expectations. You've not received such permission.

No musician of whom I am aware of overlooks the fact that entertainment is often the subtext of a work of art. But the world of jazz is a realm of delight that is simultaneously a place for artistic exploration. Dizzy Gillespie often noted that jazz is an endeavor of dedicated creative uncertainty, for which many players literally "gave their lives." Artists have the right—even sometimes the obligation—to revamp their creative approach. In my lifetime, jazz has embodied uplifting human ideals. Jazz continues to be a stimulus for racial understanding and cooperation, a force for reconciliation internationally. Jazz also carries forth the classical heritage, and expends adventurous energy on behalf of musical innovation. Think of Louis Armstrong in the 1920s, memorizing Caruso's licks on Puccini and extending them in ways no one had imagined. Consider how John Coltrane paid homage to Charlie Parker, while expounding a completely new interpretation of his music. No truly great player arrived at a pinnacle of this art without hard-won expressive renovations.

In a highly commercial, financially interdependent world where hope for cultural stability seems an aberration, a musician today is more alone entrepreneurially and imaginatively than ever before. Almost all artists, including jazz musicians, find themselves in increasingly precarious circumstances. And yet, the artist's role in society has not become less important. Comically, perhaps, I'll assert that a jazz musician is a soliloquist of sorts—but one who seeks a response. In moments of give and take, there are not two minds in play, only one. I have come to see that the purpose of art has always been to share a radically subjective understanding of everything that, objectively, binds us together. That is the source of all knowledge, or rather, of the inauguration of knowing. Although our species is ferociously territorial, this exchange of diverse ways of knowing offers a road forward.

My music is the outcome of blind groping, an incremental exploration of my life's inner mystery. What I feel in my musical search is nonnegotiable. I cannot please someone else unless I please myself. I am here to work toward my best possibilities. That's all I can do. Like all of us, I am here for only a short while. Hope and trust in the direction of my self-abandon sustain me.

I have now been back on the jazz scene for several decades, longer than most youngsters have been playing. I am still not satisfied, and I never will be. Recently, Kenny Barron told my friend Jim Merod that he believes he has not yet arrived at his peak. If that is true for Kenny, it is true for all creative people. If ever we achieved musical satisfaction, we would be finished. Nothing further creative could come forward. The secret of artistic striving resides in the profound nature of desire and longing. Spiritual hunger beckons the mind and the imagination toward private places we find irresistible, some of which have no name or definition. Longing is the exotic surplus of need—in truth, the secret of art's necessity and allure.

My various attempts at artistic self-reconstitution taxed both my wife's inner resources and my own. I realize that we have been blessed, more than most. I am proud of my successes, but I do not take them for granted. I do not believe I deserved my success more than others did. But if I had to do everything over, I would do nothing differently.

A related, technical point: I credit Freddie Hubbard and Miles Davis with teaching me that mistakes in a solo do not destroy it. I had always strived to create perfect solos. The effort was fruitless, because I'm not perfect. No one is. The notion of "perfection" is a very bad joke. Check out pianist Kenny Werner's deep observations here: often, even when the energies on a bandstand mesh nicely, nothing of deep interest takes place. This experience plagues even the greatest musicians. I recall The Jazztet at Birdland at some point in the early 1960s. We were playing Dizzy Gillespie's heavenly piece, "Con Alma." Oscar Peterson walked in just as I was preparing to take my solo. I thought something very much like this: "Okay, let's see what I can do with this amazing song." I proceeded to play a flawless, boring solo. I played like a cautious student in a high school spelling bee. I embarrassed myself. Aiming for perfection, I bombed. I should have trusted my feelings and the song's inherent glory. The reach for perfection is self-deluded and uptight. It culminates in nothing of consequence.

When Freddie played, mistakes often cropped up. That bothered me at first, but eventually I apprehended the overall "fabric" of his solos. Freddie was lethal on the trumpet, perhaps comparable in this only to Pops. No one else could touch his imaginative intensity. He played like his life was at stake, even in rehearsals; perhaps it *was*, although we never discussed this. Nothing was wasted even on a "walk through" with him. What he played was overwhelmingly creative. Mistakes meant absolutely nothing to him. Miles, similarly, told me once, "I'm famous for cracked notes." Miles was an elegant stylist who played wrong notes with such conviction they sounded perfect. Bird, Coltrane, Miles, and Freddie were daredevils of the highest magnitude—tightrope walkers without nets.

CHAPTER 47

The Blues

W HEN AUDIENCES are told the circumstances in which a particular song came to be written, or any details of its composition, I think that song takes on greater meaning and impact. Listeners feel closer to the song's creation. Such sharing lends intimacy to our brief time together in a club or jazz setting. On stage I sometimes share personal information about musicians past and present, on occasion even about those on the stage with me. I sincerely believe appreciation for our music is heightened when people can feel closer to the humanity of those performing.

Until the very last years of his life, Miles Davis made a practice of withholding information of any kind from his audiences. Apparently he felt silence increased his mysterious aura. Perhaps it did, though even Miles, near the end, began to share more with his adoring crowds, strolling the stage holding above his head placards with the names of his musicians. My feeling is that, even if one is not given to speaking to the audience, we owe it to them to at least let them know what they're hearing. That's not un-hip; it's minimum courtesy to the people who support our efforts. What musician achieves success without the support of fans and patrons? We owe them respect and appreciation. None of us are gods, though we should remember that to a young fan we may seem heroic. I remember the first time I saw Duke Ellington in the flesh, when I was a kid. Cootie Williams took me to a theater in Philly to meet him. It seemed to me obvious that this glorious man hailed from some mystical place and visited the world of humans only briefly. I was emotionally overcome. If Duke had said, tritely, "I need a band aid," or conveyed any personal information not found in album notes, to my ears it would have been sacred speech.

Jazz musicians make a point of being hip. We constantly try to inject new songs with our own musical personalities. That challenge is a big part of the jazz adventure. Playing jazz is an innocent exercise. We spend time learning techniques, chord structures, and key changes. The task is monumental, but most of us don't seem to mind. How many tunes do we commit to memory? Who knows? If we care to know a song, we learn it. Every musician's interior archive is different, and these internal treasure troves are an indelible part of what jazz is all about. The strongest musicians know by heart not only contemporary pieces, recent gems, and soon-to-be chestnuts, along with show songs and invincible jazz standards, but also obscure songs from decades back. How about "Like a Butterfly Caught in the Rain," a sweet, delicate song known by Tommy Flanagan, Jimmy Rowles, Merrill Hoover, and Ellis Larkins—and, quite possibly, by only them?

Many of us travel a great deal. Some of us speak several languages, and interact with people who speak many more that we do not understand. If you're a New Yorker, you might crave a Nathan's hot dog while you're away from home, or you might just miss the streets of New York City, their clatter and energy, their disarray and continuous turmoil. (To those unfamiliar with Manhattan and Brooklyn, that may seem odd, but it's true.) Likewise, jazz musicians carry old and new songs in our heads, Chopin études, passages from Debussy and Mahler, chord changes to every tune in Bird's classic library. The blues can sneak up on you out of nowhere, from deep artistic instincts. Walk the Ramblas in Barcelona and enjoy its colorful crazed cheer, or stroll Tokyo's crowds and smell her exotic scents, and you might still hear the blues dancing through your skull. The redeeming, aboriginal satisfaction of the blues beguiles the heart.

Not all jazz musicians feel this way, but I do. I hug the blues to my chest the way Whitman hugged the seashore. I'm talking about the *low-down dirty blues*, not some faux imitation with substitute chords obscuring the feeling. There comes a time when only the gospel-inflected, carnally tested blues can accomplish an old, down-home spiritual cure. To play the blues is to cure yourself by admitting what ails you. Songful complaint, intelligent mourning—telling it like it is. I'm speaking about the origin of blues more than a hundred years ago: the field hollers and the gut-wrenching, call-and-response of collective singing on Civil War–era cotton plantations and farms. The blues, with its three basic chords and a few authentic modifications, is thoroughly "American," the heroic source and origin of jazz. If a scholar or a hipster from outer space dropped in, demanding the keys to the jazz mother lode, you could invite your newly arrived guest directly to hear Tommy Flanagan's treatment of Billy Strayhorn's "The Meaning of the Blues." Or stop your eager visitor in his tracks with Ray Charles's "Georgia," alongside Hank Crawford and Jimmy McGriff playing "Lift Every Heart." If you want to lovingly bruise the ears of your new extraterrestrial pal, introduce him to Pops's "West End Blues," or maybe to his duets with Ella Fitzgerald on Gershwin's sublime scores from *Porgy and Bess*. When was the last time you listened to "Bess, You Is My Woman" or "I Loves You, Porgy"? And if the grease is not yet adequate, try the deepest essence of blues: Dizzy Gillespie's "After Hours," recorded for Verve in 1957 with Sonny Rollins, Sonny Stitt, and Ray Bryant. Or check out Johnny Hodges with Duke Ellington's Orchestra sliding across Rabbit's own song, "Jeep's Blues." Give a spin to Cannonball Adderley's seductive "Barefoot Sunday Blues." How about Horace Silver's "Cape Verdean Blues"? All else falling short, play Art Tatum's "Aunt Hagar's Blues." You dig?

No matter how sophisticated one's ears, sometimes one's heart yearns for the suffering and joy of the deepest roots of jazz. The blues are lyrical explorations that do not require the orthodox rigor of twelve bars. Their unrivaled emotional persuasion will never disappear from our wounded planet. As Charlie Parker insisted, in the slow drift of human history, if ever the healing balm of the blues were badly needed, "Now's the Time."

CHAPTER 48

Brielle

MY FIRST WIFE AND I had three children, all boys. I loved each of my boys—Odis, Reginald, and Robert—but I also wanted a girl. I always imagined a little girl of my own, growing up wearing frilly dresses and all the baubles girls wear that make them even cuter. Daddy's little girl: silly, maybe, but the thought always enticed me. Robert, the youngest of my boys, was eleven years old when I met Bobbie in 1958. We were married in 1959, and after we had enjoyed married life for a year and a half, she told me she thought she was pregnant. I was not disappointed, because even though I thought three kids were enough, I loved Bobbie so much, anything we shared would be magical. I would be happy to be the father of four boys. Bobbie, this child's mother, was the most amazing and beautiful wife in the world, and my best friend on earth.

Because I was not traveling extensively at the time, I was able to watch Bobbie's tummy grow larger and rounder by the week. There is something glorious about a pregnant woman who is your wife and whom you love with all your heart. Bobbie glowed; even her face looked different. I took pictures of her throughout her pregnancy, which I didn't do with my three boys. This time around, I gave it all more attention and appreciation and mature awareness. One weekend we had a small get-together at our apartment. Bobbie was serving our guests from behind a little bar we had. As I looked at her, I realized she would never be more beautiful to me than she was at that moment, carrying our child. Sometimes I would look at her and twirl inside. This woman was the love and light of my life. She was my *everything*.

When Bobbie was in her sixth month, her pregnancy progressing beautifully, I embarked on a short tour with The Jazztet. While I was away, Bobbie developed a kidney infection that could have had adverse consequences for her pregnancy. When I heard this news, I panicked. She needed to be rushed to the hospital, but it was late Sunday night, and I had no medical insurance and no way to get her the money she would need. Kay Norton, manager of The Jazztet, telephoned her fiancé, Herbert Barnett, who was president of Pepsi Cola. Herbert got out of bed, left his Park Avenue apartment, and picked up Bobbie in a limousine headed directly to the hospital. He took care of everything. I will never forget Kay and Herb for supporting Bobbie and me to such lengths. We were friends who had spent many good times together, but who expects the president of an international corporation to climb out of bed and stand in for an absent friend? I paid him back, of course, but still I owe him my eternal gratitude. Herb was there for us in a crisis, when we needed him the most.

Eight months into her pregnancy, I left on a two-week engagement. This time there were no emergencies. I remember coming back into Manhattan through the Lincoln Tunnel, feeling completely elated. Tom McIntosh, the group's trombonist, and I went to Art Farmer's apartment building and took a taxi uptown, where we both lived. As we pulled onto 90th Street, where I lived, on the corner I saw Kay and Bobbie, trying to hail a cab. I dashed to join them, and Bobbie told me that the baby, so active up to then, was not moving, and had a very faint heartbeat. We sped to the hospital, leaving Tom standing on the sidewalk with our baggage and our horns.

It was evening. They admitted Bobbie immediately. The umbilical cord was wrapped around the baby's neck, slowly choking her. There was no time to induce labor. She would need a cesarean delivery. Neither ultrasound nor any of the other sophisticated birth technologies of today were available then, so we had no idea what sex the baby was. A nurse friend of ours, Ruth Rosenfeld, came to the hospital to help Bobbie. I waited anxiously, as expectant fathers did in those days when their wives were in labor. Uselessly I tried to read a newspaper. The words on the page had no meaning to me. This was an ultimate moment of need, hope and grave alertness. Every time Ruth came out, I trembled, but the hours passed with no news. Finally, she emerged from Bobbie's room with a big smile, clapped softly, and informed me, "It's a girl!"

Her words were from heaven. I was overjoyed, delirious. Tears poured down my cheeks. I felt like screaming. Ruth gestured to the newspaper I still held in my hand and suggested we keep it: it showed our daughter's birth date, June 12, 1961. I'll have that newspaper forever.

It was two hours before Bobbie came out of the recovery room, and in the meantime our baby girl was settled in the nursery with the other newborns. I made my way to the nursery, barely able to contain myself. I was going to meet *our daughter*. The baby was in an incubator, unlike all the other babies in the nursery. I was shocked. She was so small, about as long as my two hands together. Could a baby that tiny survive, I wondered? I would have fought to the death for her then and there, but I had never seen a baby so small. Ruth said she was premature, which accounted for her small size and explained the need for the incubator. I loved her limitlessly from the moment I looked at her. She was the daughter I had always wanted. I could hardly believe she was here—in the world, with Bobbie and me. I gazed at her in disbelief, watching her wriggle. I found her beautiful already.

When I saw Bobbie, the first thing she asked was if I liked our little girl. I almost shouted: "Like her!? I *love* her!" Bobbie was too weak to see the baby that night, but in the morning I rolled Bobbie up to the window in a wheel chair to see her daughter for the first time. I had wanted to take pictures of this important moment, but the hospital did not allow flash photography in the maternity ward. In a burst of inspiration, I dashed over to Willoughby's, a big camera store on 33rd Street, the moment it opened, and I bought a Leica. That purchase not only allowed me to take the first pictures of my wife with our baby (without needing a flash); it also initiated my career as an amateur photographer. I was never as savvy as Joe Wilder or Milt Hinton, but I was launched as a picture taker, nonetheless.

Back at the hospital, I wheeled Bobbie up to the nursery viewing window, to meet our baby. Distressed, Bobbie exclaimed, "Oh, she's so small!" I assured her this was temporary. The baby would grow quickly once she came home. I began snapping pictures. I knew nothing about photography and nothing at all about how this expensive camera worked. I fumbled with the device, clever as Yogi Berra in a tutu, or Ralph Ellison preparing to scale Mount Everest with a golf club, but I managed to take all thirty-six pictures on the film roll at once, at different settings. I figured this way I was bound to get a few decent shots, and I did. We still have those photographs. It's great to have predecessors like Ellison and Yogi on your side when you need 'em.

Bobbie came home the next day, but the baby stayed for further observation and care. The charge nurse told us it was time to choose the baby's name. Bobbie left the choice to me, and I said her name was Brielle. I spelled it out. Two days later when I arrived to pick up little Brielle, I was asked why "a woman" had not come with me. They were extremely skeptical, apparently perceiving it as inappropriate for a man to bring a new baby home from the hospital. I was told, finally, to get in a waiting taxi, and they would bring the baby out to me. When they settled our gorgeous little girl in my arms, I touched her for the first time. It was like holding a part of myself, cradling a wiggling little angel. I was holding life itself. I swear on all that is true and good, I knew at that moment I would do anything to protect her, against any odds. I looked at her tiny, helpless form in my arms. She was partly hidden in her blanket. The taxi pulled briskly into traffic. I told the driver to slow down. My new daughter slumbered in my arms. I informed him, "This is my daughter!"

I pulled the blanket back to peer at her. I thought she smiled at me. If I hadn't been holding her, aware of my responsibility to protect her, I could have oozed through the floor. Back at our building, I carefully made my way to the elevator. I carried Brielle up to the fourth floor and rang our doorbell, almost wetting my drawers with excitement. Bobbie opened the door, greeting us with a huge, nervous smile. She was still weak. I took Brielle to the bedroom and laid her on our bed. I unwrapped her blanket and announced, "Here she is!" Bobbie, to my astonishment, burst into tears, and in a moment was sobbing uncontrollably. My heart almost stopped. I did not understand. This was our daughter; there was no going back. "What's the matter?" I asked, in trepidation. Embarrassed, Bobbie confessed that she did not know how to take care of a baby. I was so relieved. So that was all! I had had three boys, so I knew a few things. I told her not to worry. I would help. The next day Bobbie's mother arrived. Women, especially mothers, are extraordinary creatures. In less than two weeks, Bobbie was telling me what to do. And I did, always, as the glorious years passed watching Brielle grow. Every moment was wonderful. I drove our families crazy with my photo taking. I was compelled to document this miracle in our lives.

When she was only a few months old, we noticed something inexplicable about Brielle. No matter what kind of show was on television—high drama, western, musical, documentary, cartoons, whatever—she did not look at the screen until a commercial came on. It didn't matter what the commercial was advertising. When an ad started, she strained to see the screen no matter which direction she faced, even if she had to look backwards over her head lying on the floor. When the commercial was over, she lost interest until the next one. We still cannot comprehend that.

When Brielle was about four years old, we had the scare of our lives. While we were eating dinner one evening, a piece of meat stuck in our baby girl's throat. The morsel lodged so tightly she could not make a sound. She screamed silently, her face turning blue. I grabbed her legs, turned her upside down, and thwacked her on the back—to no avail. The situation became desperate. Bobbie's face was a mask of horror. She grabbed Brielle, uncontrollably screaming my name. I was prepared to make an incision with a razor blade just below her Adam's apple so she could gasp air. Before Bobbie could locate a blade, I tried a final desperate thwack. The piece of meat popped out onto the floor. Brielle's voice, held involuntarily in abeyance, unleashed frantically. Little Brielle knew her helpless jeopardy. We were all traumatized.

In 1965, Brielle was attending a preschool in Manhattan. A bus picked her up in the morning and brought her home around 3:00 in the afternoon. One afternoon, 3:00 came and went, with no Brielle. At 3:30, I called the school. All of the children had been picked up. Alarmed, I called the bus company. No one answered; all of the drivers had gone home. Nearly in a panic, we called the school again. The school was closed, too. I felt my life's blood draining from me. Feeling myself becoming slowly weaker, I called the police. They could not help, they told me, until she had been missing for twenty-four hours! By now, Bobbie was hysterical. Had we lost our wonderful daughter to a madman? Had a crazed, childless woman abducted her? Had she been abused, or worse? Inside, I was going crazy, but I tried not to show Bobbie, as she was already overwhelmed with fear.

It was close to 4:30 when the phone rang. Bobbie snatched it. "The police station!" she cried, nearly fainting. I grabbed the receiver. The sergeant at the local precinct asked if I had a little girl named Brielle. I believe I almost keeled over. "We have her here," he assured me drably. "Can you come and get her?" We jumped in the car and didn't stop for a single traffic light.

Thinking we would find Brielle scared to death, we prepared ourselves to comfort her. Instead, Brielle was standing on the sergeant's desk, singing, showing no fear. She was enjoying being the center of attention; a precinct-full of cops was enamored of this one cute kid. We asked how they had found our phone number. Brielle had given it to them. Thankfully,

Bobbie had trained her to memorize her name, address, and phone number. We eventually learned that a new driver on the afternoon bus route dropped off Brielle on the wrong street. Not sure what to do, our brave girl walked into a nearby building. When the doorman asked if she lived there, she said "Yes," then "Maybe." She rode the elevator to the fourth floor, but everything looked wrong to her. A door opened, and a strange lady peered at her and said nothing. The doorman, not recognizing the little girl heading upstairs, had probably alerted her.

Shortly, the elevator opened again, and a policeman asked Brielle where she lived. At the precinct, she recited her phone number. A day of terror for me and Bobbie; for Brielle, another day's adventure, singing to policemen. Today that precocious little girl is a strong, beautiful, well-educated woman; ever since then, she has always found her way "home" with style.

Coda / A NEW WAY OF LIFE

I N 1959 Art Farmer and I formed The Jazztet. We had high hopes and great ambition. Most jazz groups change personnel from time to time, for many reasons. Pianist McCoy Tyner left us to join John Coltrane. We replaced him with Cedar Walton. When Addison, Art's twin brother died, we brought in bassist Herbie Lewis. Curtis Fuller moved on, so we hired Tom McIntosh as our trombonist. I first met Tom after he left Count Basie and joined James Moody, whose group was playing at the Howard Theater in D.C. along with The Jazztet. There was something exceptional about Tom. One night, in the middle of a performance onstage, he gave me the warmest smile I had ever seen. This cheerful, sincere man, with his big, warm sound on the trombone, knew something deep and special.

Tom read the Bible constantly, an aberration for a jazz musician. He was studying with the Jehovah's Witnesses. Tom spoke about things that I associated with H. G. Wells's science fiction: idyllic new worlds with no crime or murder, no adultery, no illness—and no death. This man was clearly off his rocker. But as we continued our travels together, he demonstrated in precise detail what he had learned from the Bible. Uninformed, I assumed that his view could be found only in *his* version of the Bible. I checked my King James Version at home, in addition to my wife's Catholic Douay Bible. I realized that Tom was right; with the exception of slight differences, the Bible did say the things he told us. I was perplexed. Why had

I been deprived of this understanding as I grew up? Why are people in general ignorant about the essential knowledge that is found in the Bible?

I became consumed with wondering *why*. During the period Tom toured with The Jazztet, arguments about the Bible raged long and hard among the bandmates. We all tried, in turn, to shoot Tom down. Amazingly, he was always able to show us a passage in the Bible that confirmed what he had told us. I stayed quiet during those arguments, because I knew very little about the Bible, and because I wanted to hear Tom's insights. When I saw that he was always proved right, I began to wonder about what I had been taught in church as a boy in Philadelphia. I wondered how Reverend Lewis could have led us astray. Soon after, Bobbie and I began regular Bible study. We experienced one epiphany after another. We came to see that we had both been left in the dark because the people who taught us (or, rather, did not teach us) were themselves unenlightened.

Early in my career, in the long days on the road, I lived a life that I am not proud of. Women, not drugs or alcohol, were the bane of my miserable life. While I was married to my first wife, I was an adulterer of the highest order. Thankfully, years after my divorce, I met Bobbie, my darling wife of more than fifty years. My unquenchable love for Bobbie and my growing love for Jehovah compelled me to abandon interest in other women. I must admit that I am proud of this: Jehovah's people are known worldwide for impeccable conduct, for giving no cause for anyone to harm them. Our aim is to abide by the Bible's counsel: first, to live a life devoted to God, and second, to honor secular law. The goal is to "be peaceful with all men" and to foster respect for family values, law, and morality.

Why do I offer all this as I conclude? I want anyone who reads *Whisper Not* to know the genuine Benny Golson. My life has been about more than music. Each of us is complicated; each of us is in constant need of refinement. Without these details, my life story would be incomplete. On July 18, 1969, in Los Angeles, I symbolized my dedication to Jehovah God by undergoing a water baptism. *I am one of Jehovah's Witnesses.* My love for Jehovah, alongside my love for my family and for my music, defines my life. I look back with joy and appreciation for all that life has brought me. I can never repay the debt of my good fortune, but I attempt to share what I can as often as possible.

A child once asked me what life meant. I was not certain and told him to be observant always. Now that I understand much more, I would tell him that life is like the grass growing green and wide each spring. I would say that the meaning of life flows from respect for how fortunate we were to have been born; for the blessing of health; and for the surprising fact that a life well lived grows stronger, higher, more jubilant, as we become more aware of our obligations to one another and to the Origin of all life and meaning. I was that child, as we all were once. Our greatest fortune is living honestly, with humility and devotion to truth.

The hour is getting late. I sometimes paw through neglected manuscripts, reassessing them. Is there untouched life still there? My songs have not changed. Perhaps I have changed. How joyful to be here, undiminished, plunged in the glory and challenge of Jehovah God's creation.

What stories will the future tell about Benny Golson? Time is a tattletale, isn't it?

Acknowledgments

FTER I DEVELOPED an interest in the piano, as a kid of nine years in Philadelphia, I had no idea whatsoever that I was going to move ahead in any particular direction. My life began to take on the feeling of an adventure, moving from one learning experience to another. My life became consumed with music, but only classical literature. I wanted to be a concert pianist. However, after a few years, and later hearing jazz and the saxophone, I expressed my desire to move from the piano and the classical literature to the saxophone and jazz. Upon hearing this, my mother screamed, "Oh my God! You're going to be a dope addict." But as always, she eventually aligned herself with my desire and supported my efforts in moving in that direction. Since my buddy John Coltrane and I were like brothers in our desire to learn to play the saxophone, my mother constantly encouraged and supported both of us. She was our inspiration as she vicariously moved forward with us in our thinking. She was a great part of my incentive to become proficient.

Much later my wife, Bobbie, a former ballerina, and jazz fan, abandoned any promise of success with her own career and devoted her time and effort to helping and encouraging me in mine. When times were difficult and my spirit was at its lowest, she was there encouraging me to keep moving forward in spite of all else, always telling me it was just a matter of time. And even later when our daughter, Brielle, was born and matured into a bright, sensitive, and informed young woman, who eventually came into the spotlight and realized who her father was other than a father—she, too, became a part of the support team urging me on.

Lester Koenig of Contemporary Records took a chance on me, an unknown, by offering me my very first record date. The celebrated Nat Hentoff was my A&R man who encouraged me through the sessions, and even long after, and who is now a writer for the *Wall Street Journal*. He is also the one who brought me into the now famous photograph *A Great Day in Harlem*. And even later, Orrin Keepnews of Riverside Records took up the torch.

Great recognition in my acknowledgments must go to Temple University Press. Without the press's belief in this book, all would be academic. Without publication, there would be no dedication, no acknowledgment, no recalling of history, no focus on personalities, no memorable events—only black, empty nothingness. The folks at Temple University Press are making everything you find written in these pages known for posterity. They are heroes of the greatest magnitude because publishing is a massive undertaking. They have made everything extant—even symbolically retrieving Excalibur from the rock.

Finally, Jim Merod, whom I've known for many years, heroically came into this picture when I called upon him for what I thought would be just a bit of his talent as an editor. But as it turned out, he gave me everything with the exception of his beating heart and the life that flowed through his veins—and I think he would have done that if it were possible. He determinedly got this "monster'" up off the table and gave it the best style possible with his brilliant word-pictures. In all truth, he turned out to be much, much more than a mere editor. Because he knew me so well, he approached everything from an inside coign of vantage. So, then, my autobiography has his soul intermingled with mine from beginning to end.

As I look back and recall things, these are the people who stand out as I was striving to move forward in what would be a well-established career. I proudly and thankfully acknowledge them. Bless them all.

—Benny Golson

T HE COLLABORATION that Benny and I have enjoyed and endured across the decade that it took us to complete this book has been much more than an adventurous affiliation between friends of more than thirty years. Benny Golson has been profoundly "within" me throughout our shared endeavor. I am not the same person now that I was at the outset. Benny's uniquely deep purity—of character and soul—has brought something resembling Buddhist awareness into my everyday life. Across the span of our increasingly bonded experience, I've continuously experienced his unswerving personal illumination. I've been influenced by great teachers in my seventy-plus years: Benny Golson is doubtless the last, and most subtle, of those.

Over more than four decades, my wife and best friend, Maeve, has given me so much more than I could ever repay in kind. At Princeton, R. P. Blackmur embodied the resonant force of visionary poetic nuance; John Wheeler prevailed beyond others. At Cornell and long after, my colleague and sublime friend A. R. Ammons helped me discover where the pieces of my voice were scattered. During six traumatic years at Stanford (1966–1972), Arnold Toynbee and Bob Creeley defined an unimaginably wide cognitive spectrum. Like Ishmael, I count myself a fortunate *desperado* whose friendships in the world of jazz deepened an astonished witness of humanity's innately raucous (often manic), comic wisdom: Jimmy Rowles, Joe Wilder, Gerald Wilson, Hank Jones, Tommy Flanagan, Buddy Collette, Max Roach, Red Rodney, Bob Florence, John Hicks, Art Farmer, Nick Brignola, Stan Getz, Buddy Rich, Gary Foster and Bob Cooper (among others—counterexamples reside near at hand).

I cannot imagine a well-lived life that is not informed (perhaps obsessively) with great music. A small cadre of musicians and composers have sustained everything that I regard as best within me: Duke with Billy Strayhorn, Cal Tjader, Bill Evans, Miles Davis, Kenny Barron, Antonio Carlos Jobim, Ahmad Jamal, and two who exist beyond horizons: J. S. Bach and Beethoven, with their final, essentially ineffable creations. I'd be remiss not to thank Danny Habuki, Ed Feasel, and Arch Asawa at Soka University, who've created a university unlike any that I've experienced elsewhere: humane, respectful, and, despite our increasingly tormented world, devoted to affirmative fellow-feeling and global peace.

At the risk of overlooking someone, I'll note people who've rooted *Whisper Not* on with cheerful solidarity: most of all Joe Kubala and Steve

McCormack, Hortense Spillers, Karen Oberlander, Buster Williams, Bennie Maupin, Geoffrey Keezer, Kornel Fekete-Kovacs, Gary Tinnes, Michael Golden, Bob Magnusson, Maria Schneider, Greg Weaver, Kenny Werner, Tom Harrell, Fred Hersch, Josh Nelson, Donald Brown, Roy McCurdy, Tamir Hendleman, Michael Oletta, John Clayton, Karrin Allyson, Scott Hamilton, Jim Seeley, Mulgrew Miller, Charlie Haden, Jimmy Heath, Jaime Valle, Jim Plank, Delfeayo Marsalis, Franco Harris, Marvin Levy, Andreas Koch, Charles McPherson, Claudio Roditi, Anthony Wilson, Ron Stout, Larry Koonse, Grant Stewart, Duduka DaFonseca, Roni Ben-Hur, Dori Caymmi, Gilbert Castellanos, Ron Eschete, Joe LaBarbera, Barry Harris, Kareem Abdul-Jabbar, Peter Sprague, Gene Bertoncini, Santi Debriano, Wayne Escoffery, Harry Allen, Joel Strote, Sherry Williams, Marc Edelman, Jose Rizo, Bubba Jackson, Rick Brown, Susan Horton, Duncan Moore, Putter Smith, Adam Schroeder, Rickey Woodard, Allan Phillips, Mike Garson, Neal Faison, Jackie Ryan, Gary Carner, Mundell Lowe, Perry Chen, Dmitry Matheny, Larry Vuckovich, Ruben Estrada, Jonathan Blake, Steve Situm, Vicki Pedrini, Noel Jewkes, Reice Hamel, Jr., Humberto Ramirez, Terence Love, Ronald Judy, Chuck Perrin, Gary Koh, Norm Murphy, Rob Thorsen, Justin Grinnel, Otmaro Ruiz, Tom McIntosh, Anthony Smith, Elin Wilder, Kenneth Kales, John Kehlen, Oleg Gelikman, Clare Lorenzo, Dr. David Case, Nick Sauer, and Susan Grady. Teri Chester lent her good heart and astute skills at several important moments. She has our everlasting gratitude.

Benny and I both admire the intelligence and hard work that Sara Cohen and Ann-Marie Anderson, at Temple University Press, brought to a project that needed their special, passionate talent. Thanks, also, to Diana Winters and Susan Thomas. We consider ourselves exceptionally fortunate.

—Jim Merod

Index

Benny Golson is an NEA Jazz Master, composer, arranger, and saxophonist. After helping Art Blakey revamp his regime with The Jazz Messengers, he co-founded The Jazztet with trumpeter Art Farmer. He has composed not only jazz standards, including "Killer Joe" and "Along Came Betty," but also music for films and television, including *It Takes a Thief* and *M*A*S*H*.

Jim Merod has recorded a veritable "who's who" of jazz greats under his BluePort Jazz label. He is a Professor of Literature and Humanities at Soka University, who has also taught at Cornell, Brown, Brandeis, Stanford, and UCLA. He is the author of *The Political Responsibility of the Critic* and the editor of *Jazz as a Cultural Archive*, a special issue of the journal *boundary 2*.